Your Amazing Preschooler

*How You Can Have the Same Capable,
Confident, and Cooperative Child at
Home that Teachers Have at School*

Deb Ellsworth and Tina Charney

"It's *my life*."

— Deb's son, Zack, age 3

"When I'm sad I just sing a little song to myself so only I can hear it."

— Tina's daughter, Alisa, age 3

Contents

Preface

It was parent-teacher conference time at our preschool, and we were having a conference with three-year-old Darrin's parents. His mother was concerned about the number of toileting accidents he was having. She asked if we had any suggestions. We did. Darrin's mother enjoyed dressing her son in cute grown-up-looking outfits every day. Unfortunately, they often involved belts that were almost impossible for him to undo himself.

We reminded her that preschoolers are reluctant to leave what they're doing until the last second, until their need to go overwhelms their need to play. They just don't have time to go to a teacher to get help with that tricky belt before the floodgates open. We told her that Darrin wasn't being obstinate in not getting to the bathroom sooner; this is normal and appropriate for a three-year-old. We suggested that she dress him in pants that had elastic waistbands that he could easily and quickly take down by himself.

We could almost see the light bulb go off in her head. She was very grateful for the idea, which hadn't occurred to her. As she thanked us for helping her with this vexing problem, a light bulb went off in our heads as well.

We realized that parents might benefit from our many years of experience and our training, not just in regard to toileting issues, but in all the areas of child development.

We, Deb and Tina, co-taught for three years at St. David's Center for Child and Family Development in Minneapolis, Minnesota, where we had both been teaching for many years. Subsequently Tina moved to Arizona, where she is now teaching at the Summit School of Ahwatukee, in Phoenix. All together, we have almost 40 years teaching preschoolers — so far. This book is based on our experiences together and separately. The stories are real, although the names have been changed. As for the quotes, real kids we know actually said them.

Our belief is that children are inherently competent and capable. It is our job as teachers and yours as parents to support their hard work as they develop into the amazing young people we know they can be.

We know that, like the parents of the preschoolers we teach, you have many questions about how best to bring out these abilities in your children. In this book we share with you stories that you can relate to, and ideas that we have used in the classroom that we hope will work for you at home.

Deb Ellsworth and Tina Charney

Acknowledgements

We would like to thank and acknowledge those without whom this book would not have been possible:

- St. David's Center for Child and Family Development, Minnetonka, Minnesota

- Summit School of Ahwatukee, Phoenix, Arizona

- Our colleagues at both schools, who shared some of their own tips and experiences

- The Search Institute® in Minneapolis, Minnesota, for their concept of Developmental Assets®, which they have allowed us to cite throughout this book

- Susan Wootten, for her generous feedback and valuable advice

- Deb's family: Mike, Zack, Devin, and Alex

- Tina's family: Bill, Nathan, and Alisa

- Gloria Kamen, Tina's mother, whose career creating and illustrating books for children has instilled Tina with a love of books, and inspired her to try writing one

- Deb's parents, Dewey Kolbo and Lois Drury, who gave her the greatest example of how to be excellent parents

- The parents who volunteered to read the manuscript and gave us valuable feedback and enthusiastic encouragement to publish this book

- And, of course, all the children we have enjoyed in our classes, who continue to amaze and inspire us

1

Capable and Competent Preschoolers

> *Elsie proudly showed us how she could go backwards across the monkey bars with her eyes closed. "Did you know?" she informed us. "I'm a Master of the Monkey Bars."*

Think, for a moment, of a person you know whom you consider to be an exceptionally competent and capable person. What traits does he or she have?

Perhaps the person you're envisioning is someone like a friend of ours, a guy named Jeffrey Soderberg. Jeffrey is a person who has developed excellent people skills. At work, Jeffrey engages in collaborative problem-solving with his colleagues, producing remarkably successful results. Jeffrey is able to generate novel solutions to problems and to think creatively. While Jeffrey is a strong leader, he's also great at teamwork, and at bringing out the best in other people. But Jeffrey Soderberg isn't just successful at work—he is a person with many interests, from sports to art, which he pursues avidly. And not surprisingly, Jeffrey's relationships with family and friends are excellent.

So just who is this Jeffrey Soderberg, this all-around capable and accomplished person? Is he the CEO of a big corporation, or perhaps the successful owner of his own small business? Not quite—or at least, not yet. Jeffrey is a four-year-old in our preschool class. But we are not exaggerating when we refer to him as competent, or when we describe his terrific people skills.

Jeffrey works well with others in creating excellent structures out of blocks. He cooperates with his friends in a nice give-and-take manner when playing with them in dramatic play, considering their desires as well as his own. He explores all areas of the room, and is interested in each new thing we introduce, whether it's a monarch caterpillar in a butterfly cage, or a new musical instrument, or a machine with intriguing gears and levers, or a new set of watercolor paints at the easel. During discussions at group time, Jeffrey contributes thoughtful and interesting ideas.

When Jeffrey accidentally hurts someone, rather than get defensive, he strives to make them feel better. In preschool-land, this may mean making silly faces and doing pratfalls — but hey, it's effective!

Jeffrey is in fact very likely to grow up to be a wonderful father and husband, a good friend to many, a success at whatever occupation he chooses to pursue, and a man with many interests and avocations.

Happily, we have found many, many Jeffreys in our classes over the years. Our years of preschool teaching have taught us many things, but nothing more important than this: Young children are amazingly, astonishingly competent and capable human beings, in their own way, when given the opportunity and the tools to be so.

Preschool teachers and parents are partners in the wonderful adventure of raising young children. Generally, your goals as parents and our goals as teachers are the same. When your child is older, the focus of his school experience becomes more and more academic. But in the pre-kindergarten years, the focus is on the whole child, because the young child is learning important things in every area of development: social and emotional as well as, and even more importantly than, letters and numbers.

In this book, we would like to partner with you, to help you help your child become the most competent, capable person he can be.

Focusing on the Positives

Aubrey wanted to try using the wall-mounted manual pencil sharpener. After cranking it successfully, she proudly showed us the sharp point. She announced, "I think the first time I did it, it made me a little stronger."

Unlike many parenting books, which are all about changing unwanted behaviors in children, we prefer to focus on the many positive strengths a young child has, and to build on those. We believe that this shift in attitude and perspective is crucial.

As we at school, and you at home, give your child the opportunities and means to become more competent, we are building skills that will help him get through his (potentially) turbulent teenage years successfully, and that will ultimately help him become the successful adult—parent, spouse, worker, and citizen—we all wish our children to be.

The renowned Search Institute has created a list of 40 Developmental Assets® for Early Childhood, based on extensive research. Basically, the researchers have found that the more of these assets a child has, the more likely she is to be successful, both as a child and as an adult, and the less likely she is to engage in troubling behavior.

These include 20 External Assets® under the categories:

- Support

- Empowerment

- Boundaries and Expectations

- Constructive Use of Time

There are also 20 Internal Assets® under the categories

- Commitment to Learning

- Positive Values

- Social Competencies

- Positive Identity.

See the Appendix for the complete list with explanations for each Developmental Asset. Also see our website for the link to the Search Institute.

When we work to build these assets for our children, we focus on enhancing the positive capabilities of children.

For example, Developmental Asset 17 is "Play and creative activities: The child has daily opportunities to play in ways that allow self-expression, physical activity, and interaction with others." Asset 17 is the foundation for most early childhood programs. This is an external asset, because it is provided for the child. We—teachers and parents—aim to give our children as many external assets as we can—creative play opportunities, family support, boundaries, and positive relationships with many people.

Internal assets are those which the child possesses herself—positive values such as caring, integrity, self-regulation, and responsibility. In our classrooms, we try to help the child develop these assets.

For example, we expect the children to be responsible for cleaning up after themselves when they have finished their snack, and we teach them how to do so if they don't know how. If a child leaves her empty cup and crumpled napkin on the table, rather than just throwing them away for her, we remind her to clean up after herself, and we gently guide her back to the table if necessary. We don't do this just because we're "on her case," and we don't do it to get out of work ourselves — it would be easier to just pick up her trash and throw it away, really. We do it to help her develop responsibility, a positive trait and an asset to her as a person.

We as teachers try to be mindful of how we are building these assets in our young charges, helping them, for example, to:

- Feel a sense of purpose in our classroom (Asset #39)

- Feel motivated to master new things (Asset #21)

- Make their own decisions as much as possible (Asset #32)

- Learn how to resolve conflicts peacefully (Asset #36)

Throughout this book, we note which specific Developmental Asset is being fostered, and we discuss how you, too, can foster them at home.

Inside the Preschooler's Mind

> *Mary Lou was delighted to spot the moon in the daytime sky
> above the playground. She exclaimed, "I see the moon.
> She follows me because I'm so pretty.
> She doesn't follow boys so much."*

Another way that we accentuate the positive, as the old song goes, is by understanding how young children's minds operate. So let's take a look inside that young brain, because understanding that little person's thought processes will be the basis for everything we do to help him become more competent socially, emotionally, behaviorally, cognitively and creatively.

First, preschoolers are very **egocentric**. That means, everything is perceived and understood through the "me filter."

Here's an example. Often at school we ask, "How many children are here today?" and then count the children in the group out loud. When we get to the third child and say "three," she will often respond, "No, I'm four!" The numbers three, four and five have more meaning to the children personally (their age) than they do in a more abstract sense of quantity.

Here's another example. When Deb was drawing stick-figure pictures of people using pulleys and ramps to make a poster for a unit on simple machines, a little girl watching her draw asked, "Which one is me?"

Preschoolers take almost everything personally. When Liana was raking leaves one fall day, the wind was blowing the leaves all over, making her task difficult. Deb remarked, "That's a strong wind," to which Liana replied, "Yeah, and naughty, too!" For her, the action of the wind was personal. It really is *all about me* for a preschooler.

Developing the ability to understand things in a less personal and more general way, as well as the ability to understand another person's viewpoint, are very important cognitive skills that begin during these preschool years, and continue to grow in the later childhood years. We do see wonderful examples of empathy in these young children, particularly when their classmates are hurt or crying.

Preschoolers understand things in a physical, **concrete** way, rather than in an abstract way. Consider time, for example. The words "half an hour" mean almost nothing to a three-year-old. Seeing a clock hand go from the 12 to the 6 means a little more, but it's still pretty hard to hold onto, mentally. Seeing half the sand run through an hourglass sand timer is easier to understand.

Because they are concrete, rather than abstract, thinkers, actions speak louder than words to preschoolers. The action of holding out his coat to him will speak louder than the words "go put on your coat."

At this stage, seeing is believing. It's interesting when magicians come to our school to entertain the children. None of the three-year-olds are impressed by any of the tricks. They take at face value what they see, and as far as they're concerned, they see lots of new things all the time. By the time they're five, some will say skeptically to the magician, "You tricked us. How did you do that?" But really, for most of them, the best part of the show is when the magician makes a funny hat appear on his own head and pretends not to notice while the children are laughing hysterically. Humor for a preschooler is pretty concrete, too.

Finally, preschoolers are very **now-centered**. Unlike adults, they focus mostly on what is happening now. That's because of what we just talked about — what is happening now is real and concrete, while the past and the future are more abstract.

That's not to say that they can't remember things. Preschoolers have fantastic memories. Nor is it that they can't anticipate future events. It's just that they are very captured by the present. So they can go from screaming at a playmate one moment to being best friends five minutes later.

Being very now-centered also means that preschoolers devote their attention to what they are doing with a fullness that we adults, swamped as our minds are with a million details, cannot. For this, really, we must envy them. Their attention may not always last very long, but while they are working on that puzzle, they are totally into it. Then, when their friend comes up to them and barks like a dog, the next "now" thing captures them, and they scamper off to pretend to be puppies, the puzzle gone from their minds.

We adults need to be mindful of these traits of the preschool-aged child — being egocentric, concrete, and present-oriented — so that we don't ask them to do or understand things they are not yet capable of. On the other hand, we want to capitalize on and use these traits as we help our children learn, grow and become more competent people.

By the way, although we are generally discussing the preschool child as a three- to five-year-old, children grow and develop at varying rates. Some of what we say can be applied to two-year-olds, and much of it will still be applicable to elementary school-aged children.

PRESCHOOLERS' THINKING PROCESSES ARE

- Egocentric (it's all about them!)

- Concrete (not abstract)

- Visual (what they see captivates them and is real to them)

- Now-centered (not past or future-oriented)

All Kinds of Kids

Several children were having a lunchtime conversation about who had plans to marry each other. Then Tania decided: "I'm not going to get married." Another child asked, "Why not?" To which Tania replied, "Because I'm going to stay a kid."

The interesting thing about a preschool class, like life itself, is how many different kinds of people there are. Of course, every person is a unique individual. But we've noticed, after many years of teaching preschool, that there are several types of kids that we frequently encounter in our classes. See if any of these sound familiar.

Eight children are sitting at our art table, making collages. On the table are bits of tissue paper, pieces of foil, pasta, yarn, and many other small items. Each child has a piece of construction paper on which he or she can glue these things.

Lindsey is loading her paper with everything she can put on it, and not just from end to end and top to bottom, but in layer upon layer. She works at her art project for a long time. We wonder if her collage will become so heavy and so laden with glue that it will collapse.

Lindsey is an **All the Way** kid. She does nothing halfway. Everything she does is BIG! When she paints at the easel, she always fills all the paper with paint, often in several layers. She makes six pictures, not just one. She takes all the blocks off the shelf when she's building. At naptime, she sleeps with five stuffed animals and two blankets. She may come to school wearing, on top of the usual shirt and pants, five glittery necklaces, a vest, a scarf tied around her waist, bracelets on each arm, and a snazzy hat.

All the Way kids are frequently collectors. They bring in pocketfuls of rocks each day from the playground, and fistfuls of dandelions. Their parents find cubbies full of "treasures" at the end of every day.

Angel is carefully placing each item on the paper, putting one piece of macaroni in each corner, and laying a piece of yarn from each pasta piece so that they all meet in the middle, where she precisely places a foil circle. She is absorbed in her work as she spends twenty minutes creating a beautiful and intricate pattern on her paper.

Angel is a **Pattern Maker**. She loves to draw at the writing center, but what she draws is full of geometric and other patterns. If she draws a person, she draws alternating red and green triangles all around the edges, and alternating blue and purple circles in the sky above. Her abstract artwork can be strikingly beautiful. She has great attention to detail. When she builds with blocks, she carefully places the various shapes in a complex and symmetrical structure. Perhaps Angel will grow up to be an engineer or a designer.

Capable and Competent Preschoolers

Trey puts one big square of tissue paper on his paper and says "I'm done." He goes off to play with cars.

Trey is a **Butterfly**. He has a short attention span, and he flits from thing to thing. He will start to play a game, and leave the table after two turns. It's too boring to have to wait for other kids to take their turns. He will write the letter of the week in his letter journal once, and want to be done, even though he knows that everyone is supposed to practice writing the letter five times. He gets restless at group time after a few short minutes, and entertains himself by playing with something in his pocket, or by bothering his neighbor. He is only interested if he is the one talking or doing something. He's usually happiest on the playground, engaged in big, fast action like running or biking.

Gerald takes Trey's place. Before he starts, Gerald looks at Mariah's picture. He copies what she did with the yarn. Mariah notices this. "You should put the green tissue paper here," she says, and proceeds to direct Gerald in how he should do his art project. Gerald is happy to comply.

Gerald is an **Observer**. He isn't one to leap before looking. He's usually pretty quiet. He may not say much of anything for the first several weeks of school. But he's watching everything and everyone very closely. Only when he feels comfortable that he's got things figured out does he begin to interact with the other kids and teachers. He doesn't like to be pushed into things before he feels ready. He doesn't mind taking direction and ideas from others, but he'll also come up with his own ideas once he feels comfortable. Observing before acting is really a pretty smart way to approach things. Gerald won't be the kid who does reckless things on a dare. And he'll probably be an observant, careful driver, too!

Mariah is a **Director**. She's always telling the other kids what to do. In the housekeeping area, she will assign roles to all of the children: "You be the baby, and you be the sister, and you be the dog, and I'll be the mommy." As we're walking out to the playground, she's telling her friends exactly what they will do and where they will do it when they get there. Some kids call her bossy. Others are happy to follow her lead. She may need some help in seeing and respecting other people's point of view, and in accepting that friends don't always have to do everything her way. But if her leadership skills are developed appropriately, she's got "future C.E.O." written all over her.

Ahna notices that the color bleeds from the tissue paper onto the white construction paper a little bit. She goes to the sink and fills a small cup with water, which she brings back to the table. She dips pieces of tissue paper into the water and "paints" with them on the paper. She does not end up making a collage at all; instead, she creates a very original piece of artwork.

Ahna is an **Experimenter**. She's got a mind that sees things in a different way. She wonders about things. What happens if... Why does this do that? What if I change this? When she does art, she tries new ways of creating it. She experiments with painting white lines over the finished painting. She colors the trees orange and the sky yellow. She picks up a stick and tries out drumming on various things on the playground. When we do science experiments, she wants to carry them to the next step, and to try out more variations. Ahna is creative; she thinks outside the box. When she grows up, she may become a musician, or she may design a new application for computers, or she may direct a play that reviewers call innovative and daring. As long as she is encouraged in her creative thinking, the sky's the limit.

Brian forgets to put the glue on, so nothing is sticking. "You need to put the glue on first," the teacher says. But Brian pours the glue over the piece of pasta instead. The teacher sees that he has loaded one side of the paper with the collage materials. She hands Brian a piece of foil. "Would you like to put this shiny foil over on this side?" she suggests. Brian drops the foil, picks up a piece of yarn, and puts it on top of everything else on the full side. "Well," says the teacher. "You've left yourself a lot of room to write your name on this empty side." She hands Brian the marker. He writes his name, with much difficulty, on the full side.

Brian is a **Go My Own Way** kid. Whatever an adult tells him to do, he wants to do the opposite. If you suggest that he wear his green jacket, you can bet he'll put on his red one. His grandmother calls him stubborn. His dad says he's got a mind of his own. We know that he is fiercely independent, and we try to respect that as much as possible. Whether it's just a stage, or a core personality trait, we know that getting locked into a battle of wills with Brian won't get us anywhere. Better to work with him than against him.

Todd is working intently, his brow furrowed. He can't seem to get the piece of tissue paper to stick on like he wants it to. It keeps wrinkling up, and he wants it to be smooth. Suddenly he balls up his piece of paper and says angrily, "I can't do this!" He storms off from the art table.

Todd is a **Perfectionist**. His expectations are set very high, and his tolerance for frustration is low. Life can be hard for Todd, because, as we all know, no one is perfect. Problems happen, things can be hard to do, and life doesn't always work out like you want it to. But Todd gets upset whenever he can't do something exactly as he envisions it, whether it's zipping his jacket or making a sandcastle. We hope to help Todd learn to ease up on himself a bit, and to keep trying a little longer.

Lola is so busy talking that she almost forgets to work on the collage. She chats away to everyone at the table, telling about her new puppy, making jokes, saying she's going to her grandma's after school, and talking with anyone who responds to her. She barely pays attention to the collage she's making with a few randomly chosen materials.

Lola is a **People Person**. She is an extravert. For her, it's all about friends and talking and interactions with other people. She has a hard time listening at group, because she's so busy talking with her friends. She has a new best friend every day, sometimes every hour. She enjoys being the center of attention, and always wants to be the first one to say something at group time, whether or not it's on topic.

Philip's been sitting in the book corner looking at books by himself for forty-five minutes. We have tried to persuade him to come over to the art table to make a collage, but he refuses. Finally, when most of the other kids have made their collage and only Lindsey is left at the table, he comes over. He works quietly and carefully on his collage and smiles at Lindsey, responding to her when she talks to him about his picture.

Philip is a **Cat**. By that, we mean he is content to play by himself much of the time; he is sufficient unto himself. It's not that he doesn't like people or need people, but he gets overwhelmed by larger groups of people and lots of talking and interaction. He prefers to play with one friend at a time, and has one best friend who is always his preferred playmate. He has an active imagination, and loves to set up little figures in elaborate play scenarios. Philip is an introvert. This doesn't necessarily mean that he is shy, although some introverts are.

Your Kind of Kid

We would like to point out here that it is not inherently better to be extraverted than introverted. Both are intrinsic temperamental traits with which a person approaches and deals with the world. In her book, *Raising Your Spirited Child*, Mary Sheedy Kurcinka describes how extraverted people renew their energy by being with people, while introverted people find their energy drained by having to socialize too long, and need to recharge their emotional batteries by being alone for a while. It really helps to know which temperament predominates in your child, extraversion or introversion, and it is important to respect that.

Many children, of course, are combinations of the above types, as well as having many other personality traits and styles. We remember Elena, from our class a few years ago, who was a **Social Director** who made wonderful works of art that were highly creative and also often filled with intricate and complex patterns.

We describe these different children, because as you read this book, we want you to keep in mind that what works with an Observer might be entirely different than what is effective with a Go My Own Way kid. Think about your own child's personality, strengths, interests, and temperament. Does he resent your trying to tell him how to do something, or does he appreciate it? Does she absolutely have to put on twelve different articles of clothing every morning, and is that just something you need to make more time for, because it's part of her personality? Will he be excited to try something new, or will he need time to adjust to the idea and figure out what will happen?

Isn't it wonderful how many different kinds of kids there are? At almost every conference we've ever had with parents, they say at some point, "My children are so different from one another." And thank goodness for that! The best teachers appreciate each child for who she or he is, and they individualize their methods of helping each child. You, as a parent, love each of your children totally, but you can still appreciate your oldest child's attention to detail, and your middle child's zany humor, and your youngest child's fierce sense of independence.

In this book, you will meet many children who are *becoming* more competent. Children like Kali, whose daily temper tantrums subsided as she learned how to gain more mastery over her emotions, through use of our Bear Cave and the Feelings Wheel, and increased language capabilities. Or Nick, who learned to negotiate a problem by going to our Stoplight for Peace with a friend. Or Tia, who began overcoming her shyness about speaking in front of the class by first telling her information to our puppet friend, Gabby. Or Chun, who proudly learned to put on his own snowsuit and boots by following the step-by-step pictures on the wall.

As you read this book, mentally transform the children we use as examples into your own distinct and special child. And then think about how what we say fits for you and your child.

The Five Areas of Competence

Five-year-old Alice had the opportunity to see author Mo Willems and learned how to draw a pigeon. On Monday, Alice demonstrated her new skill to the class. She then read Willems' book, "The Pigeon Finds a Hot Dog." When she was done, one of the children exclaimed, "Alice is a genius! I want to be her!"

It may sound strange to refer to a person who knocks over his glass of milk at the dinner table most nights as competent. Competence really means skilled, so we're talking about young children being — or learning to be — skilled in ways that children of their age can be. Some young children are very skillful at making friends. Some are especially skillful at learning and using new words. Some are skilled at reading the emotional body language of their parents. We try to always see the children in our care as capable, competent people.

In this book, we discuss children developing competence in five critical areas:

- Emotional

- Social

- Behavioral

- Cognitive

- Creative

We talk about them increasing their competence rather than achieving competence, because becoming competent in these areas is an on-going process stretching from early childhood into adulthood.

We like to focus on each child's development in a positive light, as they become increasingly competent, rather than concentrating on what they don't know and can't do.

It's important to see little children as full human beings who are building and creating their own competencies, with our help. In the past, children were seen as empty vessels that needed filling by adults. Now scientists know that children, from the earliest moments, come hard-wired to construct their own understanding of language, emotions, and everything else in the world.

Children derive the specifics of the knowledge they are constructing from the culture and people around them. They learn to speak English sounds and words if they are raised in an English-speaking environment, and Japanese sounds and words if they are living in a Japanese-speaking environment. They learn the specifics of the cultural norms, such as what is considered polite, and how they are to relate to peers, family members and adults, from the people in their own culture. But they are programmed genetically as human beings to want to learn these things.

Children are driven to learn. They are driven to become more competent.

We invite you to join us as we travel on this wonderful journey, as your child becomes more competent emotionally, socially, behaviorally, cognitively and creatively, in his or her own unique and amazing way.

2

Bridge Between Home and School

Deb asked Suri why she was sucking her thumb. Her explanation was beautiful. "When I suck my thumb it makes me feel like I'm with my mama, and my mama makes me feel better."

Bethany and her mom had just arrived at school. Bethany was refusing to take off her jacket and hang it in her cubby. It seemed that Bethany was having a rough morning. Bethany's mother rolled her eyes and said, "It's been awful. She wouldn't get ready for school and she threw her cereal on the floor and then refused to clean it up. And then she had a complete meltdown. How do you do it? I can't even manage my one child half the time, let alone sixteen."

Developmental Asset #23:
Home-program connection

We see many analogous situations. Even at school, children sometimes get mad enough to throw something, refuse to put their coat on to go outside, or have a complete meltdown.

Perhaps you are thinking, though, that there are too many differences between the preschool classroom and your own home to apply the same techniques and tools. Perhaps you're wondering whether teachers and parents can—or should—approach children the same way.

True enough, there are some big differences between the needs and expectations of dealing with a class full of children versus your one or more children at home. Some differences between parents and teachers we can't and wouldn't want to change.

We're not as emotionally tied to the children as you are. We like the children and we care very much about them, but you love your child totally and unconditionally.

You have a deep, unbreakable bond with your child. It's not so devastating for teachers to hear a child tell us "I hate you." We usually respond, "Oh, I see that you're really angry right now. It's still the rule and you still have to follow it." We don't take it personally. But for you, the parent, we know those words cut deeply. Fortunately for all of us, a preschooler's anger is short-lived, but his love is boundless. When Deb's son, Alex, was just three-years-old, he yelled at her furiously, "You are the worst mother in the world!" Not a half hour later, he was snuggling up and telling her, "I love you more than food."

It's also easier for us to live with our mistakes. For you, messing up as a parent feels like you're messing up your child, and that is so hard to live with. Sometimes we teachers try something and it backfires. Sometimes we have a bad day, like anyone can, and we're a little too sharp with the children. We try something else, or we apologize to the children, and we move on.

We would like to give you permission to forgive yourself for your mistakes and move on, too. Both Tina and Deb still feel guilty remembering assorted mistakes we made with our own kids, but we're pretty sure they have long forgotten them. We're happy to report they all turned out fine. Yours will, too. Why? Because it's that same deep bond of love between you and your child that will carry you over all the hurdles.

In a classroom, we have to get fifteen or more kids doing the same things at the same time in order to function, so we tend to be more scheduled than you are at home. Home is a place to relax. But most families usually follow a schedule too: dinner at six, bath time at seven, gymnastics on Tuesdays, and so on.

In a lot of ways, the preschool classroom is not as different from home as you might think. A good part of the preschooler's day at school is spent in open-ended play. There is active play on the playground or in the gym, and what's called "free play" or "free choice" in many classrooms. The children get to choose what to do, whether it's building a castle out of blocks with their friends, or looking at books in the book corner, or painting at the easel, or whatever.

Your child has a smaller group of peers to play with at home than she does at school, but she still most likely interacts with children and adults in both places, learning important socialization skills all day, at school and at home.

Preschool teachers may seem calmer and more patient than parents feel like they can ever be, but that's because we've learned that our calm, steady responses to children make the situation better. Yelling begets yelling, so when the class is getting too noisy, you'll often find preschool teachers speaking to the children in very quiet voices, as they tell each child softly, "It's getting too loud in here. Can you turn your voices down to an inside voice?" Surprisingly, this works a lot better than if the teacher were to raise her voice to be heard over the din, and shout for everyone to quiet down. Try it with your own children when they're wild and noisy—you may be pleasantly surprised. Likewise, anger begets anger. So when a young child has lost it, and is out-of-control angry, the preschool teacher is especially controlled and calm. Again, it works.

Preschool teachers have had experience with many children, hundreds of them over the course of their teaching careers. This gives us a broad perspective. We know that behaviors that are so vexing to parents are common among children. Parents, on the other hand, generally have a smaller pool of experience to dip into. In this book, our aim is to share with you our knowledge and our experience of what is normal and typical for this age.

So, what about Bethany? Clearly, she and her mom had been having power struggles all morning. This was a good time to remember to ask ourselves whether this was an important battle to fight. We told Bethany in a reassuring voice that we trusted her to make a good decision and to hang up her coat when she got too warm in the classroom. We assured Bethany's mother that we were not giving in to the tantrum, but rather asking Bethany to take responsibility for her actions.

Teacher Tools

Our class puppet, Gabby, was sitting on a shelf. Roger marched up to her, stared into her beady glass eyes, and said firmly, "Gabby, I know you're not real." Then he turned around and strode away, unaware that his actions had belied his words.

Just as carpenters use hammers and doctors use stethoscopes, teachers have their tools. The key feature of our tools is that they are *concrete and visual or auditory*. Young children are essentially concrete thinkers and visual and hands-on learners. They learn by touching, doing, seeing, and by repetition. And they pay attention and respond to real things better than they do to words flowing from the adult's mouth in rivers of lengthy sentences.

Children feel secure when things in their world are predictable. When they see us using the same tool, such as a familiar puppet, they respond with comfort and enthusiasm.

Throughout this book, we will show this symbol to identify specific tools that we use:

Three of our teacher tools are useful in so many situations that we will introduce them here. All of these tools capitalize on the young child's concrete, here-and-now, visual thinking processes.

Puppets

Children love puppets, especially when an adult is making them talk. We love puppets because young children respond so well to them. A colorful puppet is real and captivating to a child, because it is so compelling visually. We have found, by the way, that so long as you move it and talk for it, a doll or stuffed animal serves just as well as an actual puppet. One caveat: It is probably better not to commandeer one of your child's favorite stuffed animals, because they may be upset to hear it talking in a way that they have not imagined it. Use a new or forgotten toy instead.

We have several class puppets.

Gabby (short for Gabriella Chatterbox, because she loves to talk excitedly) comes out every day to sing the "Hello" song. She is always curious and excited about what is new, and what is happening today. If she doesn't appear, the children are very insistent that she "wake up!"

Gabby breaks the ice for shy children. They will answer her, when they won't talk to us. If she makes a mistake or says something silly, the children correct her. She can be very sympathetic if a child is sad or having a hard time, but she always asks first if they would like a hug. She models respectful behavior. Often when she first comes out, a child will tell us, "I have to tell Gabby something." Then he'll say something like, "Gabby, I just got new shoes yesterday." The kids love her.

Franny and Freddy, (actually two soft dolls), act out friendship issues. So long as the doll who is speaking is also moving, the children have no trouble following, even if one teacher is working both dolls. Franny and Freddy can argue, fight, get angry, be selfish, whine, and pout, but they always resolve their dispute, show empathy to each other, and remain friends. Often, we will pause in mid-argument and ask the children what Franny and Freddy should do. They are eager to offer ideas.

Puppets are a wonderful tool that you can use at home in many situations. Don't worry that your child listens to a puppet better than she does to you sometimes. Instead, realize that you are using one of a young child's greatest assets—her wonderful imagination—to help her. And she may even tell the puppet something she can't quite tell you, even though the puppet is on the end of your arm!

TIPS AND IDEAS FOR USING PUPPETS

• Let the puppet be curious and observant. "You know what I noticed...?"

• Let the puppet be fallible and make mistakes. (Kids love to correct them!)

• Let the puppet show that he likes your child. The puppet hugs, shakes hands, "high fives," or gives a kiss on the cheek.

• Let the puppet be a confidante – it "whispers" to the child. The child can whisper back.

• Let the puppet have some of the qualities of your child – for example, shy, scared, allergic.

• It's OK for the puppet to have some qualities that are the opposite of your child's – for example, talkative, goofy, very excitable, or very calm. Your child might enjoy that.

• Children love it when a puppet is excited about something they have just accomplished.

Songs, rhymes and sounds

Children love the predictable, and also the unpredictably humorous. Familiar and personalized songs, chants, and rhymes catch their attention and pique their interest just enough to get their participation before they have a chance to think about resisting. Sometimes, joining in the game for the fun of it is a way for a resisting child to save face: He's not *giving in*, he's *joining in*.

In general, singing something rather than saying something is an effective tool with little kids. Really, it's the same technique they use in opera. Sometimes the soprano is only singing, "Oh my, I see it's raining outside," but it sounds much more impressive set to a beautiful melody. (And don't worry—you don't have to sing like an opera star. Kids aren't critics.)

We use a small wooden train whistle to signal that it is time to leave the room. We use a small bell to call the children to circle time—and they do come running when they hear it.

This may seem harder to do at home, perhaps. Maybe you feel foolish being silly. Maybe you just don't think of it, as you search for your car keys, dress the baby, and worry about being late to work. But if you can get your preschooler to put on her own coat and come promptly to the door by blowing the train whistle and saying "All aboard the Smith Family train," won't it be worth it? For years, Deb used a crystal dinner bell to signal that it was time to come to the dinner table. Her children enjoyed getting to be the one to ring it. You could use a drum for the march to bed.

In addition to songs and sounds, we use rhyming to get the children's attention by saying, "One, two, three, all eyes on me!" Or "Lunch on the plate, so don't be late." They enjoy saying the rhyme with us, and they're much more likely to comply with their own instructions! You can rhyme all sorts of things, but especially your child's name, if it lends itself to rhyming. Sometimes we use phrases that make the request more of a game. For example, we say, "Freeze. You're a statue!" Try this when you want your child to stand still for a minute so you can tie his shoes; it just might work.

And when none of this works? Then we have to vary the routine—a little surprise ending is bound to get their attention. The Clean Up song ends: "It's already clean up time." If we change that to "It's already nap time," they stop what they're doing to correct us. "Noooo, it's clean up time!" "OK," we say, "then let's clean up!"

Sign Language

Here is another tool you may find helpful: using sign language to give simple directions and reminders. It wasn't until Tina had two girls who were hard of hearing in her class some years ago, and a classroom aide who was fluent in American Sign Language (ASL), that she learned how well all young children respond to signing. The whole class caught on instantly to the signs for "stop," "sit down," "wait," "more, please," "listen," and "too loud!" It wasn't long before they were using the signs to communicate with one another.

We discovered that they loved learning how to sign the alphabet. We soon saw that even the children who did not yet understand the concept of printed letters could remember and associate the hand signs with the name of each letter. And children who were shy about speaking or singing began to join in by using signs.

We signed key words in many of our favorite songs and found that even the most reluctant singers were joining in with the hand signs, and eventually singing. Parents began asking us if we could teach them the signs—or told us that their children were teaching them at home.

You can understand why sign language is so effective with preschoolers. It's a concrete, visual language, and children are concrete, visual thinkers. Many of the signs actually look like the words they represent. For example, an elephant is signed by making a gesture with the hand that shows an elephant's long trunk. For "listen," you cup your hand behind your ear with a questioning look on your face. Facial expressions are an important part of ASL.

The biggest bonus for us is that we can sign "sit down" or "too loud" or "listen" silently without interrupting what else is going on and it is more gentle, more effective, and less stressful than repeating a spoken command that seems often to be ignored. This will be effective for you when you need to tell your child such things in quiet public places.

Interestingly, there has been a big movement to teach babies sign language, and parents are finding that their infants can sign many words long before they speak a single one. Children really respond to this totally visual language system.

> **Developmental Asset® #2:**
> Positive Family
> Communication

There is no need to be fluent in ASL, or even to try to be strictly faithful to the ASL signs unless you want to communicate with a deaf or hard-of-hearing person. Simple words, and a few phrases will be very useful. You can find ASL signs demonstrated online, or you can purchase one of many books on signing. A pictorial dictionary, lessons, and practice ideas can be found at www.lifeprint.com and other sites. See the appendix or our website for some of the signs and links.

ALL-PURPOSE TOOLS THAT CAPITALIZE ON PRESCHOOLERS' THINKING TRAITS:

- Puppets

- Songs, rhymes and special sounds

- Sign language

Finally, there's the most all-purpose, generally useful tool of all—and it's free, and it's right there outside your door! Yes, we're talking about the very simple, but very beneficial, act of spending time outdoors in nature. We can usually tell when we haven't been able to go outside due to the weather, because the children's behavior noticeably deteriorates. The fresh air, the exercise, the contact with nature and the living world, are all deeply restorative for children (and for adults as well).

The excellent book, *Last Child in the Woods: Saving Our Children from Nature-Deficit Disorder,* by Richard Louv, asserts that contact with nature improves children's lives in every way—emotionally, cognitively, behaviorally, physically, and spiritually. It calms children with ADHD, and helps children with emotional regulation issues. In fact, there is a growing movement for nature-based schools, due to the impressive research that backs up these claims. So, in regard to every area of competence that we discuss in this book, your child will benefit when you take him outside to experience, explore, and enjoy nature.

Bridge Between Home and School

3

Emotional Competence

> *"I'm as brave as a dinosaur," said Charlie to himself as he bravely faced his anxiety about going to see the live animal program with his class.*

What's the difference between the toddler having a temper tantrum in the grocery store because she didn't get a candy bar, and the office manager screaming that if his staff doesn't quit jamming the copy machine he'll take the next repair job out of their paychecks? Not much.

Except the toddler has an excuse: She's only two-years-old. Unfortunately, we all know people like the office manager, who have never learned appropriate and more-effective ways to deal with their emotions.

One of our most important tasks as preschool teachers — and one of your most important jobs as a parent — is to help children begin to learn how to manage their own feelings. In just a few short years these children will, we hope, grow from a toddler who screeches with rage and bites the child who takes her toy, to a child who calmly says, "I was still using that. You can have it when I'm done." Or, "I'm using that, but here's another one you can have. Do you want to play with me?"

Right up front, we need to acknowledge that learning to manage emotions is a difficult task that takes well more than the preschool years. (Are you thinking teenagers now? Talk about wildly swinging emotions controlling the kid!)

In fact, research now shows that the human brain doesn't finish developing until around the age of 25, and one of the last areas to develop is the part of the brain that handles impulse control. Fortunately, preschoolers don't have to handle their feelings all on their own. Adults are a protection zone for them, buffering them from their own most intense feelings, and helping them to deal with those feelings.

We once asked the children in our class what helps them feel better when they feel bad. They had lots of things to say, but at the top of everyone's list was *you!* Mommy and Daddy, holding, snuggling, cuddling, and rocking them.

Going back to our angry office manager for a moment, we should point out that he not only lacks emotional competence, he also lacks social competence. He doesn't understand that he would get better cooperation out of his staff by discussing the problem in a reasonable way, rather than yelling at them.

So the areas of emotional and social competence overlap quite a bit. When a child is angry, and screams and throws toys and kicks the wall, she is not very emotionally competent at that point. But when she's angry and she screams at another child and then hits him, she's also not being socially competent.

That's why, when we do conferences with the parents, the first part of the conference report is called "Social/ Emotional Development." Becoming emotionally and socially competent is the most important task of early childhood, the foundation upon which all other skills are built. Every kindergarten teacher we've ever talked to has told us that if a child is able to manage his emotions fairly well, work cooperatively and nicely with other children, listen to the teacher, and meet his own needs independently (such as getting dressed to go outside), he's ready to start kindergarten.

One additional caveat before we begin our discussion: generally speaking, your child will experience and display far more intense feelings at home than she does at school. That's because, as we mentioned, she has a far more intense emotional bond with you and her siblings than she has with her teachers and classmates.

> **Developmental Asset # 31:**
> Self-regulation

Also, it's safer to express really strong feelings at home (even screaming the dreaded "I hate you!" at mommy or daddy). This is because your child knows deep down that you will always love her and always care for her, no matter what she says or does. However, probably a little part of her will be afraid that she has crossed the line and will lose your love, the thing she holds most precious in all the world.

Very often in our conferences a parent will say, "Pedro has terrible temper tantrums at home. Does he do that at school?" And nine times out of ten, we answer, "No. That's reserved for you, for home, where he feels safe letting out these huge, terrible feelings. Lucky you."

And we laugh, but it's true. Lucky you, that your child loves you so deeply, so intensely, so completely. If there's one truth we can say absolutely, it's that you are the center of your young child's world. Most of the pictures the children make at the art table are for Mommy or Daddy. Most of the pictures they draw are of their family. When they get hurt or are upset, the first thing they say is, "I want my mommy," or "I want my daddy."

But just because they feel safe expressing intense emotions at home, that doesn't mean they want to. It doesn't really feel good to be in a rage. It doesn't feel good to melt down crying over every little disappointment. It doesn't feel good to whine about everything you want, and to be met with annoyance for it.

So, whatever the level of intensity of emotions, both we as teachers and you as parents will be doing our children a great service by helping them learn how to manage those feelings. The first step is helping your child to identify and describe what he is feeling.

Name It: Identifying Emotions

> *Some of the children were being noisy at rest time. Deon complained, "They're being so loud I can't even hear to sleep!" Malia agreed: "If I can't go to sleep, I'll be very disappointed."*

The therapists at our school have a saying: "Name it and tame it." What they mean is, once children can identify their feelings, they can begin to get control of them.

In our class, we concentrate for several weeks on learning about feelings, which we use as a basis for helping the children develop their emotional competence throughout our school year. Most preschoolers identify the broad categories of emotions: happy, sad, angry and scared. They are very interested to learn more-precise words that more accurately explain how they're feeling—words like frustrated, nervous, embarrassed, proud, and furious, and even words like exuberant, exasperated or enthusiastic.

Don't be afraid to use big words with little kids. Their brains are hard-wired to learn vocabulary (and other language constructs) at this age in particular. When they hear us say to them something like, "Oh, Jorge, you looked exhilarated when I pushed you so high on the swing!" the word exhilarated is planted like a seed in their brains. Using the words in context, in this case in the context of describing their emotions to them, helps them to understand the word and to recognize it the next time they hear it.

Besides identifying the children's emotions for them, adults should name our own feelings for the children. We might say, "Jonah, I'm very unhappy that you dumped the crayons onto the floor again. I'm disappointed that you didn't remember we'd just talked about that yesterday."

> **Developmental Asset #2:**
> Positive family communication

Naming your child's feelings also validates his feelings. "George, I see that you're frustrated that you can't get your dresser drawer to close all the way." "Amy, you look really proud that you made your bed all by yourself."

Tip: Use a wide variety of words to describe emotions.

It also helps if you describe your own feelings. For example, when you get something stuck in the vacuum cleaner and you can't get it out, and your child sees you struggling with it, tell him, "I am so frustrated that I can't get this vacuum unstuck!"

When you get a good job review at work, share it with your family at the dinner table. Let your child hear you say, "I'm really proud of myself for the good job I did at work." Not only will this help your child identify and understand emotions, it will also increase your emotional connection with your child as you share your feelings with him. Plus, it's very important for children to know that adults feel the same emotions they do. "Wow, Mommy gets frustrated, too, just like me."

We adapted this popular children's song to express a variety of emotions:

♪ If you're happy and you know it, clap your hands [clap, clap]

If you're happy and you know it, clap your hands [clap, clap]

If you're happy and you know it, then your face will surely show it

If you're happy and you know it, clap your hands [clap, clap]

We might instead sing:

If you're crabby and you know it, you can pout...

If you're angry and you know it, stamp your feet...

Feelings Book

One fun thing we do in our class, which you could do at home with your child, is to make a *Feelings Book*. We take photos of the children showing different emotions. Happy is easy. So is proud—just snap your child's picture when he's done something that was rather hard for him, such as writing his name, or getting all the way across the monkey bars.

Children like to pretend to be scared, so we have some fun, saying something like, "Oh no, here comes a scary monster!" They pretend to be scared, and we take the photo. You can also have your child pretend to be angry and sad. Or you can be a little bit ruthless, and snap a picture of your child the next time she's crying, or the next time he's having a temper tantrum. We've done that and, honestly, while you might think they wouldn't like it that you took their picture while they were feeling sad or mad, they're so egocentric that they usually find any picture of themselves fascinating. Other good emotions photos to take are worried, shy, lonely, surprised, excited, and of course, the funny picture, silly.

Tip: Make a photo book of your child's feelings.

Then, when you've got photos of all the feelings, you can make a simple book, with just the pictures and the names of each emotion. Or, you can take it one step further and ask your child what makes her angry, sad, lonely, happy and so on, and add what she says to the book.

You can create your own books on your computer and print them out yourself, or you can use one of the many websites available for custom-making books with your own photos and words. The kids in our class love looking at the Feelings Book with the pictures of themselves. As an added bonus, your own child's Feelings Book would also make a wonderful keepsake!

Claim It: Expressing Emotions

Shayla and Bianca were acting out their own story on the playground. Shayla came running up to us to explain: "She is the Nice and I'm the Mean. We are just doing it for the game."

Now that the children are getting a handle on identifying and defining various emotions, their next step is learning how to express their feelings in an acceptable way. When Benjy shrieks at Maria, "I'm feeling very furious at you!" and then wallops her, he has indeed identified his feeling, but he hasn't expressed it appropriately. You will be happy to know, though, that with your guidance your young child can learn to both name and tame his emotions.

Here is a vivid memory of Kali, a four-year-old who was having a very difficult time handling her volatile emotions at home and at school and was prone to bursts of anger, sadness and withdrawal.

We had been working with her for two years and she was trying hard to manage her emotions and just beginning to articulate her feelings. She liked using the Bear Cave when she needed to be alone, and she was proud to help others at the Stoplight for Peace. (See page 47 for a definition of the Bear Cave and page 92 for a definition of the Stoplight for Peace.)

When she arrived late one morning, the class was already in another room for a Spanish class. Kali refused to go join them, rebuffed all efforts to talk to her, and then ran away to huddle in a corner at the end of the hallway.

Keeping one eye on Kali, Tina went back down the hall to the door of our classroom. A few minutes later, Kali snuck over to the door of the Spanish classroom and sat down beside a kid-sized sculpture of a man in a sombrero, legs drawn up, arms wrapped around his legs, head and hat bowed down to his knees. Kali mimicked the pose perfectly, silently communicating: "I am feeling sad, a little sorry for myself, but I am calm now; and I'm almost ready to rejoin the class." This was a great demonstration of her increasing self-control, and managing and expressing her emotions. We love our amazing preschoolers.

What follows are some of the techniques we use for helping children express those feelings in our classroom that you can easily use at home.

Giving Children the Words

Perhaps you often say to your angry child, "Use your words." This is one of the big tasks for preschoolers, to move from expressing themselves physically to expressing themselves verbally. A one-year-old does not have the words to express his feelings, beyond "no" or "mine." A three- or four-year-old does have sufficient vocabulary to express his feelings verbally, rather than with a punch. But strong feelings of anger might overwhelm his recently-acquired language abilities. That's where we adults come in. It takes a lot of practice and repetition and help from grown-ups for many children to be able to "use their words."

We try to remember that it's progress when Joey actually stops himself from hitting the child who took his toy car and screams "That's mine!" right in his face, instead. However, once little Joey has gotten better at consistently expressing his anger verbally rather than physically, we might then coach him on how to say it less aggressively: "Joey, try telling Luis, 'I didn't like that when you took my car.'"

Direct coaching of kids works very well. A child will almost always repeat what we say in the same manner. Doing this time after time, the child finally learns how to express his anger constructively rather than destructively. We continue the coaching with the other child. "Luis, instead of grabbing the car out of Joey's hand, you can tell Joey, 'I want a turn with that car.'"

Modeling

Model a calm expression of emotions yourself. When we teachers occasionally need to express neg-

> **Developmental Asset #14:**
> Adult role models

ative feelings to the children, we use a tone of voice that matches the feeling. If we're sad about something, we tell them so, quietly. When we are angry, we use a serious voice, and the child can hear in our voice and see in our face that we are upset. But we don't yell. We don't scream at the child.

Why not, when that might be an honest expression of how we're feeling at the time? Inside our head, we might be yelling "AAARRGH!" But we need to show the child that we can manage our angry feelings and express them appropriately, which means not attacking another person, either physically or verbally. And actually, yelling is counterproductive: all you get is a defensive reaction. You get a scared child who can't hear the words you're saying; she can only hear the screaming.

Use Puppets to Demonstrate Feelings

We often use our puppets to help the children see how to appropriately express feelings. If you want to talk to your children at home about something that has happened in which they hurt each other out of anger, you may find that they pay better attention when you use puppets or stuffed animals to reenact what happened. It may engage their attention better, and it makes the starting point for the discussion a little more neutral. It's Stubby Bear screaming at and hitting Purple Bunny, and that's not very nice. It may be easier for your children to understand if they see it happening to two stuffed animal friends, rather than if you ask them about their own expression of anger. That's likely to prompt a defensive recitation of why each was justified in feeling angry and how the other one started it, and it was all his fault.

Feelings Wheel

Our Feelings Wheel is another very effective tool for helping children identify and express their feelings. It is a circle about the size of a paper plate. Around the outside are drawings of faces with different expressions:

- Happy
- Excited
- Scared or Worried
- Angry
- Sad
- Sorry

- Frustrated

- Proud

We punch a small hole in the middle and, using a brass fastener, attach a paper arrow that says "I feel" to the middle of the circle, so the arrow can turn.

We give one wheel to each child, and while we're learning about emotions, we put all the children's Feelings Wheels on the bulletin board in our room. We then practice using it, encouraging the children to go to their own Feelings Wheel and turn the arrow to show how they're feeling.

We might say something like, "You just did a hard puzzle. I bet you're feeling proud. Would like to turn the arrow to 'proud' on your Feelings Wheel?" Or, if a child says to us, "I miss my mommy," we might respond, "You look really sad about that. Would you like to turn the arrow on your Feelings Wheel to 'sad'?"

They always do. The kids really like using their personal Feelings Wheel to express their emotions. Soon, we see them going over to their Wheels on their own and turning the arrow. One day as we were in the hallway getting ready to go outside, Jayson said, "I helped Brian snap his jacket. I'm really proud of myself. I'm going to go turn my arrow to 'proud'." And into the room he went to do just that!

The Feelings Wheel is useful for children who are reluctant or unable to verbalize their feelings. For example, a child who has accidentally hurt another child may feel too upset or too guilty about it to say the words "I'm sorry," but he may be able to go to the Feelings Wheel and turn his arrow to "I feel sorry." A child who's nervous about going on a field trip the next day may not be able to explain that to his mother, but he can turn his arrow to "I feel worried."

Feelings Wheel

Eventually, the children take their Feelings Wheels home. We've heard from parents of past students that their children used their Feelings Wheels at home for years after they were done with our class! Note: for older school children, you can add a second arrow, as they are able to understand and express two emotions at once: "I'm happy that my team won, and proud that I scored the winning goal." For years Tina's children turned their Feelings

Wheels to "excited" and "worried" the night before the first day of school.

We encourage you to make a Feelings Wheel for each of your children to use in your home. You can download and print a Feelings Wheel from our website.

So, we're now helping the children to identify, understand, and express their feelings appropriately. We hope they are learning that we all feel lots of ways every day: excited, worried, shy, friendly, angry, scared, confident, contented, interested, silly... It's all part of being human.

HELPING YOUR CHILD TO EXPRESS HIS FEELINGS

- **Use direct coaching**—Give your child the words to use and give her a chance to try them out in that situation. Help her to resolve the problem peacefully.

- **Be a good model**—Express your own emotions clearly and calmly

- **Use puppets**—Let the puppets act out a similar situation and the inappropriate behaviors and your child will want to help them act more appropriately

- **Make a Feelings Wheel**—Create a wheel with your child and practice using it frequently. Soon he will want to use it to show you how he feels.

Emotional Competence

Tame It: Managing Emotions

One day, a highly-flammable five-year-old put a small, white, ornate Bible in her cubby. She went to it a couple of times during the day, telling herself: "I have to check the Good Book, to see how to be good." Pretending to read it aloud, she said, " 'Go sit on the carpet. Be quiet. Listen.' OK." Then she did.

The third leg of the emotions stool upon which children metaphorically perch, in addition to identifying and expressing feelings, is managing them. Can young children not only learn to talk about their feelings, but to deal with them? Can they learn how to get themselves out of an unhappy state and make themselves feel better?

First, we must say that there are no magic bullets here. You can't always make your child go from crying or enraged to smiling and happy with a quick trick. Nor would you necessarily want to. These negative feelings that children have, as do we all, are legitimate. It's OK, and necessary, for these emotions to be expressed and acknowledged. But eventually a person, whether a child or an adult, wants to move on and to return to a more benign state.

If she is upset about something and you want to help her to feel better, remember the power of your child's imagination and sense of humor. Sometimes we can surprise a child who is upset and angry — let's say, because Daddy didn't put the right kind of sandwich in her lunchbox — by inviting her to imagine: "Wouldn't it be fun if we had our own sandwich shop right here in our classroom, and you could make any kind of sandwich you wanted? What kind would you make today?" Suddenly, you and the other children are conjuring up fantasy sandwiches and Sophia is eating her tuna with pickles.

Of course, there is a range of negative emotions, and a range of causations for them. We are not talking here about how to deal with a severely depressed, or a chronically angry child who frequently hurts or bullies others. These children probably need professional help, and if you have such a child, we urge you to seek a referral from your physician, school, or social service agencies.

Rather, we are talking about the kinds of negative feelings that children experience every day, at school and at home: feeling sad, mad and bad. Let's look at the kinds of unpleasant feelings that children typically have in our class, and how we help them manage these feelings.

Sadness

Usually, preschoolers feel sad when they get hurt, or when someone won't let them play, or when they miss their parents. It's a rare day in the preschool classroom when no one cries. The first thing a crying child does is to seek adult comfort, which is a very good strategy for feeling better. A teacher's lap and some sympathetic words do wonders. Likewise, your tearful child seeks and receives comfort from you. What your child doesn't need at that point is dismissal of her feelings, from us or from you. When adults say, "Oh, that wasn't so bad," or when we assert, "You're OK," when clearly she is not OK at that moment, we are telling her that her feelings are wrong, or invalid.

On the other hand, if we see a child who is running on the playground trip and fall, we'll usually watch to see what she does, rather than rushing over while gushing "Oh, poor Lucy, did you get hurt?" That's a sure cue for tears from the child, where there might have been none if we'd just let her deal with it herself.

It's a natural impulse to feel sympathy for the child, but in many cases, the first tears are more in reaction to the event of falling down than to the actual injury. We often see the children looking around and checking to see if anyone noticed them fall down; if they don't spot an adult looking concerned, they may just get up and go back to playing.

If we have a child who is prone to tears over every little thing, we tend to offer brief comfort and then assure her in a very matter-of-fact way that we believe she will be feeling better very soon. We then either turn her attention to something else, or turn our own attention away, or maybe turn the situation around with a little humor.

 ## Bear Cave

When you are unhappy, do you ever just feel like being alone? Do you sometimes resent people trying to cheer you up? Do you head off to the bathroom, or go take a walk? Children feel the same way. They need a place to be quiet, to be alone, to calm down, to recharge, to get away.

We have a special place in our room for a child to use if he feels sad or bad and wants to be alone. It's called the Bear Cave. It's just a small two-foot by four-foot space between the back of a bookshelf and the wall, where we've put lots of pillows, some stuffed bears, and a poster that shows children's faces displaying different emotions.

> **Developmental Asset #31:**
> Self-regulation

It is strictly a one-person place, reserved for this purpose only. Outside the cave, there is a two-sided picture hanging on the wall. One side says "I want to be alone" and shows a sad face; the other side says "I feel better now" and shows a happy face.

The children quickly learn to use the Bear Cave appropriately. One day Marla's friends rebuffed all her efforts to play with them. She rushed off in tears to the Bear Cave, furiously turning the sign to "I want to be alone." Peeping over the top of the shelf, we saw Marla scrunched down among the pillows, clutching a stuffed bear, and talking to it tearfully about how her friends were being mean to her. Since she was also pointing to the pictures on the feelings poster, we could almost literally see her mentally working through her feelings. After ten minutes, Marla emerged from the Bear Cave, stopping to turn the sign over: "I feel better now." And she did.

The Bear Cave is a wonderful tool for helping children realize that they can be in charge of their emotions, that it is OK to be sad or angry or lonely or upset, and that they can handle these emotions. There is no time limit on how long a child can spend in the Bear Cave; when he feels ready to come out, when he feels like he has regained his emotional equilibrium, he can come out.

Think about whether you could set up a Bear Cave in your home for your children to use. Even if they have their own room to go to when they want to be alone, where they probably have several things to help themselves feel better, they might appreciate a small, cozy spot specifically designated as the place to which children in the family can go when they feel sad or angry and want to be alone, a place where they can feel sure that no one will bother them. And please remember that even little children need their space sometimes. It's natural for adults to want to rush to their child when he's upset and try to help him by asking what's wrong and talking about it, but often children can't talk when they are consumed by their feelings.

Learning how to soothe oneself is a very important part of Emotional Competence, and even young children can begin to do this. As we mentioned earlier, when we asked the kids what made them feel better when they felt sad, Mommy and Daddy ranked at the top of the list. But also high on the list were the self-soothing items: the special blanket, the pacifier, the thumb. They also listed things that took their minds off of being sad, such as looking at books or watching videos.

Separation Issues

A common cause of tears in the preschool classroom is separating from the parent at the beginning of the day. Many children don't want mom or dad to leave, and they let them know that quite clearly. Nothing is harder for a parent than to have their crying child taken out of their arms by the teacher, and to walk away as the wailing sound of "Mommy, don't go!" follows them down the hall. It's hard on everyone: parents, teachers, and children.

Of course you know, because you've been told by the teachers, that five minutes after you're gone little Julian will be smiling and happily playing with his friends. And that's true for most kids. Remember, children are very now-centered. When you're there, they really do want you to stay, so they're using their most effective means to get you to do that. Once you're gone, they soon accept the new reality and get busy playing. But that thought only helps *you* a little bit, since the last thing you see — the image that stays with you your whole day at work — is Julian weeping miserably.

What we have found to be most effective in helping the children manage the separation from their parents is establishing a routine. We ask parents to develop a routine with their child: "Remember, Julian, when we get to your class, I'm going to give you three hugs and kisses. Then I will blow you a kiss from the door. Then you can go to the window and watch for me, and I'll wave to you before I get in the car."

There are three key things here that must be followed for leave-taking to be a success, whether you're leaving your child at preschool, or at his grandparents' house, or with the babysitter in your own home. First, do not deviate from the plan. Be assured, Julian will at first cry for that fourth kiss and hug—and if you relent, the fifth and sixth and however many more he can get from you. Please be firm and cheerful, tell him you're sticking to your goodbye plan, and then do it.

Second, don't say you're leaving until you are really ready to do so. If you're dropping Julian at Grandma's, and you start the goodbye routine, but then continue chatting with your mother, this is very confusing for him. Then you have to go through the routine again, only doing it again means maybe you really aren't leaving, because you didn't the last time, so maybe he should try wailing a little louder.

Finally, be cheerful and confident in your manner. Let him know that you're confident he can do this, and that you think this is a good place for him to be. Even if you're feeling anxious inside, because you don't want to see your child unhappy, or maybe because a part of you feels guilty for leaving him, please don't let him see that. It will convey to him that you don't think it's such a good idea that you're leaving him here. And if you don't think it's a good idea, why should he?

HELPING YOUR CHILD WITH SEPARATION PROBLEMS

• Develop a consistent goodbye routine

• Leave quickly when it's time to go

• Be confident and cheerful

• Give her a picture of yourself to look at

• Ask him to draw a picture for you while you're gone

Frustration

Sometimes we adults forget what it's like to be little and to *not* understand so many things, and to *not* know how to do so many things that it seems like bigger people can do so easily, and to *not* know what's expected of you in new situations, and to *not* have people understand what you're trying to say. No wonder their little faces and little hands get bunched up into *knots* of frustration!

Think about sitting in a traffic jam. Besides annoyance, you probably feel frustration because there is nothing you can do to make the cars ahead of you move, and no apparent way for you to get out of the jam. Little kids get stuck in "traffic jams" for all sorts of reasons. We adults try to help them out of these jams in various ways.

Often we give them the words they need but can't come up with. If one child is frustrated because he can't get another child to play the way he wants to, we might suggest what he could say to his playmate to explain more clearly what he wants to do.

Sometimes we break things down for them into little steps. Young children can be overwhelmed by tasks that seem easy to adults, such as putting on socks. It's such a routine for you that you don't even think about it, but many two- and three-year-olds are confounded by socks. So we coach them through it one step at a time, demonstrating as we go.

When introducing a new skill, we show them the process and let them practice it. For example, at snack time, we have the children pour their own milk from small pitchers into their little plastic cups. But we don't just put the full pitcher and the empty cups on the table the first time and say, "Pour your milk," or we'd have milk all over the table and frustrated kids saying, "I can't do it! You pour my milk, teacher."

We first have a lesson, using water in a pitcher, with a demonstration of how to hold onto the cup while pouring so it doesn't tip over. We inject a little humor into the demonstration by pretending to get distracted and looking away while we keep pouring, so that the water flows all over the tray underneath. The gales of laughter from the kids tell us we effectively made our point. Then we let them practice.

We put a pitcher of water and a cup on a tray, to catch the overrun. Only after a few days of this do they get to pour their own milk at snack, which they do successfully. More than one parent, joining us for lunch, has been amazed that her little tot is pouring milk (from a pint-sized pitcher) with such skill and confidence.

Tip: Use pictures, demonstrations, and small steps to teach a new task to your child.

We will help the children when they get stuck on something, but only after we make sure they've really tried their "hardest, longest, and best." A little frustration is fine; too much is just aggravating. So, while we usually express confidence that they can do something if they keep trying, we also want to be realistic.

The other thing that we need to do is have patience ourselves. It takes little kids a long time to do things that they're just learning, whether it's zipping a jacket or writing their name. Please don't step in and do it for them just because they're struggling. Count to ten, then count to twenty, then turn your attention elsewhere.

Wait until they ask for help before you give it — and even then, suggest that they try again, or just give them a little help. Get the zipper started, and let them finish pulling it up. Suggest that they try turning the puzzle piece another way, rather than putting it in yourself. We know this is hard for many adults, but your patience will be rewarded with a beaming look of accomplishment.

Fear

We must respect and even appreciate children's fears. Fear is what keeps them from jumping off the top of a high slide.

Little children can have some unusual fears, and often they can't explain why something is scary to them. In general, we never dismiss children's fears, nor push them into something they're not comfortable with, such as touching a snake when the lady with the petting zoo comes to school. Instead, we will demonstrate to the child that it is OK, and even interesting, to touch the snake.

If your child is experiencing fears at home, we suggest that you use his imagination to deal with them. On our intake forms, we ask about the child's fears, and

| Developmental Asset #20: |
| Time at home |

the most common one is fear of the dark. Along with that goes fear of the monsters that your child is convinced live in his dark room.

Dismissing your child's fears of monsters with a "monsters aren't real" spiel won't help very much the next time the lights go off, because in fact monsters are very real to your child in his mind. Instead, you can ask your child what might help keep the monsters away. Deb's son, Zack, at age four, liked to sleep with a fan next to his bed to blow away the monsters. This is a good example of how competent young children can be, since he thought of this idea all by himself!

Tip: Your child's imagination is a great help in dealing with fears.

Some kids like to sleep with superhero toys next to them to help defend them. You can sprinkle magic "anti-monster" dust that you pull out of your pocket (or a can that you label Anti-Monster Dust). You can tell your child that monsters are afraid of themselves, and put a mirror next to your child's bed that will scare away the monsters when they see themselves in it. A little humor might help lighten the situation, so if you feel like hamming it up, pretend to be a scary monster who sees himself in the mirror and then runs away.

Fear of monsters and bad guys extends to the movies and videos that children watch. Just as we have found that the children cannot quite convince themselves that our puppets are *not* real, we have observed that preschoolers believe that anything they see on TV or movies *is* real.

They may say that they weren't scared, but later tell us about nightmares, fears, and concerns about something they watched at home. In our experience at school, even a movie that seems innocuous may have parts that are frightening to many young children. We know that, at home, it is sometimes convenient to let younger children watch videos with their older siblings, but we feel that only G-rated (or a few PG-rated) family movies are appropriate for preschool children. Save those thrills and chills for when they can better handle them emotionally.

Anger

Does your child need "Preschool Anger Management" class? We work hard as preschool teachers to help kids learn to manage their huge angry feelings now, so they don't grow up to be the guy who rages at his wife and his kids and his employees and who, furthermore, thinks this is normal and justifiable.

Some children have explosive tempers and really need help learning how to manage these overwhelming feelings of rage. While it may be normal to feel angry when another child takes your toy, it is not within the normal and acceptable range of behaviors to screech in that child's face, push him over, kick him, and then run around the room hitting every kid who gets in your way while knocking toys off the shelves.

If you happen to have a child who has problems with explosive rage, who is making life miserable for your family, we recommend an excellent book called *The Explosive Child: A New Approach for Understanding and Parenting Easily*

Frustrated, Chronically Inflexible Children by Dr. Ross W. Greene.

Dr. Greene offers a clear and useful explanation about how these children are not willfully disobedient. Rather, they have an inability to mentally process and deal with changes or small problems (such as finding out that their favorite shirt is in the laundry) that most people can handle.

Dr. Greene explains: "An explosive outburst—like other forms of maladaptive behavior—occurs when the cognitive demands being placed upon a person outstrip that person's capacity to respond adaptively." Or, as one of his young patients put it, it's like he has "brain lock."

Most kids can learn to tell other kids when they're angry with them, and to tell them why. This is a constructive way to deal with anger, which often leads to positive outcomes. When it doesn't, most kids can learn to manage their angry feelings in their own way, whether it's stomping off to the Bear Cave for a few minutes of alone time, or telling the other child, "You're not being nice! I'm not going to play with you!"

But for some children, instead of being able to control and manage their anger, their anger overwhelms and controls them. Every year we seem to have one or two children in the class who have frequent explosive outbursts over what seem like small problems to us. This doesn't feel any better to these children than it does to everyone else in their path. So we start from this point, believing that they want to learn to manage their anger as much as we want them to do so.

Using physical means to express themselves when anger overtakes them can be helpful for a little child. We don't mean hitting things, not even pillows. Acting in this way used to be considered helpful for an angry person, but is now recognized as just fueling the angry fire.

Rather, we use concrete physical imagery to help them express their anger by saying to them things like, "Show me how big your angry feelings are now. Are they this big (holding our hands about a foot apart) or THIS BIG (holding our hands way apart)?" Or we might say, "I wonder if you are feeling like an exploding volcano" while gesturing a volcano blowing its top. This gives them a visual picture that expresses the enormity of their feelings and how they are, at that moment, unable to control the explosion of angry feelings. Then we might add, "Pretty soon the lava is going to stop blowing out of the volcano so hard. Should we help the volcano calm down?"

Therapists at our school talk to children about their "engine." How fast is their engine running? Then they try to help the furious child slow his engine down.

We use proven and well-established coping and calming techniques with the children. It helps for you to do them *with* the child, guiding him and having him copy you, rather than just telling him what to do. These techniques include things like counting slowly to ten or twenty, pressing your hands together firmly, or pressing hard against a wall, and doing muscle relaxation work. Some children calm down when we massage their shoulders or arms with gentle deep pressure. Taking 10 deep breaths with the child seems to work especially well. If he's still upset, take ten more deep breaths.

For some children, holding their hands and jumping up and down with them while counting, breaks the hold anger has on them. Even chewing gum sometimes helps, because the rhythmic action of chewing a piece of gum often helps a child pull his whole body into a calmer, more organized state.

A child who's been overtaken by anger is in a state of deregulation. His feelings are like a river being forced over rocks in a narrow channel—wildly turbulent and unpredictable. We want to help move his emotional river into a wider, calmer channel. These techniques help the child to slow his body down and become regulated.

- **Get the child out of the situation**—We might ask the very angry child if he would like to go for a walk. By the time we've gone once around the school and are back at our classroom, he has usually calmed down quite a bit. The physical exercise of moving his whole body also helps him to feel better.
- **Be calm and quiet**—The whole time we are trying to help the child who is having an explosive outburst, we keep our own voices and body movements very calm and quiet. Yelling at an angry child only feeds into his anger and escalates it. We want to model calmness for him, and hope that this "quiet in the eye of the storm" will expand and seep into him.
- **Surprise the child**—Sometimes, it helps a child who is in the midst of an explosion for the adult to surprise him with something that breaks the cycle and takes him away from his rage just because he wasn't expecting it.

  For example, one day when Sean was having a meltdown in the hallway, lying on the floor screaming and kicking and refusing to move, Deb knelt down next to him and whispered in his ear, "Tell yourself—Sean, you will get up and walk to the room." He stopped in mid-meltdown, looked at Deb with surprise, and said loudly and firmly, "Sean, you will get up and walk to the room." Then he did.

- **Give the child some space**—Another time, Sean was screaming and fighting because he didn't want to leave the gym at the end of gym time. While another teacher took the rest of the class back to the room, Deb stayed behind. Any attempt she made to interact with Sean seemed to escalate the meltdown, so she said, "Sean, I

Emotional Competence

think you need me to leave you alone and give you some space. I'm going to go out of the gym. I'll be right here on the other side of the door. When you're ready to go, knock on the door." Keeping an ear and an eye (through the gym door window) on the situation, Deb stood on the other side of the door. About a minute later, she heard a knocking on the door. She opened the door, and Sean came out and calmly took her hand as they walked back to class. Much better than carrying a screaming, flailing child down the hallway.

- **Don't try to reason with the child** — It is important to note that we don't try to reason with the out-of-control child. The angry storm that is raging within him does not allow for rational discussion. Only when the child has calmed down can we figure out with him what went wrong and what he should do about it.

Children are unable to handle complex verbal interaction when they are in a rage. Picture their brain like a cup, and their rage like hot coffee; their rage has filled the cup to the brim, and any cream that we add (words such as "You know it was Julian's turn to have the scooter") only causes the cup to overflow.

- **Use empathy** — The only things we say to a child in the midst of an explosion are words of empathy: "I see that you're feeling really angry that you had to give the scooter to Julian. You wanted to keep using it." We don't lock horns with the child when he is in the throes of his rage.

- **Don't assert authority** — We don't need to make sure that the child understands that we're "the boss" and he must do as we say. He already knows that, and we know he knows that. It does neither of us any good at all to get into a "You will!/I won't!/You will!/I won't!" battle. If Joey is raging around the room dumping over toy buckets and knocking over chairs, it will get us nowhere to insist that he pick up the toys and chairs right now. He is not capable at this point of rational or compliant behavior.

- **Make the child responsible** — One day Cory exploded at clean-up time and dumped over a trashcan. Another child, trying to be helpful (since it was clean-up time and she was in clean-up mode) went over and picked up the can and put the trash back in it. Cory angrily dumped it over again. This happened again. Finally, we had to tell the other children, "Thank you for helping. But Cory would rather clean this up himself when he feels ready."

It was almost like the dumped-over trash can was a visual metaphor for Cory's feelings. His brain probably felt like the trash of angry feelings was spilling out of it — and he needed to express himself that way. Cory did eventually pick up the trash quite calmly, even though it didn't happen until an hour later. In this case, he was ready to be calm and rational again after he'd eaten snack. We suspected that hunger — low body fuel — might have been one contributing factor to Cory's rage, so rather than insisting that he first pick up the trash can in order to be able to get snack, we let him eat first. After snack, we reminded Cory that the trashcan still needed picking up, and he did so without any protest at all. Were we giving in to Cory? Not at all. We were working with him, understanding the state of his body and emotions, and helping him to eventually rectify his misdeeds.

Of course, we don't let raging children destroy property or hurt other people. We say firmly, "We can't let you hurt anyone or anything in our class. You may feel angry, but

> **Developmental Asset #37:**
> Personal power

you may not hurt someone else and you may not wreck the things in our class." If the raging child is hurting others or breaking things, he must be removed from the immediate vicinity.

And eventually — once the explosion has subsided — he must make amends. If he has hurt other people, we ask him to check on them to see if they are OK. If he is feeling remorseful, he may want to apologize. (See the discussion on saying you're sorry in the on Social Competence chapter on page 81.) If he has broken something, we will ask him what he thinks he can do to fix it. If he's thrown stuff all over the room, we ask him how he can fix that problem.

When the solution is chosen by him, he will feel some control of the situation and some ownership of the problem, rather than just having to go along with a solution imposed on him by adults. It is better for him to actively and constructively repair any damage he has caused. If he can't think of anything, we will then help him. He must realize that he is accountable for his destructive actions.

We will also discuss with him why he went off the deep end in the first place. Does he remember what he was thinking and feeling? ("Really mad!") How does he think the other kids felt while he was exploding like a volcano? ("Scared.") Is there a better way he could have expressed his anger? What could he have said? He may try to divert the blame to the other child ("It was all his fault! He started it!") We don't let him do that; rather, we bring it back to him. "We're talking about you and what you could have done."

Whenever possible, of course, it helps to avert the crisis before the anger explodes uncontrollably. That means keeping an eye on what that child is doing, and stepping in immediately when we see something happen that might be a trigger.

For example, one child accidentally knocks down the block tower that another child has just spent ten minutes carefully constructing. Some children happen to have easy-going temperaments, and are likely to just pick up the blocks and start over. Others, we know, are likely to go ballistic. So we quickly move to their side and put our arms around them and express our sympathy. "Oh, that's so sad that your tower got knocked over. You were working really hard on that. Would you like to ask Jimmy to help you build it back up again, or would you rather do it yourself?"

Many things can bring on emotional meltdowns, but the commonality between all emotional meltdown situations is that the young child becomes overwhelmed by her negative feelings. She is swamped, and it's up to adults to help her learn how to keep her boat afloat even in turbulent emotional waters.

Temper Tantrums

There is a difference between the emotional meltdowns that all children sometimes have and temper tantrums. We've all experienced a child falling apart emotionally because she's tired, hungry, or stressed for some reason. Adults sometimes fall apart emotionally too, for the same reasons.

Temper tantrums are motivated by the child wanting something she can't have, whether it's candy at the grocery store or staying up later to watch another TV show. Temper tantrums are aimed at adults, not other children, because it's the adults who have the power to give her what she wants. And therein lies the key: You've got the power. You can say no. You can stick with no.

HELPING YOUR CHILD COPE WITH ANGRY FEELINGS

- Use visual imagery (for example, a volcano or a storm)

- Use body-calming techniques, like deep breaths and muscle relaxation

- Use rhythmic body-regulating techniques

- Use as few words as possible during the heat of the moment

- Try to relieve the underlying factors (such as hunger or discomfort) before asking the child to clean up or remedy the effects of his out of control actions

- Use distraction and a change of scenery

While toddlers are prone to tantrums, at school we less frequently see children older than three having tantrums, because it just doesn't work for them. As teachers, we make decisions that we think are correct and then remain firm. When we tell the children they can only have two cookies at snack, we don't get children throwing a full-blown tantrum to have a third. They know that they can't. That's the rule. Preschoolers are very attuned to the idea of rules.

Generally, we are more likely to see tantrums at school when the parents are picking their children up in the evening. Here's an example: it was five o'clock, and Jolene told her mom, who had just come to pick her up, that she wanted to go to Dairy Queen. Mom said no, it was too close to dinner, and they had to go home. Jolene threw herself on the ground, kicking and screaming.

After a few minutes, we heard her mother say in an annoyed tone, "OK, but you can just have a small ice cream cone." We realized that Jolene's mom was exhausted after a hard day's work, and didn't have the emotional energy to deal with her child. But unfortunately, that meant it was likely that Jolene would be having more tantrums at pick-up time in the future.

At the beginning of the school year, sometimes a child who is used to exerting power through temper tantrums tries it on us. When Akbar got angry because we didn't let him do something he wanted to do (such as work on the computer when other children were waiting for a turn), he would grab things from other children and throw the objects across the room, then look back at us defiantly, waiting for us to say "Don't!" so he could yell "I will!" If that didn't work, he would escalate the damage, running up to another child and pushing him, again looking back at us to get our reaction.

What was most effective for us with Akbar was not allowing him to suck us into a confrontation or power struggle. We consistently, calmly, told him that we could not let him hurt other children in the room, but we didn't discuss it. Then we calmly removed him from the situation.

Tip: Don't get into an extended discussion with your tantrumming child. State your position once and be done.

We were amused, later, when Akbar ran up to the writing center, grabbed a notebook, and ran away. When he turned back to get our reaction, hoping we would chase him and try to force him to put the notebook back, Deb said calmly, "When you're done feeling angry, you can put that back on the writing table." Then she turned her attention to another child. Akbar gave her an exasperated look, stalked back to the writing center, and put the notebook back. We could almost hear him thinking, "Well, rats, that didn't work."

Temper tantrums may seem like the biggest, most difficult anger problem to solve. In fact, it's the opposite, because you, the adult, can control the outcome. If the outcome of the tantrums is that they don't work — if you stay calm, if you don't get sucked into a discussion or negotiation, if you just state clearly that the answer is no, and you don't give in — eventually there will be no tantrums!

Now we'd like to add a caveat: we know that tantrums are not easy to live with, and that they don't magically go away after a few firm stands by the parent. But with consistency and patience, they will.

Deb's son, Devin, went through a period, just before he turned three, where he had several full-blown screaming, hitting, raging tantrums every day. They were in response to anything that thwarted his will, even when we consistently stuck to the same rule: only one video per day, or, no more than two cookies. He even threw a tantrum over not being able to drive the car down the street! Clearly, logic and reason had nothing to do

> **Developmental Asset #11:**
> Family boundaries
>
> **Developmental Asset #12:**
> Boundaries in child-care and educational settings

with it, nor did they do any good in trying to quell the outbursts.

We can learn two things from this personal story.

One: parenting and family life are more complicated than school life. As Devin was approaching three, not only did the dentist insist that he had to give up the pacifier immediately, which was very traumatic for him, but Deb was also seven months pregnant with Devin's little brother. Two factors collided — extra stress, and feeling the need to assert himself and be powerful, which often is very strong at that age.

Two: It helps to take the long view. The fact is, Deb had completely forgotten about this tantrum phase that Devin went through (even though it lasted for several months, and was really stressful for all concerned at the time) until recently, when she was looking through the journal she'd kept about Devin. Happily, Devin developed into a very easy-going, laid-back child, and that's still how he is as an adult.

It helps to keep in mind, as you struggle to remain firm and consistent in the face of tantrums, that you are doing your child a favor, as well as yourself. Preschoolers know that they're little children. They don't really want to be the ones with the power in the family. They feel scared when they see that they have such power over their parents.

We're not saying you can't let preschoolers make decisions and that you have to exert your authority over them at all times. Far from it. It's fine for them to pick their own clothes to wear to school. It's great for them to decide which friends to play with and what they want to play. But many things aren't negotiable, and many decisions that you make they just have to live with, including whether to go to Dairy Queen right before dinner. You explain once why you've made this decision, and if they keep arguing, you tell them you're done talking about it. And then you are.

Self-regulation

As children move from infancy through their toddler years, and then through their preschool years, they are moving along a line from impulsiveness and a lack of self-regulation, to increasing self-control. This is part of being able to manage feelings, as well as being able to get along with other people.

Scientists call this executive function, which means the ability to stop and think, to plan and solve problems, to focus and pay attention, and to control one's behavior. Teachers try to enhance young children's executive function by doing things like playing Simon Says, clapping hands in various rhythms that children must imitate, playing "What's missing?" games, and playing games that require turn-taking and attending to what others are doing.

Anything that requires your child to stop, pay attention, and think will help him develop his executive function. Sorting tasks, especially those that require paying attention to more than one thing, are great. Jobs like unloading the dishwasher (the small spoons go here, the big spoons go there), sorting laundry, and sorting toys are wonderful.

Think of activities that require your child to wait and to pay attention to what others are doing, such as waiting to eat dinner until everyone is sitting down. Playing games in the car ("Spot the blue cars"; "I'm thinking of an animal in the ocean"; "Something in this car starts with the letter T"), rather than passively looking at videos, is helpful. On our website, we list some sites that have tips for parents to help their children increase their executive function.

Music is especially useful, both at school and at home.

Music for Self-Control

Music can be used to help a young child with his self-control. Music involves being able to calm himself, get wound up and then wind down, stop when appropriate, listen, and follow directions. These skills help form a good foundation for your child's growth toward self-control, self-help, and problem-solving.

Music is very compelling for young children. The music teachers and music therapists at our schools use simple musical and game-like techniques that you can also use to foster self-control skills. Here are a few of their ideas, which you can vary and build on. You can use these as party games for preschool children when you want to keep the group moving and laughing, but in control.

♫ Make your own music

If you have maracas, shakers, or tambourines, use those. If you don't, have fun creating maracas from empty plastic water bottles with caps. Partially fill them with sand, pebbles, or beans. Cover and test the sound. Tape the cap on securely! You can decorate them by gluing on colorful tissue paper or bits of wrapping paper and ribbons.

Using your "shakers," join your child (or children) on the floor. First have them shake the instruments loudly and quickly—to get their wiggles out—and then ask them to hold the instruments still and make them be quiet. Do it with them, gently calming the noise and motion as you cradle your own shaker.

Ask them to play *with* you as they listen to your words and do what you do. Chant, as you shake the instruments in rhythm to your words: "You shake, and shake, and shake, and STOP!" Repeat several times and give them a "great!" or "thumbs up" when they stop on cue. Next: "Raise them up and shake them high. Shake, and shake, and shake, and STOP!"

As long as the fun continues, vary the commands: shake them fast, then slow; make them loud, make them soft; tap them on your knees, shake behind your back; close your eyes and see if you can copy the rhythm. These can all be done sitting on the floor or standing up. Start on the floor, because it is easier to focus on the specific movement, and thus helps the child to stay in control.

Without realizing it, your child is learning vocabulary and concepts, listening to and responding to directions, and learning that he can use self-control (stopping or changing what he is doing, in the middle of doing something fun).

♪ Use Recorded Music

Children can develop similar skills by playing "Stop and Go" or "Music Freeze" games. Choose a good piece of music (or several). It could be classical, marching, lyrical, jazz, reggae, whatever. Explain to your child that she should move the way the music makes her feel, but she must stop and freeze like a statue or drop to the floor when the music stops.

Play the music repeatedly for a short and unpredictable time (5 to 30 seconds) and abruptly pause it. You will soon both be laughing. You might let your child do her own creative movement or suggest different ways to move: like a train, like a plane, like a boat, a bird, an elephant, a snake, a windstorm, a feather, a dancer.

Hint: In a room full of children (as in our classroom or your living room), one music teacher, Miss Michelle, asks each child to blow a big, invisible bubble and to stay inside it, so they don't pop anyone else's bubble! This is an effective way to practice self-control, awareness of personal space, and to avoid crashes.

We talk more about music in the Music Creativity section on page 287.

MUSICAL ACTIVITIES TO FOSTER SELF-CONTROL

- Make music with your child while you model, and they practice, keeping a rhythm, following your verbal directions and actions, using controlled levels of activity, and stopping on cue.

- You might also have fun, first, making the music makers.

- Using recorded music, play musical games, inviting your child (and her friends) to join in, and modeling the ability to control your actions and to stop.

- Listen and move to music of various genres, and encourage your child to move in different tempos, using all his large muscles, while still remaining in control.

Managing Difficult Temperaments

When another child gave Ronnie a toy he wanted, Ronnie was too shy to say "thank you." Instead he used sign language to convey "thank you" to the boy.

Some people see the glass as half full. Some people see the glass as half empty. And some people not only see the glass as half empty, they are also sure there's a crack in it and all the water will leak out.

If you happen to have a child whose core personality is Sunny Optimistic, enjoy it. Many children get over hurts and disappointments quickly and bounce back to their normally cheerful state. But for others, it's not quite so easy.

So far, we have talked about helping children manage those transitory emotions that come and go for all of us. But some children seem to have personality traits or temperaments that are like they're permanently stuck in one of those negative emotions.

How do we help those children who seem to be in a constant state of anxiety rather than a temporary state of fear? How do we help them when their occasional frustration at being unable to do something well enough seems to have evolved into a frequent state of dissatisfaction with themselves? For that matter, how do we help ourselves co-exist with a little person whose nickname could be "Glowering Gus"?

Again we refer you to Mary Sheedy Kurcinka's excellent book, *Raising Your Spirited Child* that we discussed back on page 14. In it she discusses kids who are *more* — more intense, more persistent, more sensitive, and so on. She not only helps us to understand these kids and to deal with them, she also, wonderfully, helps us to appreciate them.

In our classrooms, we work with children who have temperaments that just make life a little more difficult for them. Here we discuss what we do to help them, and what you can do if your child has such a temperament.

Perfectionism

Some children, like some adults, have a perfectionist streak. They may set the bar unrealistically high for what they think they should be able to accomplish, and they have a very low tolerance for frustration. These children don't want to attempt to do anything unless they can do it well.

If they're having trouble with something they can't yet do well, their frustration overwhelms them. They rip up the picture they're trying to draw, even when you think it looks pretty good. They make one mistake in writing their name on a piece of paper and throw it in the trash, even if whatever else is on the paper is fine. They're halfway through a hard puzzle when they get frustrated trying to find where one piece goes, and then suddenly throw all the pieces on the floor. They crumble into a little ball, crying with angry despair, "I can't do it! I'm no good! I'll never be able to do it!"

Children with a perfectionist streak tend to notice failures more than successes. And they have an all or nothing attitude—either something is completely good, or it's completely bad and worthless. So we try to help them see the grays, and the colors, in between the black and the white.

We try to notice small steps that they have done successfully, and to point this out to them: "Look, you got your shoelaces crossed. Making the X is the first step to tying your shoes. Good job! Give me five!" Of course, we don't go overboard and praise every little thing they do effusively. They'd see through that in a New York minute, and their trust in our opinion would plummet.

Our job is to help them understand that no one does anything perfectly when they first try it. Trying again or trying a different way is how we learn things. We tell this to them many times and in many ways. No doubt, if you have a perfectionist in the family, you've done the same. Here are some of the things that have worked for us.

We may point out to them that their daddy couldn't always drive a car; he had to learn how when he was a teenager, and it was really hard to learn, but he kept trying and trying until he got good at it. This is often a surprise to them.

We let them see that adults make mistakes, and it's no big deal. When we spill some milk, we say, "Oops, I spilled the milk. I'd better get a towel to wipe it up. No problem. Even grownups spill sometimes."

We really try to stick with the perfectionists, urging them to try again, or to keep at the task even when it's hard, rather than letting them off the hook. "I believe you can do it." Or, "That was a good try." Or maybe, "Let's look at this together. Do you think if you drew this circle a little smaller, you'd be able to fit the whole flower on the page?" Or, "Let's be creative and turn that paint drip into something new. Could it be a bee, sitting on the flower?"

When a child negates everything he's done because one little thing went wrong, we try to help him see the big picture. For example, Weston had glued at least thirty tiny mosaic squares to his paper for an art project, carefully placing them in a straight line. But it was hard work, and when a few went awry, he fell off his chair to the floor, sobbing, and insisted that it was no good and he wanted to quit.

Tina stuck with him, getting him to calm down and sit back on his chair. She pointed out to him all the mosaic squares he'd put on so carefully. "You wanted these to be in a straight line, and you did a nice job putting them on. Do you think you did a good job on these?" Weston admitted that he did. Then she asked him, "Do you want to try to move these squares that are crooked, or do you want to take them off? Or do you think they're OK the way they are?" He decided to take off the ones he didn't like. "Are you happy with your picture now?" Tina asked. Weston smiled. "Yeah." He let Tina put it on the drying rack and went off to play happily.

If you've got a little perfectionist at home, use plenty of words and actions that tell him: no one does everything perfectly all the time. It's easy to give in to his tears, and natural to feel sorry for the frustrated little guy. But tying his shoes for him the moment he says "I can't do it," or letting him give up on learning to ride a bike the first time he falls over, does him a disservice.

We adults need to keep expressing our cheerful confidence that we know he can learn to do it if he just keeps trying. Don't get into a pitched battle, though. He may need to let your words sink in. Come back to it in a few minutes, or hours, or days.

> Tip: When your child says, "I can't do it", don't jump in immediately to do it for him. Express your confidence, and have patience.

Let's face it. It's frustrating for us, and for you, dealing with perfectionist children. It's difficult to have to keep countering their negatives with positives, and it feels like an uphill battle sometimes. Plus, it's heartbreaking when they keep putting themselves down. But it is a gift we give them, these rose-colored glasses that we hope to get them to try on. Maybe, one day soon, they'll be able to see themselves a little more realistically, and a little more positively.

Shyness

Were you painfully shy as a child? If so, it may be particularly hard to watch your shy child and to feel her discomfort. We tend to want to protect our children from going through what we went through. But try to remember it's often the pressure to participate that the shy child fears most. And, on the other hand, our expectation that she won't participate can make it even harder to overcome. So how can you help?

Shyness is common in children. Many children feel overwhelmed by social situations.

We try to give the shy child time to adjust to new situations, and to become comfortable with new people. If a new child won't tell us her name, we prefer that the parent not push his shy child to start talking to us right away. We know that this child will warm up eventually. In the meantime, pushing her just makes her worry more.

When all the other children at a birthday party are happily playing and your child is still hiding behind you, refusing to answer the host mom's friendly "Hello. What's your name?" you may feel embarrassed for your child. But there is a middle ground between pushing your child to participate and doing all the talking for her. Neither pushing too hard nor babying her helps your child. Instead, you can simply say to the other mom, "Janie's feeling a little shy right now, but she'll be ready to play soon." Then quietly express your confidence to your child that she will join her friends soon, when she feels ready.

Sometimes it helps the shy child if he prepares ahead of time for whatever situation is coming up. For example, if you know he's often shy with his out-of-town grandparents when they visit, you can prepare him by showing him pictures of them, and asking them to send a letter to him telling him that they're looking forward to the visit. Prepare the grandparents as well, asking them to not take his lack of exuberance at their arrival personally. Suggest that they begin in a low-key way, perhaps by reading a special book that they bring for him.

If your child is going to be standing in front of the group at school, you can prepare him the night before. He can go over what he wants to tell his classmates with you.

You can even write it down for him and he can bring it to school. Having that piece of paper in hand, and maybe having the teacher prompt him from it, can be very reassuring. Similarly, you might prepare your daughter for a new social event, such as a birthday party. You can tell her who will be there and what they will be doing at the party. As long as you speak confidently about the event, conveying that you think it will be fun for her, this preparation should help her.

Tip: Prepare your shy or anxious child ahead of time for new social situations or events.

Shy children often feel more comfortable when they're pretending to be something or someone else. We've had a few kids who wear capes or costumes to school day after day for weeks. Parents sometimes apologize to us for that, but we're fine with it. Again, these children are using their wonderful preschool imaginations to successfully deal with their problem. So if your shy child feels better about going out in public in his Batman costume, don't worry about the looks you might get. He is literally putting on a superhero persona to help himself, and that's great!

Interestingly, some shy kids really sparkle when they get to act in a play. They're not nearly as nervous about all eyes being on them when they're pretending to be someone else. Some of the most wonderful performances we've seen in the class plays that we put on every year have been by some of

---

our shyest kids. Afterward, the parents tell us, "Wow, I can't believe she did that!" And if a child just can't face being on stage this time—even at the last minute—we offer him a role behind the scenes: prop master, scenery mover, or assistant director. And they are usually pleased and proud to do it.

Shy children often prefer to play with just one friend at a time and probably need some help in joining groups for play. (See the chapter on Social Competence.)

Shy children also need their time alone. So if we notice that Hope has been sitting apart and drawing by herself for some time, we don't necessarily push her to join other children at play. We may ask her if she'd like to, but if she says no, she just wants to draw by herself, we respect her choice.

Shy children have taught us that, with a little help (and given a little space and time) they will find a way to participate that makes them feel comfortable and confident. Letting the other children see our acceptance and confidence in the shy child helps them to accept and welcome her as well. On the other hand, if we push, and battle, and express disappointment, the other children perceive this and are likely to regard her negatively, thus increasing her reluctance to join them.

We've heard that shy people often go into teaching. That may be true, because both Deb and Tina were very shy children!

Anxiety

We all feel anxious sometimes—usually in new situations, such as the first day on the job or the first day of college. Some of us worry a lot, and some of us feel nervous about trying new things. But for some children, a heightened sense of anxiety frequently floods their minds, to the point of impeding their ability to do everyday things.

Most years, we have at least one child who becomes overwhelmed by anxiety over every change in the classroom routine and every new situation. Even things that seem routine, such as singing songs with the group, are hard for that child. It's not just shyness. In fact, some of our anxious children are not especially shy with their friends, although they may be shy with strange adults. For them, it seems to be more of a general state of extreme worry.

These kids are worried about the unknown. They're worried about doing something wrong. They're worried about bad things that can happen. They're worried about changes. And just telling them to relax doesn't help. The worries are still there.

Fortunately, we have found that there are some things we can do to help ease their anxiety.

Not surprisingly, having a set routine and sticking with it really helps these children relax. If you have an anxious or worried child, it is helpful if you follow a routine in your family life. If he goes to bed at the same time, and you follow the same bedtime routine, he feels reassured. On the other hand, if you live a somewhat variable or even chaotic lifestyle, he will be in a frequent state of anxiety. Do whatever you can to make his life more predictable.

The anxious child likes to check the daily Picture Schedule that we use in our class to show the children what's happening that day. But when he sees a star, which indicates a special activity, he does not experience the pleasant excitement that his classmates are feeling. The star induces in him a feeling of dread. Anxious children do not like changes, and they do not like surprises. So we prepare the anxious child with as much detail as possible.

After preparing him, if your child still seems anxious, ask him what he's worried about. Some of the things that small children think of would never occur to an adult. Often the anxious child will not be able to articulate why he is feeling so, and may not know himself. But we never dismiss his feelings. We respect his concern, and give him a serious answer. We try to reassure him that we believe that the thing he is worried about will be safe.

Tina remembers when her son, as a toddler, consistently refused to sit down in the bathtub, especially when she tried to make it fun with a bubble bath. For a long while, she was unable to find out why, but she never forced him to sit down when he was so afraid to do so. Eventually, she discovered that he couldn't see the lower part of his body under the bubbles, and that made him really worried.

We have noticed that many of our anxious children have also been self-conscious. In dance class, they don't dance. At group time, they don't sing. Or if they do, it's very quietly, and only the really familiar songs, and almost never with gestures. Everyone else's Itsy Bitsy Spider may be climbing up the waterspout, but not theirs. We assume that this is because they're nervous about doing something wrong and having people see them, because occasionally they will loosen up a little and join in the song movements, until they catch us looking at them. Then they freeze up. So we try to give them ways to feel more comfortable, such as singing from the back of the group, or dancing with a pretend partner if they don't want to have a real one.

Sometimes children invent or adopt their own coping technique. Children who are highly anxious are sometimes helped by having a talisman—something concrete and re-assuring that they can hold onto: a small stuffed animal, a tiny plastic fairy, even a special rock—whatever makes them feel more confident in the face of the unknown.

Tip: A talisman or a special saying can help relieve a child's anxiety and give him confidence.

Some children like to share their worries with one of our puppet friends. Some children use special words to boost their courage. We had one very anxious child whose parents told him to say "I'm as brave as a dinosaur" over and over when he felt nervous. This really helped him.

Giving an anxious child some control over the situation also helps. One child became completely unnerved about

> **Developmental Asset #37:**
> Personal power

having the job of Line Leader, to the point of falling on the floor clutching his leg and saying it was broken so he couldn't be the line leader. We consulted with one of the therapists at our school, and she gave us an excellent idea.

The next time his name came up on the job chart to be Line Leader, we told him he was in charge and could choose how the kids would walk down the hallway. "How would you like them to walk?" we asked. "Hmm," he said thoughtfully. "How about backwards?" When it was time to go to the gym, he strode confidently to the front of the line, and we said, "DeMarcus has decided we'll walk backwards today." The kids loved it, and the problem for DeMarcus was solved!

In general, whether you are dealing with anxiety, perfectionism, or any other temperamental trait that makes life more difficult for your children, do your best to acknowledge their concerns, while helping them to find their own personal ways to cope and make life a little easier for them.

4

Social Competence

> *One little girl was overheard confiding to another, "In sixteen days is my wedding, don't tell all my friends."*

Perhaps you went to an Early Childhood parenting class and you nodded in agreement as the facilitator said, "Don't think of your child as a reflection of yourself," but it's hard not to. Really, we wish that we could claim "that's not my child" when our son whacks the little girl next to him in the sandbox (while we are getting acquainted with her mother), or when our daughter imperiously demands "give me my dessert" in the middle of dinner with Uncle Henry. When she is the one child in the gymnastics class who keeps pushing in front of others to get her next turn on the balance beam, prompting the instructor to tell her to go to the back of the line, it's hard not to cringe and take it personally.

We wonder how our child will ever find friends when she fights with the classmate we invited for a play date. We fear she will be sent home from kindergarten when she tells the teacher "I won't do that!" We cringe when she whines, "That's not fair!"

Learning the social skills we all need to become an enjoyable friend, a cooperative student, a good host, a collaborative worker, and an effective leader, is a task lasting well into adulthood. But, as you know, it begins in toddlerhood and is a primary focus in the preschool years.

Social competence is foremost in the minds of parents and teachers. Many parents list "learning social skills" or "making new friends" as their priority for their child on the preschool admission form. Social competence is a complex set of skills that have as their core being able to interact successfully with other people. For young children this includes learning how to:

- Pay attention to others' feelings and needs

- Enter into an on-going play situation

- Invite others to play (which does not come naturally to all children)

Social competence is something that must be practiced and learned. As children approach kindergarten (and especially if they are at the younger end of the age range for starting kindergarten), many parents and teachers debate whether the child has the emotional and social competence necessary to be successful.

Let's start with the topic that always seems the most urgent: resolving conflicts.

Conflict Resolution

> *Two children grabbed a shiny red car at the same time, and neither would give it up, both asserting, "I had it first." Finally Xavier stated firmly, "If you don't give it to me, you can't come to my birthday party." Daniel burst into tears, sobbing, "Xavier says I can't come to his birthday party!"*

Conflict is a normal part of life. It's certainly a normal part of childhood. Conflicts occur anywhere two or more human beings are gathered. Learning to manage them is a part of childhood, too. The issue, at home and at school, is how to resolve the conflicts that are inevitably going to occur.

At the preschool level, conflicts are pretty basic. More than 50 percent of the time, they're about possessions: You've got something I want. They also occur over social interactions: you want to play something that I don't want to, or you won't let me play at all. These friendship issues will be further discussed later in this chapter.

As soon as a toddler comes in contact with another toddler (or a sibling) the question of possession leads to conflicts. "Mine!" is the universal cry of two-year-olds. Before she has words, all she can do is hold on tightly, grab it back, yell, cry, or even bite.

This pattern is so well established that—even after she becomes more verbal—grabbing or hitting is, for a time, the primary response. It's simple for us to say, "Use your words!" but this reminder is only helpful to the child if she knows the words to use; if she has evidence that this will be effective; and if she has the maturity and temperament to stay calm enough to use the words before one or the other of the children takes a swipe.

If you are spending much of your time trying to mediate conflicts or feel as though you are going over the same ground again and again, rest assured that we do too. Children learn some things lightning fast, but when their emotions and self-interest get in the way, their impulsive response kicks in first (well, that's true for almost all of us).

Yet we can expect that our children sometimes — and with increasing frequency — will use words to avoid and resolve conflicts. But first we have to give them the tools. What "tools" are we talking about?

Giving Children the Tools

Teachers have some good techniques to help children learn to resolve conflicts peacefully, such that all parties are satisfied. Young children don't necessarily care whether the other party feels satisfied, but that's something else we try to teach — to care about the others in your environment. You will see, as we describe them, that you can use these techniques at home as well.

Most teachers use direct coaching, as we do in helping children learn how to express their emotions appropriately. We tell each child in the situation what he can say to the other. So when your son's friend yanks a toy right out of his hand and a wrestling match ensues, after you break up the fight, you can say to your child, "Tell Bobby: I don't like it when you grab stuff from me." As you say this, demonstrate the strong, firm voice he can use. Hopefully, your son will then say this to his friend.

Developmental Asset #36:
Peaceful conflict resolution

Tip: Don't expect your child to know what those words are when you say "Use your words." At first, you will need to give the words to her.

We are impressed with how often we overhear one child say "I don't like it when you..." to another child at school. Clearly, after repeated coaching by all teachers at our school, many children really do learn to "use their words" in a positive, assertive manner.

Let the Puppets Help You

Other times, we use an indirect approach, doing short, impromptu puppet shows — little "morality plays" for the young set — dramatically enacting what happens when one puppet grabs a toy from another. In an instant, the children are drawn in, wanting to stop the puppets from arguing.

For the youngest children, we might just suggest a solution and have the puppets agree, shake hands, and go off to play. But most of the time we solicit opinions from our young audience on how the puppets could have resolved their dispute. Amazingly, even the children who tend to grab and hit will tell the puppets: "Don't fight. You have to share," or "Use your words!"

At home, you will probably find this fun and effective, too. If you don't have puppets, two soft dolls or stuffed animals work as well. If you want to portray a recent dispute your child has been in, change the source of the argument slightly so it doesn't hit too close for home, substituting a refusal to eat spaghetti for an argument over scrambled eggs, for example.

Let the argument between the puppets keep going until your child (or you) tries to stop them. Ask your child what they should do. Then ask the puppets if that will work. Sometimes the puppets can say "no" and start arguing again, so that you can come up with another option.

By the way, sometimes a child protests that "It's just *you* talking," and we reply "It's my voice, but [name of puppet] is talking." That often satisfies.

Use Sign Language

Sign language is an effective conflict resolution tool for both children and adults. For the teacher or parent, it's a great way to get the kids' attention, visibly showing what you're trying to say quickly and without having to yell over their yelling. The sign for "WAIT" is useful, as is the sign for "STOP."

Another useful sign when conflicts become verbally heated and kids are screaming is the one for "TOO LOUD." The accompanying facial expressions really convey their whole message clearly. Children also like to use these signs with each other. Kids who misbehave when their senses get overloaded (a common problem) find it useful to show us with the "too loud" sign. In Appendix B, we include pictures of these and a few other signs that we, and the children, find useful. On our website, we give you links to basic sign language sites, as well.

Good Choices Cards™

When children are having a dispute over using the same toy, we can help them to see some alternatives by using our pictorial Good Choices Cards, which depict various ways they can resolve the conflict. This is especially useful for children who still have limited vocabulary and language skills, but works well with verbal children, too. How does this work?

A picture is worth a thousand words, especially when two children are too upset or too locked into a verbal battle to process those reasonable but complex

> **Developmental Asset #15:**
> Positive peer relations
>
> **Developmental Asset #32:**
> Planning & decision-making

explanations you want to give. Seeing their own situation in simple stick-figure (and therefore neutral) drawings allows them to switch gears and to see the situation from the outside. Consider this example from our classroom.

Ty and Charley have been working hard at making race cars with LEGOs® so they can use them on the big ramp they have been building with blocks. Finally, Ty makes a really cool car. He has used all the good wheels and connected them so they are staying together. Charley is frustrated because his keeps falling apart and now he wants to use Ty's car. Ty is proud and possessive of his creation and says "NO!" It is late afternoon, when both are tired, and very quickly the two of them are at a standoff over the car. Charley is begging and sobbing, while Ty is repeating, "It's my car!" and looking like he is going to cry too.

This is what we did. Tina approached them and said, "You are both very unhappy. What is the problem?" Ty replied defensively "I made this car and he wants it." She realized that explaining to Charley that Ty made the car and is not ready to share it, or expecting Ty to let Charley use it with the risk that it will fall apart as he sends it down the ramp, would not go over well. Tina took their hands and said, "I want you to see something. Come with me. You can bring the car." She brought them with her to get the set of cards we keep on a ring, and then they all sat down at a table.

Tina read the top card: "Two children want the same toy. What should they do?" (Here is a problem for Ty and

Charley to help solve – it does not say: "What should *you* do?") She flipped to the next card: a stick-figure drawing of two children with angry expressions both pulling on a toy truck. "They don't look very happy to me," Tina said. "Why not?" "They both want the truck," the boys replied. Tina showed them the next card: stick figures of the two children each playing with an identical truck. "We don't have two cars that are like this one (indicating Ty's car), so you can't both have one," Tina commented. "No," they agreed.

She flipped to the next card: The stick figures were smiling and playing together with one truck. "Do you think you could play with it together?" "No," they agreed. But Ty immediately suggested, "We could get the timer and take turns." "That's on the next card," Tina said, showing them the picture of one child playing with the truck, with a clock on the wall, while the other child stood nearby. Charley got up and brought the five-minute sand timer back to the table, and Ty said, "You can use the car until the sand runs out, then you have to give it to me."

Taking their minds off the battle and focusing on solving the problem in the pictures allowed Charley to stop crying and Ty to let go of his concerns over his car. Making the decision themselves, rather than having the solution imposed on them by an adult, left both children feeling satisfied.

If Ty had still been unwilling to give Charley a turn, we would have gone on to the next two cards. One shows the two children working on a puzzle together, with the truck on a shelf behind them. The other shows the two children playing separately, with two different toys, with the truck on a shelf behind them. We would have cycled through the choices once more until the children chose a solution, or Tina would then have put the cards down and asked, "Well then, can you think of another idea that everyone can be happy with?"

If they were not already both smiling as they walked away, we would suggest to the happier one, that he thank the other one for whatever he gave in on and ask them to shake hands because they found a solution and are still friends. After using the cards once or twice, some children will want to refer to them each time to choose a solution. Others may file the solutions in their heads and just need to be prompted to "make a good choice so you both will be happy."

You can download and print your own copy of the Good Choices Cards from our website.

KEY ELEMENTS THAT MAKE THE GOOD CHOICES CARDS™ WORK

- No assignment (or even discussion) of blame about who started it or who is wrong

- Pictures are neutral – stick figures could be any child and the situation is a familiar one

- The adult can ask questions in a neutral way, allowing the children to respond to the situation and come to their own conclusions

- Children have a sense of control

- While the children feel that they have solved their own problem, in almost all cases, they have made a choice that is acceptable to the adult

---

Visual Timers

When we suggest taking turns for five minutes that's because five (or sometimes 10) minutes is about as long as one child can remember that his turn is limited, and about as long as the other can wait.

We use a large five-minute sand timer so that the children can monitor their own turns, and because it is a visual, concrete way to track the time. Other classrooms use a visual timer that shows a red area that gradually gets smaller as the time goes down. Sand timers and electronic visual timers can be found at teacher supply stores or online.

We like using a visual timer better than a standard kitchen buzzer because it is a gentle and silent reminder rather than an insistent buzzer, and the end of the time doesn't come as a surprise, since the children can easily watch the time counting down. Furthermore, it keeps us from being the enforcer—the timer is the arbitrator. Invest in a visual timer. It will pay you back in five minutes.

Not all disputes, of course, are about who wants what or who had it first. Sometimes it's hard to know just what the trouble is about. In fact, it's important to remind ourselves: Don't assume that we know what's up!

One day, it looked like a fight was brewing over a toy horse. Oliver was yelling and crying. Tina asked him why. "Lili says it's a horse! It's not a horse; it's a Bucking Bronco!" Oliver insisted. Aha! After Tina calmly explained that a bucking bronco is "a kind of horse," Oliver calmed down and both children felt redeemed. And we were reminded to stop and listen before trying to resolve a dispute.

- **STOP** (both children and adults need to pause and take a breath)

- **LISTEN** to each of the children

- **REFLECT** their concerns back to them. (Tell them what you are hearing them say, without making a judgment.)

- **COACH** the children in finding a solution

Here is another example of how, like many preschool teachers, we use a careful process when we step in to help with a problem.

Nadia and Chelsea were doing a puzzle together. Suddenly, they were both screeching and Chelsea was trying to pull a puzzle piece out of Nadia's hand.

Keeping the four steps in mind, Tina approached them calmly. Using the simple ASL hand sign for "stop," she simultaneously signed and said: "Please stop." She put her hands on top of both of their (still grabbing) hands.

To take their attention off the puzzle piece in question, Tina said, "Look at me and take a deep breath." After she had their attention, she said, "It looks like you are having a problem," at which point they both started to yell about who did what. Tina asked them to speak one at a time. After listening, Tina reflected their concerns back to them. "OK, it sounds like you both want to put that piece into the puzzle. Now how can you solve this?" At this point, they began asserting their own rights again.

"Stop," Tina said and signed it once again. "I think it's time to go to the Stoplight for Peace."

Stoplight for Peace

We developed the idea of the Stoplight for Peace based on an idea from *The Optimistic Classroom: Creative Ways to Give Children Hope*, by Deborah Hewitt and Sandra Heidemann. It is nothing more than a two-foot-long strip of

---

Developmental Asset #36:
Peaceful conflict resolution

---

black paper with a red circle at the top, a yellow circle in the middle, and a green circle at the bottom. We made it more important-looking with the title *Stoplight for Peace* at the top and some glitter on the three circles. It's a very effective tool for conflict resolution. As you might imagine, the stoplight colors have meanings:

- **RED:** means STOP (fighting, shouting, crying) and TAKE A DEEP BREATH

- **YELLOW:** means LOOK at and LISTEN to each other

- **GREEN:** means GO. When they have found a solution, they may leave the Stoplight for Peace and go back to playing, hopefully in a much calmer and happier state

First, one child talks (without shouting) about how she sees the problem. The other listens, without interrupting, and then the second child talks. They continue talking until they come up with a solution. The adult may offer some alternatives to help move the conversation along— impartially. But the conflict must be resolved by the children. Eventually, no adult is needed!

Our Stoplight for Peace hangs on the back wall of the classroom. Let's go there now with Chelsea and Nadia. They are not yet veterans of this method, so Tina talks them through the steps.

We need to wait patiently, as we expect them to do, while they each express their interpretation and feelings. Often, we are surprised by an alternative solution that they suggest. Chelsea offers, "I could put it in the puzzle and take it out again so you can put it in." Interesting idea, isn't it? Our adult mind thinks the process is done when the puzzle piece is placed in, so this solution would never even occur to us!

When they seem to be in basic agreement, Tina asks: "Are you ready to GO now?" Yes, they happily nod. To cement the idea that they have together worked out a good solution, we ask them to shake hands or to thank each other.

The Stoplight is another concrete and visual symbol — a place to go, away from the scene of the conflict, and a symbol of the steps to take in resolving the conflict. This is something you can also try at home.

Are you thinking that the contentious siblings at your house would never do this? It will take some practice, like all new skills, and you'll have to help at first.

Are you thinking that this was a very long solution to a very simple problem? It will take some time to lay the groundwork, and you may have to facilitate their efforts from time to time, but you'll be surprised how quickly the children catch on, and how satisfied they feel afterwards.

Your reward will be the day that your child makes the suggestion to go to the Stoplight for Peace, and your warring children walk away minutes later, smiling at having found their own solution! It might not be the solution you would have chosen, or even the one that you think is fairest.

But that's OK! It's *their* conflict, so it's best if it's *their* solution.

To make your own Stoplight for Peace to use at home, either print out a photo of a stoplight, or cut out 3 circles from red, yellow and green paper. Glue them onto a strip of black paper. Print out these words to paste on the circles:

- RED—stop and take a big breath

- YELLOW—look at and listen to each other

- GREEN—when you find a solution, go

Let the Children Find the Solution

As our story of Nadia and Chelsea shows, we are often surprised by the solutions children suggest, and how calmly they

> **Developmental Asset #37:**
> Personal power

agree on one. Because of this, in a dispute between children, we try not to insist that they choose one of our options (although we do sometimes limit their options when it is important that they comply with our requests). They gain much more satisfaction, and competence, by coming to an agreement on their own. It allows them, also, to save face.

One of our colleagues gave us a tip: When children come up with ideas on how to resolve conflicts, she writes their ideas down and posts them on the wall. That way they see that they are capable of finding solutions, and they have ownership of the solution. This is a good idea that you can also use at home.

Tip: It is best when children come up with their own solutions to conflict.

We have been surprised by the children's own solutions so many times that we would like to share some of the stories with you that demonstrate the different ways young children use their own strengths and competence to solve their problems:

- **Imaginative reasoning**—Jayden didn't want to share a big dinosaur and two little ones he had been playing with. "These babies need a mom," he objected. Deb told him that class rules said that everyone who wanted one could have a turn, so he would have to relinquish them in five minutes. A minute later, Jayden gave the big dino to Tory, saying, "They're grown up now. They don't need their mom anymore."

  We have noticed that once a child makes the decision that she will share a toy, often she hands it over much sooner than the agreed-upon time. This is because of the young child's now-centered thinking process. The new reality that she has agreed to becomes the now reality in her mind.

- **Good compromise**—Erin and Analise were working out a dispute at the Stoplight for Peace over a doll with a wheelchair. Analise currently had the doll and wanted to play with it first. Both acknowledged that Erin had picked it up first. Analise, trying to convince Erin to go second, said: "Second is more better than first. First is the worst, that's what I say." Erin countered: "Well, I want it back." Analise: "Then I'll put the baby in and you drive it. Can I have it after you?" Erin: "Yes."

- **Choosing a new way to play** — Tess and Lamar were arguing over a Beanie Baby® toy they each wanted exclusively. After calming down at the Stoplight for Peace, Lamar suggested that they share it by throwing it to each other. We reminded them to throw it gently, and watched them go happily off to play catch.

- **Face-saving justification** — Vanessa and Janie were fighting over a play camera and who had it first. Janie insisted she had put it down and Vanessa had taken it. Rather than admitting she had taken the camera that Janie had put down, Vanessa gave the camera back to Janie, explaining: "We don't need it because we're working with tools and it's not a tool." Vanessa had just cleverly defined the camera as "not a tool" so she could justify not needing it.

Saving Face

The International Online Training Program On Intractable Conflict defined face-saving like this:

Face saving (or saving face) refers to maintaining a good self-image. People who are involved in a conflict and secretly know they are wrong will often not admit that they are wrong because they don't want to admit they made a mistake. They therefore continue the conflict, just to avoid the embarrassment of looking bad.

To avoid this problem, it is important to allow one's opponents to make concessions gracefully, without having to admit that they made a mistake or backed down.

Adults (not to mention national governments) prefer to resolve conflicts in a face-saving way, rather than by giving in to someone else's demands. So do children.

Even very young children learn to avoid admitting mistakes. Helping children to solve a situation without directly admitting their fault can often be a fairly simple way to break through a standoff.

We often use our puppet, Gabby, to help the child save face. "Let's ask Gabby what she thinks." We get Gabby and ask her: "What would you do, Gabby, if your friends' beautiful castle got knocked over?" "I would help them build it back up," Gabby replies. The offending child can now say, "Do you want me to help you build it up again?" without having to admit that he caused the collapse.

Here's another example. Abby's special rock disappears from her cubby. (Or at your home, it might have disappeared from Abby's room). She starts to accuse another student (or at home, a sibling) of taking it. We say, "Let's give it a little time to come back. Maybe a kind person or invisible fairy will put it back before naptime." That calms Abby for now.

After a short while, if it hasn't reappeared we'll quietly say, to no one in particular, "I think that kind person or invisible fairy is thinking about putting the special rock back now." Then we engage the children in a quiet activity away from the scene of the crime. If it doesn't reappear, it may be that Abby just lost it and she'll have to accept that. If it does reappear, the "borrower" will have saved face.

Dealing with the Guilty Party

While children get caught up in accusations and blaming, we emphasize solving the problem rather than assigning guilt. Sometimes, we even allow the clearly guilty party to rectify his mistake without having to publicly admit guilt. But perhaps you are thinking that it's not right for the guilty one to get off scot-free, especially when the conflict escalates to serious name-calling or physical violence. We agree that children should take responsibility for their actions. But the question is, what is the role of the adult—teacher or parent—when stepping into children's disputes?

Tip: Let your child know that the objective is to solve the problem, rather than to determine guilt.

Let's take a look at a scenario that might occur at home between siblings, to see why determining guilt is not the primary objective of the adult.

Robbie is pulling Julie's hair again, and Julie is whining and tattling, and Robbie's cries of "She started it!" are making you want to tear out your own hair. You were busy elsewhere and didn't see it start. As soon as you enter the "combat arena," both Robbie and Julie try to out-yell the other as they list their sibling's grievous wrong-doings: "He called me a poopybutt!" "She stuck her tongue out at me!" and on and on. You sigh wearily; you've got no idea who started it or who is more at fault.

So, here's the good news: It doesn't matter, because the adult's role in these situations is not to be the judge and jury, determining guilt and innocence and then meting out justice. We try to think of ourselves as mediators. Even in real life situations involving adults, such as disputes between neighbors, it's better if a mediator can help the two parties resolve their problem to their mutual satisfaction, rather than taking it to a lawsuit that determines which is the guilty party, thus leaving the neighbors forever alienated.

Of course, we have to break up the fight if they don't stop when we enter the scene. Robbie can't keep pulling Julie's hair, and Julie has to stop kicking Robbie.

But once things have settled down, we turn aside all pleas of guilt and innocence with the statement, "You are both involved in this dispute. It doesn't matter at this point who started it. What matters is getting it resolved." "But," responds Julie indignantly, "He called me a baby!" So, we remind them that name-calling hurts people's feelings and is not allowed. And then we get back to the business of helping them to talk it out and figure out solutions for the future.

Here's an example that occurred on the playground: five-year-old Robert hit his friend Kirsten, who came running to the teacher, crying. Robert followed close behind, saying "She keeps putting sand back in the hole I'm digging!"

We think we may have seen the start of this conflict, but even if we did, there may be a longer history leading up to the outburst. We may know that, typically, one of the children tends to be the aggressor. But is the quieter victim also good at provoking an attack? If we agree to assign blame, the other child takes that as reason to absolve himself or herself of any responsibility or, worse, to gloat. It is natural for the child or children involved to avoid the admission of guilt, especially when they know there will be negative consequences. The instinct for self-preservation is strong, and children will avoid admitting their part.

Instead, our message is: "Your actions are inappropriate. They are not helping to solve the problem. Let's figure out how to solve it so you are both happy." (Aside: "Appropriate" and "inappropriate" are big words that little kids are proud to learn, and soon use themselves.)

Since there was hitting (with a sand shovel!) involved, we attend to the immediate physical injury, if there is one. As soon as possible we ask, with both children present, one or more of the following questions, always leaving time for the children to think, and then respond:

- "I see Kirsten is crying. How is she feeling? Can you ask her?"

- "Is it OK to hurt someone?"

- "What is a better way to show or tell someone that you are angry?"

- "What can you *say* so she knows what you want her to stop doing?" This is a good question to ask all children involved, because each child should be empowered to tell the other what they don't like.

Here is a reminder of words you can teach your child to use to avert a brewing conflict. You may recall that these are the same phrases we taught them when learning to express their feelings in the Emotional Competence chapter.

PHRASES WE ENCOURAGE THE CHILDREN TO SAY WHEN HAVING A CONFLICT INCLUDE:

- "Stop. I don't like it when you do that."

- "Stop. You are hurting me."

- "No! I am NOT a _____." (in cases of name-calling)

- "I'm not done using this yet. You can have this when I'm done."

Even when we do witness a conflict, there is no point in assigning blame publicly. If one or both was clearly deliberate in hurting the other child, we will di-

> **Developmental Asset #16:**
> Positive expectation
>
> **Developmental Asset #36:**
> Peaceful conflict resolution

rect them to sit, a short distance apart from the action, to calm their bodies down. A few minutes later, we will ask them privately (or provide suggestions) about what they could have done differently and should do differently the next time. We may express empathy for their feelings.

The children come to know that we respect them, even though they behaved inappropriately, by letting them know that we'll listen, letting them save face, and gently helping them arrive at good solution. This allows them to feel safe enough to own up to their responsibility, at least to themselves.

When children habitually deny all responsibility and instead blame someone else, we have visions of the adult they could become: blaming their boss, their spouse, and their kids for all of their problems and mistakes. Of course, they aren't even in kindergarten yet, but we believe that we have a responsibility to plant the seeds of responsible behavior at a time when they can become deeply rooted and start to grow.

Tip: Children can more easily learn to take responsibility for their actions if they are not put on the defensive.

So take a deep breath and a step back. Not having to be the judge is a huge benefit for you as a parent, and an even bigger benefit for your children. This way, there are no "winners" and therefore no "losers": no triumphant child gloating over the defeated sibling; no feelings of sibling rivalry when mom or dad deems one child righteous and one child guilty.

Always, our goal as teachers and your goal as parents is for the children in our care, or our family, to view one another as allies, friends and compatriots. This is much more likely when we don't encourage them to establish positions as rivals.

RESOLVING CONFLICTS

Our goal is to help the children resolve their own conflicts (not to prevent them entirely). To do that, we must:

- Give them the tools to use: Good Choices Cards; sign language; visual timers; Stoplight for Peace

- Give them the words to use to express their feelings and their choices

- Coach them on how to use these words and tools

- Allow them to save face

- Work on the solutions, rather than determining guilt

- Show confidence in their ability to solve the problem

Children can learn that their actions have consequences, that they can affect their own happiness and that of others, and that they can contribute to having a peaceful classroom, or a peaceful home. They can come to understand the consequences of their actions, and learn that there is more than one side to a disagreement. Not all at once of course, and probably not today, but they will. These are critical components of Social Competence.

Establishing a Positive Social Environment

> *The children were working as a group, coming up with a long list of possible rules for the class. After about 15 rules like, "No hitting" and "No throwing toys," sweet little Marcie raised her hand. In her high-pitched voice, she offered, "No cutting off people's fingers."*

Let's start with a few rules. No one likes to be told that they've broken a rule they didn't know existed. Four- and five-year-olds are at a stage where they're very rule-oriented. Rules are rules, and they like to know what the rules are. "It's the rule" carries a lot of weight with a preschooler.

Developmental Asset #2:
Positive family communication

Developmental Asset #5:
Caring climate in childcare & educational settings

It will help your household function more smoothly if you discuss and create family rules that everyone agrees on. You can also add rules that you as parents think are important, such as "only one hour of TV per day."

We as teachers also must impose some rules that the children would never come up with on their own, such as "walk in the hallways." We try to keep the list of rules short so the children can remember them. The kids make a lot of suggestions—mostly "don'ts." "Don't hit. Don't run. Don't be mean." We help them boil it down to a few *positive* rules: let's say what we *should* do, instead of what we should not.

Let's create a set of rules that will help create a peaceful and happy environment, whether at home or at school, and explore in more depth where each rule leads us. For example:

We Share

How often have you had to say, "You need to share"? Pretty frustrating, isn't it? Well, children can learn to share, and they can also learn to do it willingly (most of the time). But not just because we tell them so. Remember the Good Choices Cards we described earlier in the chapter? They work because they are a visual reminder of some options, rather than a verbal command to "share." We want children to learn to voluntarily share with one another because this is an important social skill. Children who share toys in a welcoming way with their peers are more likely to have friends who like them. Children who hoard toys are often resented.

When we tell a child to share, many children believe that they have to give up whatever they have immediately (which may make them cry, hold on ferociously, or give up their turn altogether). The other child, also believing

> **Developmental Asset #33:**
> Interpersonal Skills

that "share" really means "relinquish," demands that his friend give the item in question to him right now.

To increase children's willingness to share, it is important that they feel fairly treated, and therefore it is important to talk about what sharing means. Here's how what we do in the classroom translates into what you can do at home.

Toys at school are for the whole class, and therefore everyone is allowed to use them. At home, you will have some family toys for all the children to share, probably kept in a common playroom. A good idea, at holidays, is to give some group gifts for all the kids in the family to share, such as large block sets, pretend housekeeping toys, and dress-up clothes. This fosters sibling play and lessens the "me-first, me-only" mentality.

Toys brought to school from home should either be kept in the child's backpack or cubby, or the child should be willing to share them with everyone. One teacher uses "treasure boxes" where children can keep a special object they brought to show, but not share, safely. At home, children may keep their own personal toys in their own room or on their own designated shelves in a shared bedroom. Each child may decide whether to take out and share those toys with siblings or not. If an older child feels that a younger sibling is interfering with, or breaking, his toys, you can suggest that he play with it when the other child is napping, or when you have time to occupy the sibling with something else.

In our class, if the toy, object, or computer, is wanted by several children, a reasonable five- or ten-minute limit is imposed, and a visual timer is used.

And now an important caveat to what we just said: Children should not *always* have to share. If they want to work on a puzzle or project alone, they should sometimes be allowed to do that. We would be denying the children the satisfaction and pride that comes from accomplishing something all by oneself if they always had to work with others.

Further, a child may have a particular vision in mind when creating something, and he may not want to have another child come into his project midway and change it.

Finally, sometimes we let the child's individual work remain for a time even after she's done. If Annie has created an amazing structure out of blocks that she is very proud of, it's not very respectful to tell her, "Now that you're done, Susie can use those blocks." At which point, Susie knocks down the wonderful structure that Annie worked so hard to build. So, maybe we should amend the first rule to: "We usually share."

Take a Photo

Cameras are a wonderful tool for fostering sharing when a child doesn't want to give up something she's worked hard on, or that she likes. In the above example, when it's time to let someone else use those blocks, if Annie is still reluctant, we will take a photo of Annie standing proudly next to her structure. Then, she usually doesn't mind if someone else knocks it down and starts building anew, since it has been preserved photographically. Likewise, if your daughter has transformed herself into a princess with all the fabulous items in the dress-up box in the kids' playroom and doesn't want to let her sister have a turn with the gown and the crown, the jewels and glittery shoes—take her photo as the beautiful princess.

We Treat Each Other Fairly

Does your child frequently wail, "It's not faair!"?

In our view, fair does not always mean equal. Let's say it's time for music and we are distributing various percussion instruments. When one child objects to what he was handed, the children will often chorus: "You get what you get and you don't get upset!" Of course, sometimes one child gets to do something special for a good rea-

> **Developmental Asset #28:**
> Integrity

son. If it's someone's birthday, she gets two jobs that day — leading the line, and putting the birthday cake sticker on the sticker chart. If a child needs a few extra column blocks to hold up the bridge she's constructing, we might ask another child to give some up.

Fair means:

- You get what you need most of the time

- Sometimes you give something up

- Other times you get something extra

We always try to make sure that the children understand this reasoning. With some simple explanations, and after they, too, have had a turn at receiving a privilege, we find that the children support this idea.

Fair doesn't mean that each child is treated exactly the same.

In our classrooms, for example, if a child wears leg braces, she might sit in a chair at circle time even though everyone else has to sit on the floor.

In families, older children get privileges and responsibilities that younger children don't — later bedtimes, PG movies, time spent with Dad working on homework. What is fair is that the younger children will also have these rights and privileges when they get older.

Preschoolers, being now-oriented and self-centered, have a harder time understanding that. So, if one child is getting a lot of something—attention, gifts, and so on—it can be helpful to give the other children a little something, too. Deb's husband came up with the idea of giving the other two siblings a small present on their brother's birthday. Each time, we said "Congratulations on having a great brother like Devin (Zack, Alex)." They all loved this tradition!

Tip: On each of your children's birthdays, give your other children a little gift as well.

WHAT WE MEAN BY "FAIRNESS"

- Fair does not always mean equal.

- Fair means that you get what you need most of the time, and that sometimes you give something up, and other times you get something extra.

- "You get what you get and you don't get upset."

- Children deserve, and will respect, a simple, matter-of-fact explanation of a special circumstance. It is helpful if they, too, are acknowledged with some kind of special circumstance at another time.

We Treat Each Other Respectfully

This is essentially the Golden Rule, used nearly universally over time to ensure smoothly functioning, moral societies. For children, it means we don't hurt each other, either verbally or physically. It means we don't make fun of each other. It means we try to be kind to one another.

Note: The Golden Rule is a two-way street. In our classrooms, the adults treat the children with the same respect they wish to be accorded by the children. We listen to what they have to say respectfully, and we try not to laugh if they unintentionally make a mistake or say something funny. Just before lunch, one little girl said, "I feel like a grandmother because I'm so hungry!" Stifling a chuckle, Tina responded, "Oh, what did you bring for lunch?"

We do not ever make fun of the children or shame them. When Pedro has spilled his milk for the fifth time in two days, we don't tell him he's clumsy. When Joey has hit another child three times in the last hour, we don't call him a bad boy.

Instead, we try to respond to the feelings behind the actions, as well as to the facts of the situation. "Pedro, let's put your glass in a safe place so it doesn't fall over," we say as we move it above his plate. "Joey, you are hurting the other children in the class. We need all the children in our school to be safe. What can we do about that?"

Tip: Treating your child respectfully leads to better behavior, better parent-child relationships, and a healthier family life.

The bottom line is: How can we tell the children not to call each other bad names or use hurtful words if we do that ourselves? Teachers and parents have a crucial job to do, modeling for young children how to treat everyone with respect.

A Sign of Respect

Respect encompasses many things. When we use the word respect, we also use a hand signal. In our class it is the ASL sign for the letter R: Hold up one hand, cross the middle finger and pointer finger, with the thumb holding down the other two fingers. This hand sign is a visual reminder to children to be quiet when others are talking, to listen, and to wait for a turn. The children use it, too, to remind one another.

Using the "R" sign for respect would be a gentle, effective tool for you to use at your dinner table when your preschooler is interrupting others, or when you are talking on the phone and she is tugging insistently at your shirt. It tells her that you are acknowledging her desire to speak, but that she must be respectful to others and wait for her turn.

We equate respect with being polite, but also with taking care of people and things so they don't get damaged or hurt. We respect the books and toys by treating them carefully, putting them away in their proper place, not stepping on them or throwing them. We point out when children are listening respectfully to someone else, and thank them.

Manners

An important component of being respectful is learning to use good manners. Preschool children can easily learn the social conventions of their culture, and are interested in doing so, because they are intrinsically motivated to try to fit into their social group.

There are some very humorous children's books about manners … bad manners, of course, but that leads to some good discussions. This is a great place for puppets, too. One teacher we know had a puppet, Rude Ruby, who occasionally came out and spoke rudely to the class and had terrible manners. The children loved to chastise her and correct her, providing an indirect and non-scolding reminder to the class about their manners. Our classroom puppet friend, Gabby, covers her ears and puts her head down when the children are all talking at once and not listening.

We reinforce table manners in our classroom by pretending we're at "The Quiet Restaurant" at lunchtime. We lower the lights, put some electric candles on the table, put on some music (often a request from the children), and expect quiet conversations so we can hear the music and each other.

We teach the children to ask their tablemates to please pass the milk and to use good table manners. At the end of the meal, they must ask to be excused.

Each child is expected to push in his chair, throw away his trash, put away his lunch box, and leave the table to play quietly. The children are proud of their manners and independence, and genuinely enjoy the music. Do you find it amazing that we expect this of the children? No, it is the children who are amazing.

GOOD MANNERS FOR PRESCHOOLERS

- Use the words please and thank you

- When someone is talking, wait for your turn to speak

- Sit at the table and speak in a conversational tone

- Ask to be excused from the table

- Push in your chair when you leave the table

We all take responsibility

At clean-up time, we sing the "clean up song" ... and Raya walks away from the large floor puzzle she's just been

> **Developmental Asset #30:**
> Responsibility

doing. "Wait, Raya, it's your job to put away the puzzle before we go to the gym," we remind her. "*You* can do it!" she replies, helpfully. So we explain: "I *could* do it, and then *I* can play with it tomorrow. But if *you* do it, then *you* can play with it again tomorrow." We remind Raya "if you were playing with it, you need to put it away." Sometimes we ask if she would like us to help her.

It helps children to take responsibility for their actions if they can directly see the results of those actions. We can talk until the kids tune us out about not walking on the toys strewn over the floor, and we can remind them five times a day to put toys away so they won't get broken (sound familiar?). But it doesn't make much of an impression . . . until the day that we find a Playmobil® pirate with his legs broken off. We tape the broken toy to a sheet of paper, draw a sad face and write: "I got stepped on." Then we hang it on the wall in the play area.

Children ask what happened, or ask us what it says. By the way, "I got stepped on" is more neutral than "Somebody stepped on me," which prompts most kids to proclaim, "I didn't step on it." Later, they come back to look at it and say, "That's sad." We refer sadly to the broken toy when reminding them to "watch where your feet are going," or to "please put away the toys that you are done playing with." They still need to be asked to clean up, but now they know why.

A mother shared a tip with us. She encourages her children to play barefoot or in socks. Then when they step on a small hard piece of plastic they can feel it—and learn the logic of watching where they step, and of not leaving all the toys out where they are playing.

By the way, "responsible" and "responsibility" are two more big, important words that your child can add to her vocabulary.

Taking responsibility includes not only responsibility for one's own actions, but also a general, shared responsibility for the well-being of the group. When we ask a child to help clean up the building blocks, and she responds, "But I wasn't playing with them," we will say, "Yes, I know. But we are all working together to get our classroom cleaned up so we can go to the playground. I'd really appreciate your help." At home, you can remind children that they are part of the family and you are all working together. Thanking your child for helping shows that you respect them.

Helper Heroes

One of our colleagues was delighted to find several of her students cleaning up a mess of paper in the bathroom, without being asked. To celebrate their responsible behavior, she slit the front of a T-shirt (leaving the collar intact) to create a slip-over-the-head cape and had the children decorate it with drawings and the words "Helper Hero." At first, there was some competitiveness to earn the cape, while some children worked together to do a helpful job, so she created two or three capes. The kids liked the recognition. Now, whenever a child voluntarily does something to help out their classroom, they get to wear a Helper Hero cape! You may want to try this at home.

Being a Community

In our classroom community, as in a family, we emphasize feeling good about each person's accomplishments, rather than comparing and competing. Competition may be a positive thing for older children in certain settings, but young children cannot handle it, and it only fosters bad feelings between classmates.

We don't compare children to each other. If, for example, we said: "Carter, look at how nicely Weston is standing in line. He's not touching anyone. Can you be more like Weston?" it would only make Carter resentful of Weston, and more likely to pester the other children in line. In families, it is crucial to foster the feeling that all family members appreciate and support one another, and that siblings are not in competition for their parents' positive attention.

Tip: Foster camaraderie, not competition, between your children.

We want children to understand that every member of the group—whether in the classroom or in the family—is responsible for the general well-being of the group. We strive to foster a group identity—The Ladybugs Classroom or The Andersen Family.

We work to create that sense of community in our classroom, where respect and cooperation are valued, and we push the concept of teamwork heavily. Children love the idea of teamwork and will readily come to help when we call out: "We need a team here!"

As you can tell from the examples throughout this book, we don't have a perfectly cooperative, perfectly respectful, polite and congenial classroom. But we're pleased that the sense of community grows rapidly and joyfully through the year—as it can and will for your family, too.

Saying "I'm sorry"

Finally, let us consider whether taking responsibility for your hurtful actions or words means having to say you're sorry.

We have a tendency to think that *saying* "I'm sorry" means that we *feel* sorry. As adults, we usually do. But when we tell children to say "I'm sorry" they may not know what that really means, and they probably don't feel it—certainly not in the heat of the moment.

When a child is angry and hits another child, he most likely intended to hurt that child, so demanding that he apologize immediately is asking him to lie, essentially. You get that grudging "I'm sorry," accompanied by an angry, resentful look that says, "I'm not really sorry." Rather than insisting on those words, we try to notice later, after they've cooled down, when they are feeling sorry and identify that feeling for them.

Here is one approach. In this case, the action was intentional: Tatiana is sitting at the bottom of the slide, sobbing. "Raha pushed me. She's mean. She's not my friend anymore." Raha looks worried, and is whimpering.

We start with Tatiana: "Raha looks very sad, too. I think she's worried about you. I can see she feels sorry that she pushed you. Raha, would you like to ask Tatiana if she's going to be all right?" Raha may (or may not) ask Tatiana. So we ask for her: "Tatiana, are you going to be all right?" We can drop it there, because Raha clearly did feel bad, or we can encourage Raha to "tell Tatiana how you feel" or "that you won't push her again."

Often, a child finds it very difficult to admit that she is sorry. They are afraid to take responsibility or sometimes they just feel too ashamed, worried, or sad. But we can catch her feeling empathy, and model how she can show her concern.

By asking children to parrot us by saying, "I'm sorry," they soon learn that they can satisfy adults by tossing off those words without truly feeling any responsibility or concern.

What happens when a child *accidentally* knocks over another child's block structure, or bumps into a child and knocks her over? Here is an opportunity to teach children the social norm of apologizing when one accidentally hurts someone else. Most likely, the hurt child will be angry and will react as though the first child had done it deliberately, because preschool-aged children rarely understand the difference between intentional and unintentional.

Remember, young children are egocentric and are still just learning to see things from someone else's point of view. All they understand, especially when strong emotions are involved, is what they see and feel: a knocked-down block structure, or a knocked-over self. It helps to coach them and help them understand. "Jacob, you didn't mean to knock over Paul's blocks, did you? Usually, when people accidentally do something they didn't mean to do, they say 'I'm sorry' to the other person. Would you like to tell Paul you're sorry, and that you didn't mean to knock over his blocks?"

In guiding children to pay attention to the feelings of others, we are teaching them *empathy*, because only by em-

> **Developmental Asset #26:**
> Caring

pathizing with another will they actually feel sorry. In the meantime, we are teaching another useful social skill by asking the offending child what he could do to make the other child feel better.

We think it's best for children to take responsibility for their hurtful actions or words by offering to fix the damage they caused. If Raul knocks down Kirsten's block structure, we will suggest that he ask Kirsten if she would like his help to rebuild it. If Raul resists, we ask Kirsten directly. We tell her we're sorry it happened and then let Raul know that she is being very kind if she replies that she doesn't need his help.

Teaching children about apologizing is much easier if we do it ourselves, if we model it for the children. We make it a point to sincerely apologize to students when we accidentally hurt them. "Oh, Tyesha, I'm sorry. I didn't mean to step on your foot. I didn't watch where I was stepping, did I? Are you all right?"

RESPONSIBILITY AND COMMUNITY

- Children more easily take responsibility when they are reminded of the results of their actions (such as seeing the stepped-on broken toy)
- They enjoy being part of a team and like the concept of teamwork
- Foster a sense of community by naming your family or team, and agreeing on shared responsibilities
- Look for fun ways to acknowledge help and cooperation (as in the Helper Hero cape example), but don't set up expectations of rewards
- Help children learn to express their concern and empathy for others, and to recognize when they feel sorry. Showing concern is better than just saying the words "I'm sorry" before they feel it or understand it.
- Model ways to express your own concern and empathy

Non-verbal Ways to Say "I'm sorry"

Here is another situation where sign language helps. If a child is truly feeling sorry for hurting someone, but can't bring herself to say the words, she might find it easier to make the sign for "sorry." The sign is simply rubbing her fist in a small circle over her heart, usually with a sympathetic expression. Or, if she's near the Feelings Wheel, we will suggest that she might like to turn the arrow to "I'm sorry."

Friendships

Jeremy was digging in the sand on the playground. A boy from another class came over and knelt beside him, and helped him dig the hole "to find treasure." Later we asked Jeremy who he'd been playing with. "He's my best friend," Jeremy said happily. "Oh? What's his name?" "I don't know," Jeremy answered.

Friendships are very important at any age, but what little children mean by "friend" may be very different than what we adults mean. Tina remembers the day her two-and-a-half-year-old daughter asked to "call my best friend Sammy because I want her to visit me." How can a two-year-old already have a best friend?

Remember our mantra: Young children are very now-centered? That is, if you are playing with them right now, you are their friend, maybe even their best friend if you are having a lot of fun. But five minutes later, you might not be their friend anymore.

Why are friendship issues so worrisome—to parents, and sometimes to the children? The ability to form friendships is important because we all want and need friends, but, by the very nature of their strong emotional content, friendships are fraught with ups and downs.

Most of us have struggled with an issue of friendship, by moving to a new school and trying to find new friends, or being rejected by a best friend or by a group we wanted to fit in with. We have an impulse to protect our children from that struggle. In fact, it is not uncommon for their child's friendships to be a bigger source of anxiety for preschool parents than it actually is for their child.

Here's a tricky piece of advice: We encourage you to be observant about your child's friendships, to listen and express sympathy, to help her navigate the ups and downs. But don't help her wallow in misery or try to fix all her friendship issues. It will only make her feel more dependent and less resilient. Focus on helping her understand others, as well as herself.

Making friends and keeping them requires some social skills, some practice, and a lot of emotional commitment. But making friends is not something that someone else can do for you — or fix for you — no matter how much we might wish to do that for our children. The best we can do is to help them gain the social skills, generosity, empathy, and experience needed to attract others, understand others, and share with others.

Even before the school term begins, on visiting day, parents anxiously ask us, "Are any of my child's friends in this class? Shelby and Nazia are so close. Shelby is going to miss her old friends so much." Unspoken, perhaps, is the parents' fear that Shelby will have a difficult time making new friends. "We'll be sure to help Shelby make new friends in our class," we assure the parents, "and we're sure she'll see some of her old friends on the playground."

In fact, if Shelby is already a close friend of Nazia, finding opportunities for them to be together at school or at home will help them stay friends for a long time. By the same token, if Shelby has already successfully made some friends, she is very likely to make new friends in our class. But give it time. Friendships form, grow, change, and mellow over time. We don't expect Shelby to have a bunch of new friends the first week.

OK, school starts and we watch the children enter the room. Many are tentative, some clinging tightly to their parents Some are curious but watchful, quietly exploring the room. And then there is Prabhat, heading straight for his favorite area (the Sensory Table) and immediately chattering with the boy who is already there. By the end of the day, he tells us: "Shane is my new best friend!" By the end of the week, Shane and Prabhat are indeed friends and have already had at least one fight.

The more-shy, watchful children have found their favorite activities and are either contentedly absorbed in solo play or are playing quietly side-by-side with another child whom they are carefully observing as they prepare themselves internally for future interaction.

Shelby has been playing happily with several of the girls and at least two boys, but has not decided that any of them can be called her friends—because none of them quite feel like the relationship she has with Nazia. Hearing this, Mom may be worried that there is no one in this class who will become Shelby's friend. But Shelby is on her way to discovering that you can have many different friendships.

We've noticed that children intuitively adjust to such things as energy level and choice of activities in order to find a way of connecting with different children as they form friendships. The ability to form friendships with all different kinds of people is a social skill that will serve children well, and it starts in preschool.

What Do Children Mean by "My Friend"?

"Zoe won't play with me. She's not my friend anymore!" sobs Lara.

"You can come to my birthday party," Abdalla cheerfully tells the child who just joined our class today.

"Tony keeps following me. I don't like him. He's bugging me." complains Ned.

Chelsea declares, "Everyone is my friend!"

For children, their awareness of others is growing and changing, just as their awareness of the world around them evolves from birth through adolescence. As babies, they may be content to play with their toes and to get attention from adoring siblings and other relatives. As toddlers, mostly they are absorbed in solo play, barely noticing the child beside them, unless they want whatever that child has, which is most of the time.

At age three and four, children are beginning to learn the skills and values involved in letting something go, sharing, and asking for something back. And as they continue to develop their own personalities and interests, they will find that shared interests, whether it's dinosaurs, dolls, or playing with balls, lead to friendships.

As we've said, all preschool children live, work, and play in the immediate here and now. Their thinking goes like this:

- He's playing with me right now so we must be friends. Maybe we'll be friends forever.

- She doesn't want to play with me right now so she's not my friend.

- I want to play with him, so if I stay right next to him, he'll see I want to play and we'll be friends.

- I'm happy playing with a different friend right now, so if my best friend from yesterday is following me around, he's bugging me.

Of course, all preschool friendships aren't transient. Many four- and five-year-olds form special friendships that endure over the course of the whole school year and beyond. These true friendships can be especially rocked by those hurtful words "You're not my friend anymore."

Around age four, children become more verbal and more interested in the interactive forms of sharing, cooperation, and role-playing activity. When this happens, it is time to help them understand how to:

- Be a friend

- Enter into play situations

- Include others in their play

- Deal with moods and rejections.

This is a process they will continue to refine through adolescence. So what do we do in our classrooms to help children navigate the swells and tides of friendships?

Many Ways to be a Friend

As teachers, we make a conscious effort to help our young students understand the nature of friendship and develop their friendship skills. Sometimes teachers may tell children that "we are all friends," but of course not all children feel as though they are friends with all the other children. Perhaps a better way to say it is "We all need to behave in a friendly manner to each other." This makes sense for families, too. Our goal is to have our children become friends with their siblings, and remain best friends in adulthood.

As adults, we can help children understand that there are many types of friendships and many ways that we can be friends. We discuss the following friendship topics with our students:

There are friends who:

- Like to do lots of things together

- Just like to do one kind of thing together

- Like playing with just one other friend

- Like being with three or four friends at a time

Friends can:

- Be the same ages or different ages

- Look alike or look very different

- Live near each other or live far apart

- Go to school together and see each other every day

- Have different things that they like

- Be better at doing some things than you are, and not so good at other things

Friends can sometimes:

- Want to play with someone else for awhile

- Want to be alone for awhile

- Get mad at each other for awhile

- Have a hard time sharing things that are very special to them

- Forget to be polite

Friends are special because they:

- Laugh about the things that you laugh about

- Like to help you when you need help

- Usually understand what you are feeling

- Try to make you feel better when you are sad

Of course we don't present this as a lecture! We might have some conversations, asking the children for some of their ideas. But more often we read books about friends, sing songs about friends, and play games that involve sharing, taking turns, and solving problems together. We use teachable moments to talk about aspects of friendship. Eventually, we might make a chart with the children, including some of the ideas mentioned above. Or we might post and learn a poem about friends.

Their concept of friendship is developing in all areas: in school, at home, and in their neighborhood. Oh, by the way, good news: In our experience, siblings are often best friends and seek each other out at school to play with and to hug joyfully.

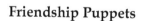 **Friendship Puppets**

This is a great opportunity to use our puppet friends again, the two soft dolls we've named Franny and Freddy. At circle time—or at home maybe at rest time or before bedtime—Franny and Freddy might come out to talk to the children about what they like about being friends. Or they might act out a short scene about a particular type of friendship or a friendship issue that has come up.

Sometimes this requires bringing out a third puppet, to demonstrate meeting a new friend, or including another friend who wants to join in their game, for example. The puppets might ask the children questions, or ask the children for advice.

Fanny and Freddy have become good friends of the children, and the children really do care about helping them to resolve their problems! This is something you can easily do at home, and you will be surprised how quickly the puppets or dolls become family friends. It may be best if they live in your room, a closet, or up on a shelf so that you remain the puppeteer. We also find many young children begin role-playing with their own toy dolls or animals, and speaking for them as they learn to think through their own problems and concerns.

Books about Friendship

What could be better than having a young child climb onto your lap or snuggle beside you to listen to a story? From infancy through elementary school (and even beyond) this is a special time to share with a child. Parents love it; grandparents crave it; even teenage babysitters enjoy it; and we teachers treasure it.

Books are our friends in this sense: there are so many excellent and engaging children's books that show the many faces of friendship.

> **Developmental Asset #25:**
> Early literacy
>
> **Developmental Asset #26:**
> Caring

In *Don't Need Friends*, by Carolyn Crimi, a rat and a dog who insist that they don't need friends come to realize that sometimes they do.

In *My Friend Bear*, by Jez Alborough, a little boy and a big bear learn what they have in common, and become friends.

In the classic *Friends,* by Helme Heine, a rooster, a mouse and a pig demonstrate some traits of good friendship as they go through their adventurous day.

Farfallina and Marcel, by Holly Keller, tells a touching story of a friendship that survives a long separation while the caterpillar and the gosling change and grow up, until they find and recognize each other again.

Then there are the delightful friends series, such as the George and Martha books by James Marshall, and the Frog and Toad books by Arnold Lobel. There are dozens, if not hundreds, more. Please see our website for more of our favorite books on friendship.

Friends Work and Play Together

We work on cooperating and taking turns all day, every day, all year. And, yes, the children do get better at it. Here are some of the techniques we use to teach the fun of cooperation.

We read aloud some engaging stories that explore the values of generosity and cooperation, and we engage the children in talking about it. We ask:

- "Why do you think he . . .?"

- "Why didn't she want to . . .?"

- "What would you do if . . .?"

Again there are many good books to use for this technique, including:

- *The Giving Tree,* by Shel Silverstein

- *Milo and the Magical Stones,* by Marcus Pfister (which shows the consequences of two possible endings)

- The classic *The Little Red Hen*.

An easy game that encourages turn-taking is *"What will you do next?"* One person starts a drawing of an imaginary creature such as a monster, an alien or a fairy. Children take turns adding to the picture.

Games that foster turn-taking and cooperation include:

- Jenga®, Pick Up Sticks, and similar games, in which you try not to let the pile fall or collapse

- Building the tallest tower. Take turns adding the next block, box, domino, or whatever to build a tall tower. The only consequence of it falling over is laughter.

- Simple board games and card games that require turn-taking

Teamwork

We love teamwork and give children a high five when they have successfully worked together to do something. We have stopped many squabbles with a call for teamwork. Example: Leah, Kerry, Jack, and Allen were all pulling on a big box of LEGOs and yelling at each other because they each wanted to be the one to put it away.

We said, "Wait a minute. I don't know if it is possible for all four of you to work as a team and carry it together all the way to the LEGO shelves. That might be difficult. Do you want to try?" Yes, of course, they took the challenge and proudly worked like an eight-legged spider to get it put away.

Teamwork is a life skill. It is simple enough that kids can do it, and important enough that adults must practice it. It is crucial for cooperative learning, friendships, conflict resolution, family harmony, and being productive at work. Teamwork increases accomplishments and fosters pride and confidence. Businesses provide workshops on teamwork and look for employees who under-stand it. We encourage teamwork every day in every way possible at school, and there are

Developmental Asset #6:
Parent Involvement in Childcare and Education

many things you can do at home to encourage teamwork. Your children can work as a team to make a sign for Grand-ma's visit, to pile all the blocks as high as they can reach, and to carry the recycling bin to the curb.

Your family can be a team that plans a family trip together, cleans up after dinner together, and designs and plants the family garden. Be playful with it: make a family crest that symbolizes what your family is all about, and refer to yourselves as "Team [your last name]."

We always have a team cheer for our class, which we do before clean-up each day. "We are the kids in 201; we like to have a lot of fun! We use good teamwork—and we get the job done!" If you sub in your family name in the first line—"The Anderson family is the best"—you can motivate your kids and turn things from negative to positive, and you can reinforce the "we're all in this together" concept in a fun way.

COOPERATING AND TAKING TURNS

- Look for good, engaging children's stories about friends cooperating and working together
- Play games that encourage cooperation and teamwork. For example, create something together by adding to it, one person at a time.
- Play games that require taking turns (quick turns with not too much waiting time)
- Take turns using your imagination and demonstrating different ways to do something – like shaking a shaker, or wearing a scarf, or walking in Mommy's high heels

Helping a Child Enter a Group

Parents are often very perturbed when they perceive their child playing alone, having a hard time joining a group, or being rejected. Both as parents and as teachers, we recognize and understand your concerns. From our experience with our students and families, we think we can help. Let's think about several factors, to provide a good perspective.

First of all, it is true that some children go through a period—it may be as brief as a particular play period, or as long as some months—when they just don't want to play with another child. It may be your child, or the other children, who are making this choice.

But, let's imagine that your child is having a play date at your house, and one of them complains that the other won't play with him. You can help them find a way to play together.

You may propose an alternate activity: an adult's gentle intervention in helping to find an activity that they will enjoy doing together may help.

You may suggest a new role in the game: you can ask the children who are already playing, what role the outside child might take on to join in the game. If it is dramatic play, we might ask: "Does your family need a grandmother (or little sister)?" Or you may suggest that "Annie wants to build a house, too. Maybe she could be your new neighbor and build a house next door." Or, "It looks like there was an accident on that race track. You'll need to call Annie, the ambulance driver, to take the people to the hospital." The children often embrace this as a way to include someone else without intruding on their own roles, and they may come up with their own ideas to welcome the child.

Or, you may state that sometimes it is OK not to want to play. It may help to make an open, verbal acknowledgement to both parties that it is OK to sometimes not want to play with someone. That does not mean that they are not friends. You can remind Henry that not wanting to play right now doesn't mean that Andrew won't want to play with him ever! Maybe tomorrow, or maybe after lunch, they will play together again, because he is still your friend.

Of course, even young children have strong personalities and they just may not mesh well with one another. In this case, it may be that they will be happier finding a child with a more similar temperament.

We need to acknowledge that we often telegraph our own concerns to our child. We do this by being too sympathetic, or asking him too many questions, or intervening too quickly, or trying too hard to fix the problem. This can make the child more anxious, or make him feel there is something wrong with his personality, or that he is disappointing you. We suggest that you stand back for a while and give the child/children time to decide when they are ready to join in. It can be helpful to make an occasional, gentle intervention such as those we suggested above and then step back and give the children time to work out their relationships on their own.

Bullying is a different issue. And so is a persistently rejected and depressed child. Whether your child is the aggressor—yes, sometimes it is our own child—or the victim, you should speak with the child's teacher, doctor, or a counselor to address the situation. If you speak with the other child's parent, make sure you acknowledge the hurt or the provocation for both children. Address the situation in a way that enlists their help—and yours—to resolve it.

Keep in mind that what may look like bullying to adults, when a child consistently teases or harasses another child, sometimes happens because the young child simply doesn't know another way to get that other child's attention or initiate play with him. In these cases, we help him learn a better way to make a friend.

What the Children Teach Us

One advantage of a multi-age classroom—or your family and neighborhood—is that there are children of various ages, who can mentor, model, and learn from one another. We can often count on an older child to take our hints and model a desired behavior, or help out a younger child with encouraging words or an invitation to play.

Sometimes, though, a couple of children have an understandable reason for not wanting to include another child. It may be that they have a complex game already in process, or that the other child has a

> **Developmental Asset #9:**
> Service to others

disruptive and annoying way of attempting to join their play. For all children once in a while, and for some children much of the time, an attempt to join others already at play presents a problem they don't really know how to cope with. This requires our guidance.

Here are a few scenes from our playground.

One morning, Sharifa tells her friend Lydia that she doesn't like her and she won't play with her. Some variation of this is a daily occurrence at our school. It worries parents, and teachers too, when a child is being unkind to another child. First, consider what is a logical consequence for Sharifa? We say "Sharifa, do you think that other children will want to play with you if you are being unkind to them?" "I don't want to play with her anyway," she replies. We turn our attention to the other child and help her to find something fun to do, leaving Sharifa to play by herself for a little while. This is a message that may not sink in right away — because right now she really doesn't want to play with Lydia, but when her bad mood clears and she wants Lydia to play with her, she may have to work a bit to convince her.

We mentioned earlier that we don't insist that children *always* have to play together. But consider Raya, excluding Angi from the climber. We insist that they share the space, and we enlist the children in figuring out how to do that. Often, this actually brings them to invent a way to play together. Today, they decide that Raya is the gymnastics coach and Angi is her student.

A shy child, or one fearing rejection, may welcome an offer to come with you to ask the others if you can join them. We might talk for her to initiate the contact: "Sandy and Carol, that looks really fun! Allison would like to join you. How about inviting her to help you to build the zoo, too."

Must We *Always* Play Together?

The question of whether children should be allowed to say "you can't play" to another child is one that we as preschool teachers struggle to resolve. On the one hand, we want an environment where all are welcome to play and no one is excluded. On the other hand, we respect the feelings of children

Developmental Asset #5: Caring climate in childcare and educational settings

who are fully engaged in an ongoing activity and find it hard to open it up to bring in another. Some children just play better one-on-one. We believe that you have to assess each situation and try to respect the needs of each child. There is no one size fits all solution. To sum up, here are a few guidelines:

- Listen to the children's points of view

- Observe to see if there is a pattern of behaviors that you can help to mediate

- Look for ways to help a child approach others in a more acceptable way if her manner is awkward or annoying

- Always support the idea of inclusion, rather than exclusion

- Try to help the children find a way to modify their game, if necessary, to include a new character or role (as in the examples given earlier)

- When the circumstances just are not right for one child to join the others, your words of sympathy for her feelings, a brief explanation, and reassurance that you will help her join in next time will go a long way.

Social Competence

And then you can offer to play with her yourself or help her find something else to do. But don't overdo the expressions of sympathy and telegraph your concerns, as we counseled earlier.

The following story, which occurred over several days in our classroom, illustrates several of these issues and several of our responses that ultimately helped.

Harvey was a loving and sensitive four-year-old, trying to be as tough and independent as his big brother, and he desperately wanted some friends. Almost daily, Harvey was rebuffed in his attempts to make friends — and we saw him set his jaw, cross his arms, drop his head, and go fuming off into a corner, mumbling "NOBODY will be my friend," bravely holding back tears.

It was heart-breaking, even though we knew that Harvey had a tendency to react dramatically to every hint of perceived rejection or criticism. Harvey, we realized, needed a little help in his approach to the other children, and he needed a lot of help to understand and cope with the perceived rejection. But first, we needed to understand just what he was experiencing and feeling.

We watched Harvey closely as he tried to join a group on the playground. We noticed that he picked out some of the slightly older boys he admired and boldly went up to them and asked "Can I be your best friend?" The two boys, close friends, were ready to ride off on trikes to the adventure they'd been planning, and immediately answered: "No, we don't want to play with you." When Harvey persisted, they rejected him with: "We never want to play with you!" Harvey went off in a funk.

The next day he approached Branson, a quiet and very self-absorbed boy, the same way. "Can I be your best friend?" Branson is self-aware and knows that he can only cope with one friend at a time. "No, I already have one friend. You can't be my best friend." Harvey tried once more, approaching him in the sand area. Harvey then came to us to report: "Branson said he HATES me. And then he said I'm his 'worst nightmare.'" Here we had two kids with conflicting concepts of friendship.

Tina talked first with Harvey, then with both. She explained to Harvey that not everyone can be a best friend. "Best" sounds like you have to be better than the other friends, so if they already have a best friend they'll say

| Developmental Asset #15: |
| Positive peer relationships |

no. How about asking if you can play and be one of his friends? He liked that idea and approached Branson again, who was more receptive to this approach. Tina sat down and watched as Harvey and Branson started to play.

A few days later Harvey was again having problems finding a friend willing to play with him, and we saw that this time he was approaching two children already digging in the sand and asking "will you be my friend?" They said no. We coached Harvey to ask instead, "May I play, too?" This time they said yes, and happily handed him a shovel.

Modeling and Rewarding Empathy

Empathy, or the ability to understand and share the feelings and viewpoints of others, is a critical asset for being a good friend or member of a group, whether the group is a family or a class or a workplace. It is a quality that some children display from a very early age. Others learn empathy when they see us modeling it ourselves.

Understanding that other people have their own experiences, viewpoints, and needs is a major developmental task of early childhood. Toddlers will cover their eyes and assume you can't see them, because they can't see you, and they can only experience the world from their viewpoint.

Three-year-olds will start talking about a person you have never met and assume you know who they're talking about.

But we see the beginnings of empathy when a baby hands her mother something she is eating for her mother to try, or when a two-year-old toddles over to a crying companion and gently touches her face with a concerned look.

Empathy is a core social skill that appears to be hard-wired into human development, so we are really helping the children begin to develop the empathy that is naturally a part of human life. This is when children can really begin to understand that other people may have different experiences and feelings than their own.

As adults, we express empathy every time we listen to and soothe a child. It allows us to reach out and open up to others, to recognize the feelings and needs that we have in common. With empathy, we can make friendships and learn to value other human beings on a personal, community, and global scale.

> **Developmental Asset #26:** Caring
>
> **Developmental Asset #27:** Equality and social justice

Here is a lovely example of a five-year-old expressing her feelings of empathy, in this case for another species. The children at lunch were discussing roadkill one day. Apparently, one of them had seen a dead animal alongside the road on the way into school. One child said that it would be OK to run over a baby coyote, because coyotes are bad animals. Madison vehemently objected: "Baby coyotes have families. They have a heart."

We have already talked about how we encourage children to ask another child whom they may have hurt, "Are you OK?" We say to the child who has hit another,

"Look at her face. How does she look? Is she upset? How do you think she feels?" We encourage them to comfort a child who is hurt or sad, to offer to help them, to share a toy, to read to them, or just to give them a hug. We'll ask: "What could you say to him to make him feel better?" We might explain to another child that "Suzy is sad because she misses her Mom, just like you missed your Dad when he went on a business trip."

A major benefit of being in the preschool at St. David's Center for Child and Family Development is that children with special needs of all kinds are students in our classrooms, and all the children interact with them every day. They all recognize that some children's bodies work differently or that they may need a walker, or hearing aid, or may even need a special teacher to help them control their behavior. But these differences become less important than the fact that they can be friends. We observe that the children in our classes often exhibit empathy, generosity, and caring toward these children and we help them extend those feelings toward others. Parents tell us that they are thrilled to see this warmth and acceptance in their children.

Learning about other cultures and other families' customs is also a terrific way to help children see that others may live in different circumstances, but have many things in common. We invite parents, other teachers, and community members from other cultural backgrounds to visit. From their stories and from some wonderful books, we learn that children all over the world play with dolls, go to school, and enjoy many styles of music and dancing. We learn to sing some of our favorite songs in Spanish, French, or Japanese. Of course, we encourage you to seize opportunities to do the same. We return to this idea in Chapter 6, in the section *Learning about the Human World*.

There is a children's book, called *Heartprints*, by P.K. Hallinan. Hallinan defines a heartprint as "the impression left behind by a deliber-ate act of kindness" and illustrates them in the book as little heart out-lines floating in the air.

> **Developmental Asset #33:**
> Interpersonal Skills

This gave us the idea of recording heartprints when we catch children doing something kind—on a blank poster board on our wall, we add a paper heart with a note about the kind act. The children like the recognition and some-times ask us to remind them what we wrote on the hearts. This is something you might want to try at home, too.

Boys and Girls as Friends

Have you heard: "No boys can play here"? In our classroom, our message is: "There are no 'girls only' or 'boys only' areas in our room. Everyone can play here." We may add: "If it's too crowded, you may say that no more children can play here right now, but that goes for girls, too."

One day we heard some boys declare that "girls can't be astronauts." We jumped right in on that one. "Oh, yes, there are some girls who became astronauts." The boys' eyes widened. We continued, "Did you know that there are women who are scientists, and firefighters, and soldiers, and doctors?"

The boys were surprised. "Are there really girl fire-fighters?" We assured them there are. Later, we heard Sophie telling someone else: "Girls can be astronauts and doctors and any job they want!"

In the examples above, children are experimenting with gender identity (appropriate for this age), exclusion and rejection (social and emotional issues), and limits (testing the limits of acceptable behavior).

Preschoolers are very interested in defining themselves by their gender, and figuring out what that means. So, sometimes, they feel like they need to define themselves as a boy or a girl by identifying and rejecting what they are not. A five-year-old boy defined gender identity this way: "Boys are strong, and they buck up, and they don't care. And they don't get their fingernails painted."

To have a peaceful and respectful classroom or home, we must help children to deal with these issues in appropriate and respectful ways. When children are old enough and mature enough to be thinking this way, they are usually verbal enough to have a conversation about it. Or several conversations.

And usually, day to day, we find that boys and girls play together as friends and playmates quite naturally. Four-year-old girls like to get boisterous and silly, and four-year-old boys like to play house and tend to baby dolls.

Your Socially Competent Preschooler

Together, we can help all our children become responsible, respectful, empathetic, and kind, young people, with the social skills to navigate successfully through life. And your child will benefit not just by having happy friendships and positive relationships, but in every aspect of his life. Studies show that social competence is key to academic success in school. Remember our young friend, Jeffrey Soderberg, the boy we introduced you to on the first page? His greatest strength was his social competence. This was the foundation of his success in our classroom and at home.

5

Behavioral Competence

> *Aaron was making faces at himself in the mirror when he should have been washing his hands. "I can't help it," he explained. "I keep imagining things that are distracting."*

Remember those dreaded kindergarten report cards of old, the ones satirized in every movie or TV show about the '50s? One side was about the academics, but the other side was all about behavior. So there's poor little Beaver, looking miserable and scuffing his shoes as Dad peers at him disapprovingly over the report card, reading: "BEHAVIOR: NEEDS IMPROVEMENT."

The difference now is that our focus has shifted away from bad behavior and how to fix it. We now focus on the positive be-

> Developmental Asset #16:
> Positive expectations

havior that we're trying to help the children achieve, believing that these young children want to become behaviorally competent. "Good" behavior is intrinsically rewarding to a child, because it naturally results in more positive interactions with adults and peers. Of course we try to keep in mind that just as with any other skills to be learned, there will be progress and there will also be setbacks.

When we talk about good behavior, we don't simply mean automatic compliance with adults' requests and expectations. There's a lot more to being a well-behaved child.

The skills we promote that lead to a child who is all-around well-behaved and a pleasure to be with include:

- Independence

- Cooperation

- Rule-Following

- Responsibility

First, we're working on increasing **independence** in the child. Our goal is to have a child who is able to do things for himself, like clean up when he's done with his snack, use the bathroom, and get himself dressed to go outside, mostly without adult help or reminders. We want our children to be able to figure out for themselves what they want to do and how to do it, and to try to solve their own problems first before going to an adult for help.

Second, we're looking for **cooperation**. Everything shouldn't be a battle.

Third, we're hoping to see the child increase his ability to understand and **follow rules**, and to begin to take **responsibility** for his part in the smooth functioning of the classroom, such as cleaning up toys and doing jobs.

And of course, we're hoping children's social competence — the ability to get along with other children — leads to good behavior, and good friendships.

And what about the child who misbehaves? What do we do with Mikey, whose misbehavior frequently gets him into trouble? That's where the techniques of *positive discipline* come in.

The one common thread to our discussion of developing positive behavior in children — the independence, co-operation, and responsibility that we're looking for — is *consistency*. Children understand things a lot better if they are repeated and predictable. Remember, their young brains are trying to make sense out of so many things in the world: what is the difference between yesterday and tomorrow, and what happens when they go to sleep, and why does

| Developmental Asset #11: |
| Family Boundaries |

the moon follow them everywhere, and what happens if they push their sister, and what tastes good, and on and on.

After lots of experience and repetition, they finally learn that tomorrow means the day after they've had their long night's sleep. Similarly, after several experiences of their parents saying "No, you can't have candy" at the grocery store and then not giving it to them despite their sincere begging and heartbreaking tears, they learn that there's no point in crying, begging and whining. They stop doing it.

We're not saying you have to be 100 percent consistent. No one can be. We'll let you in on a little secret: even we preschool teachers aren't 100 percent consistent. Sometimes, it's five minutes until gym time, and clean-up isn't going so well, and we know we've got to get to the gym, because it's raining outside and the kids really need twenty minutes of big physical activity. So we scoop the toy animals up into a bucket, and we hang up the clothes in dramatic play, even though it would have been better for the kids to clean up themselves. Because one need (gym time) trumps the other need (developing responsibility). Or maybe just because we're tired that day. We're all only human, after all.

Of course, on many behavioral issues, we are clear and consistent at all times with the children. It is never OK to call another person a bad name, or to hurt another person. Ever.

So just keep in mind, as we go through this section, that it is far easier for children to behave well if they know what is expected of them every time.

Let it be a mantra for you as a parent: *consistency, consistency, consistency.*

Independence

> *When reminded, long after the other cots were put away, to put away his nap things, one very practical young boy replied in an exasperated tone, "Why didn't someone do it for me?"*

We have a class of 16 preschoolers. Imagine the logistics. Let's say little Pedro has to go to the bathroom, but he needs an adult to take down his pants, which are being held up with a belt he can't undo. And he wants a teacher to sit there with him (like Mommy does) while he's trying to go, encouraging him, and keeping him company.

That leaves the other teacher with 15 kids. Suddenly, Mala trips and falls, hitting her head on a shelf. She's bleeding, she's wailing, she needs all the attention of Teacher #2. So where does that leave the other fourteen kids?

Yes, all teachers face this kind of situation sometimes, and they do have ways to deal with it. But the point is, it's in the preschool teacher's best interest, in order to have a smoothly-functioning class, to have the children manage as independently as possible.

Having an independent, self-sufficient child is in your best interests, too. Do you really want to be putting away your child's toys every evening? Do you have to get off the phone so you can accompany your child to the bathroom? When it's time to leave the house, wouldn't it be helpful if your child could get into his jacket and hat himself, while you're gathering your briefcase and turning off the lights?

Sure, it's going to take a little patience at first, as he struggles to get his arm in that sleeve, when you know you could have the jacket on and zipped in ten seconds. But it will pay off. Imagine the morning when you say, "C'mon, pal, time to go to school." And two minutes later, he's there by the door, ready and waiting while you search for your phone. "C'mon, Dad, what's taking so long?"

Luckily, and most importantly, independence is in the child's best interest as well! We as preschool teachers don't just encourage independence to make our lives easier. We know that it is a good thing for little children to develop their self-help skills. In fact, that's one of the primary tasks of chil-

Developmental Asset #38:
Self-esteem

dren, a task that begins when they take those first walking steps. If we as teachers, and you as parents, have done our jobs, when they take those final steps out of the home and into the bigger world, whether into the college dorm or their first apartment, they will feel confident that they can do it, and do it well.

No doubt you've heard your child say to you many times, "I can do it myself!" Rejoice in those words! Tina's daughter's first sentence was "I do dat!" The more your child can do herself, the more competent and capable she will feel. The self-esteem movement is very big these days, but educators know that true, meaningful self-esteem comes from knowing you did a good job, not from empty praise.

Preschool classrooms are designed to facilitate the young child's independence. First, everything is arranged so that the children know where things are and can find them and use them when they want them. They know exactly where to find the pencils and the paper when they want to draw, and so on.

Second, we make things accessible to the children. They can't wipe up their own spills if they can't reach the paper towels.

Third, we provide materials that are usable by the children without adult help. For example, the painting smocks are hung on a wall by the easel, and can be put on and fastened in the front without the teacher needing to help.

Take a stroll around your house and stop to consider each room from the vantage point of your small child. Which items are too high to reach, or stuck in a difficult-to-open drawer, that you really would like your child to be able to access on her own without needing to get you? Which items and tasks can be modified so that she can do them herself? When he's thirsty, can he get his own cup and fill it with water himself, or does he have to ask you to do it for him?

Tip: Pay attention for a week to what your child frequently asks you to do for him, and ask yourself — "Could he do this himself if I made it easier for him to do so?"

Teachers are so used to being around three-and-a-half-foot tall people, that they just don't seem so small to us. But we think it's a good thing, that we don't perceive these kids as little, and therefore helpless. We treat them as competent people who are able to help themselves and do things for themselves, and consequently, that's usually how they behave.

Now, you as parents have a different perspective. You have known your child since he was a completely helpless and dependent infant. What distinguishes the day he can put on his own jacket from the hundreds of days before that, when he couldn't?

Sometimes parents need to step back and take a fresh look at their child. Has she grown up more than you'd realized? Is he capable of doing more than you've asked him to? Does she want to do something for herself, and you're not letting her just because it's easier to do it yourself?

We'd like to share with you a few more ways we encourage independence and self-help skills at school.

Toileting Independently

A three-year-old in the bathroom called out: "I need help!" We asked, "What do you need help with?" Not wanting to put the toilet seat up, he replied, "I need you to touch all the germs." As this child reminds us, the first thing we teach children in the bathroom is how to wash their hands, with the help of a small step-stool and a picture or diagram to remind them.

The next step to being independent in the bathroom, of course, is getting out of diapers and into underpants. Some preschools require three-year-olds to be toilet-trained to enter the preschool class, while others, such as ours, allow kids in diapers at any age. But whether your child's school requires this or not, we feel it is a good idea for your child to be trained sooner rather than later when he's part of a preschool class.

By the time children graduate from the toddler class, they are much more aware and observant of one another. They notice who is still wearing diapers and who is proudly wearing underpants. We encourage children to be proud of their steps toward bladder control and wearing "big kid underwear," but we don't compare them or worry them or shame them.

Nevertheless, we might hear three-year-old Kristen ask Elliot why he still wears pull-ups. "Are you a baby?" she'll ask, not to tease him, but out of genuine curiosity, because in her mind, babies wear diapers and pull-ups. And maybe that's not so bad. Maybe a little peer pressure can be helpful in encouraging that last step into toileting independence. We add a bit of encouragement by telling the child who is reluctant to give up diapers that we have great confidence that he can do it.

Right now, some of you are thinking, my son is almost four years old and he still shows no interest in using the toilet. The first thing we would say is, get rid of the pull-ups. Preschool teachers dislike pull-ups because they just encourage the child to urinate in his underpants, which is essentially what pull-ups are — padded underpants. If your child shows the signs of being ready to be toilet-trained and you believe he could do it, then he should go into underpants. The unpleasant feeling of wet pants is an incentive to use the toilet in a way that having wet pull-ups is not.

We have found that even children who really don't seem to care that they are still wearing diapers as they near age four are very proud of themselves once they achieve underpants status, and are quite eager to tell us which cartoon character is on their underpants.

Inevitably, of course, when the child is first wearing underpants, accidents happen. When they do, we treat them very matter-of-factly. With a change of clothes and some wipes at the ready it's not a big deal, and the child's ultimate success is worth the inconvenience.

The next step is making it as easy as possible for the child to use the toilet independently. We ask parents to send their children in clothes that can be quickly taken down or off by the children themselves, since we know that children often wait until the last second to go to the bathroom.

Imagine your little one valiantly trying to make it to the potty in time, fumbling with a belt, tight buttons, uncooperative snaps, a stuck zipper, a one-piece outfit, difficult shoulder straps, or a frilly skirt that keeps getting in her way!

The best pants for preschoolers are those with elastic waistbands. If dressing your child in adorable outfits is a priority, we ask you to consider sacrificing a little style for convenience, or finding cute clothes that are also manageable.

Ditch the belts. Fashion can wait. The potty can't.

Dressing Independently

Which shoe goes on the left foot? We tell the children that their shoes are friends. We place the shoes in front of them, side by side as a pair. "They are next to each other and they look like friends." Then we reverse them (right shoe on the left side). The toes point slightly outward. "They look like they are angry at each other, don't they? The toes are looking away from each other like they are saying 'humph.' They don't look like happy friends. Make them look like friends again." They get it. Then whenever they ask us: "Is this how my shoes go?" we just ask: "Do they look like friends?"

Like Aesop's fable about the Tortoise and the Hare, where slow and steady wins the race, we have found that when children are successfully dressing themselves they can seem like a tortoise as we impatiently wait. When getting ready to go outside in the winter, we block out fifteen minutes for our class to put on their snow pants, jackets, hats, boots, and mittens.

Let's start with getting dressed in the morning. Exasperated parents frequently tell us of those early morning battles. If this is a problem for you, here are a few suggestions.

- Allow enough time for your child to do most or all of it herself
- Cut out the distractions. Turn off the TV.
- Engage your child in helping to choose her outfit, but do it the night before so it will be laying out for her in the morning
- Some children are overwhelmed by too many choices. If so, it helps to offer them only two or three choices.
- Please remember that there are bigger battles to fight than whether the top matches the shorts
- If your child insists on wearing short sleeves when it's twenty degrees outside, you can just bring a sweater to school, and if she is cold she will put it on (once you are out of sight)
- A special plea from your child's teacher: Please make sure that they have footwear that is appropriate for active play
- Purchase clothing that is easy to pull on and off
- If your child is balking at wearing particular clothes, he may not know how to tell you that certain fabrics, tags, and so on irritate his skin. Many children have sensitivities to tags, seams or some textures.

Now it's time to walk out the door. Let's deal with the outerwear.

Preschool teachers have two tried-and-true methods they teach their young charges for putting on their own jackets. For jackets with hoods, the child can put the hood on his head first, with the jacket hanging down from there, and then reach back fairly easily to slide his arms into first one sleeve, and then the other. The second method is sometimes called the "dip and flip".

Putting on a Jacket Using the "Dip and Flip"

1. First, lay the jacket on the floor, inside up

2. Next, squat by the top (or hood), and put your hands down into the armholes

3. Flip the jacket back over your head and slide your arms into the sleeves

Zipping is tough for preschoolers. It takes patience and lots and lots of practice. But it's something they want to be able to do, and something they're very proud of once they achieve "I zipped it myself!" status. We often start the zipper for the children, and let them finish the zipping.

For those of us in colder climates, boots, mittens and snow pants present extra challenges.

First, we have to practice the *order* in which the outdoor clothes should go on: snow pants, then boots, then jacket, then hat, then mittens. Children learn better with visual cues, so we have made a chart of the sequence for them, rather than just repeating it in words. We often see the children go to this poster to check what they should put on next. This really helps them to be self-sufficient in dressing. To make this yourself, you can use clip art or other online images, and put them in order on the poster, left to right. You could post such a chart on the inside of your closet door.

Again, it's important for parents to test out these clothes with their child when they're buying them. Can your child pull on the snow pants himself? You won't be surprised when we say that elastic-waisted snow pants are much easier for the child to manage than snow pants with straps that need to be fastened, and they work just as well. How about the boots? Can she slide her feet into them and pull them on by herself? If it's too tight, or too complicated, it's bound to be too frustrating, too.

As for mittens, that's exactly what we're looking for. Gloves are very frustrating for little kids — trying to get each finger into the right slot has caused many a meltdown! And since mittens are warmer for hands than gloves anyway, let's stick with mittens. Again, please make sure your child can put them on himself. Of course, if the mittens are too big either they won't stay on, or little hands become as cumbersome as big paws.

This is a tiring process but it is worth it because the children are so proud of themselves when they master it. And remember — when they get to kindergarten, their teacher most definitely will not be helping them with any aspect of the dressing process, including putting on and tying shoes.

Eating Independently

One day, Christopher announced to his lunch-mates: "I'm already a grown up. I'm six now. Because I ate a lot of food." Lee had a slightly different take on the subject: "I think my [younger] sister's going to turn five before me because she always eats all her lunch." At another lunch table, we overheard the ever-practical Dante explain, "I'm going to sell my Game Boy for money, because I love money and I'm going to ask for a Nintendo from Santa." Another day, Manuel started a lively conversation by saying that he wanted to have 100 children when he gets married.

We enjoy the social aspects of lunchtime at school. It is a great time for conversation. One of the things that makes lunchtime enjoyable is that our preschoolers learn to manage their mealtimes independently, and that leaves time for relaxed conversations. Here are some things that help:

- Make small plates, napkins and utensils accessible for the children

- We encourage parents to send food in easily-opened containers

- The children can pour their own beverages from small pitchers. We teach them to hold the glass firmly on the table with their other hand.

- We teach children to put their glass in a safe place, away from the edge of the table

- We recognize that children can regulate the amount of food they eat when we are not telling them how much they "have to" eat. As doctors tell us, young children do not voluntarily starve themselves.

- Children as young as two years old are capable of feeding themselves, so we don't spoon-feed the children. Even if your child eats really slowly and it drives you crazy, we urge you to let your child wield his spoon and fork himself.

Conversation

Do you find yourselves talking with your child at mealtimes primarily about what she has or hasn't eaten, and how many bites of each item she should eat? This isn't pleasant for either of you. Our advice: let it go. Talk about other things with your child, maybe a story about one of your pets, or something interesting that you saw on your way home from work. When you drop the power struggle over eating, you might find that your child actually eats more and eats better. Bonus: family dinner conversations increase children's social skills and vocabulary.

> "Researchers at Harvard in 1996 looked at the types of activities that promoted language development. Family dinners were more important than play, story time and other family events. And those families that engaged in extended discourse at the dinner table, like storytelling and explanations, rather than one-phrase comments, like 'eat your vegetables,' had children with better language skills, said Dr. Catherine Snow, professor of education at Harvard and the researcher of the study." (Tarkan, *The New York Times*, 5/3/2005)

Treats

Now here is something that may surprise you: we don't make the children eat their "healthy food" first. We assume that parents send the food they want their child to eat, but the order doesn't really matter. So when a child asks, "Can I have my treat now?" the answer is always "Sure, eat it whenever you choose." But the key is that we ask parents, if they choose to send a treat, to send only a very small one—a small cookie, for example. We never hear the children complain about the treat being too small, but then they are still hungry, so they go on and eat the rest of their lunch happily. No conflict. In fact, we are convinced that they eat better when they can have their small treat first. When they are required to eat three bites of healthy food first, we've noticed that they eat only those three bites. Then they eat their treat, pack up their lunch and are done. Remember, young children are very now-centered. Delayed gratification is not their strong suit.

Why not try it for an experiment? When you next set the table for dinner, include dessert with the other dishes — making sure that the dessert portions are very small. After all, why shouldn't something sweet be the appetizer, to whet the appetite for the main meal to come?

A Quiet Restaurant

Now for the other eating issue that plagues families: staying at the table. One fun thing we do that helps the children sit quietly at the lunch table is to have a quiet restaurant.

If we notice that the children are particularly rowdy as we get ready for lunch, we announce that we're going to be eating our lunch at a fancy restaurant. Then we turn the lights out, so that only the light from the windows illuminates the room. Many studies have shown that lowering the light level calms children (and adults, too).

We set electric candles on the table. We turn on beautiful classical music, and remind the children to speak in their quiet voices so that we can hear the lovely music. Of course, this also has the benefit of exposing the children to classical music. We always tell the children the name of the composer and the musical selection, and they soon begin to request them by name.

The children love to have a restaurant at lunch time, and often ask for it. If you try the same thing at home — putting on beautiful music, turning out the lights and eating by candlelight or low ambient light — you may get excellent results. Maybe you will put out your good dishes and a centerpiece. Even a few flowers in a small vase will enhance the attractiveness of the table and encourage your child to stay there — especially if they happen to be the dandelions she so lovingly picked for you!

Growing Independence

As you can see, all of the areas we've been talking about — toileting, dressing, eating — are aspects of a child's life that concern his own body. Helping him function independently in these areas is important. As long as we remove the obstacles, provide a little coaching, a chart or two as reminders, and some patience, these little people will amaze themselves, and you, with their growing competence.

And as they grow older, they will become independent in more areas beyond the simple self-help skills. Learning to trust themselves and to believe that they can take care of their own needs will serve them well throughout their journey to adulthood.

Transitions

We were talking about bed times one day, and four-year-old Isabel chimed in with: "When it's the crack-a-dawn, owls go to sleep."

Scene #1: Three-year-old Sasha is happily driving her toy train around the track she's put together as you think about what to make for dinner. You realize you're out of a number of things: milk, hamburger, Sasha's favorite cereal. So fine, guess it's time to go to the grocery store. You can't leave Sasha home alone. But when you tell her to put away her toys so you can go, Sasha refuses. You try to entice her with a promise of a treat from the store. She whines, "No, I don't wanna go." You get firm. "Sorry, but we have to go or we won't have anything for dinner. Let's go. Now." "NOOOO!" she wails, and launches into a full-blown tantrum.

Scene #2: Bedtime. It's been a busy day in the back yard for little Jimmy, and he needs a bath. He's watching a movie he's seen a hundred times before. He can stop watching it and have a bath, can't he? But no, your insistence that he can finish watching it tomorrow, because it's getting late and he can't go to bed filthy, meets with resistance. Soon, you and Jimmy are locked in a battle of wills, and you know the only way this is going to end is with you picking up a screaming Jimmy and carrying him upstairs to the bathroom.

Scene #3: Breakfast is done. Four-year-old Katie is putting together a fifty-piece puzzle while you bustle around gathering your things for your workday and Katie's things for preschool. You hurry to finish making her lunch, realizing that you're running late again. You put everything by the front door. "OK, Katie, time to go. Let's go see your friends at school." Her response? "I want to finish this puzzle first." You tell her you're late, school's going to start and she doesn't want to miss Morning Circle time, does she? Well, she doesn't care. She wants to finish the puzzle. Sighing, you sit down on the floor and start putting in puzzle pieces as fast as you can. Katie yells, "I want to do it myself!" and dumps the whole puzzle out, starting over. You tell her you have to go now, and Katie has a full-blown meltdown.

So, what was the common thread in these three typical situations? *Transitions.* Parents often find themselves locked into head-to-head battles with their children at those times when the children are asked to change from one activity to another. This is when meltdowns are most likely to occur.

When preschool teachers have children in their classes who are having a hard time, we sit down and evaluate when those difficulties usually happen. We have noticed that nearly every time, transitions turn out to be one of the hardest things for those children.

Why is that? Mostly, once again, it's because young children are very now-centered. Whatever they're doing now is what they want to be doing—now. When Katie is doing a puzzle, her whole self is focused on that puzzle. Unlike adults, who are frequently planning for the future and thinking about the past, young children are immersed in the present. A promise of a treat at the grocery store isn't tangible yet, while the train Sasha's playing with is real and fun and here right now.

So the first step is to understand the experience from the child's point of view, and even to admire her for her ability to be so fully absorbed in what she's doing.

To a small child, if the transition must happen immediately and without her expecting it, the effect is very disconcerting. Since we as adults are usually keeping track of time and are aware of what's coming next, we forget how it seems to a person who can't do that.

But let's put ourselves in the child's frame of mind for a minute. Imagine yourself taking a Sunday afternoon to finish reading a book you are really enjoying. You're coming to the big climax of the book, when your spouse walks in and says, "We've got to go to the Johnson's for the barbeque now. Let's go." You are surprised. "Oh, yeah, I forgot to tell you. They invited us over for a barbeque this afternoon. I said we'd go. We're actually a little late, so we've got to go now." You really want to finish your book and you're not at a good place to stop. "Sorry, but we've got to go," your spouse says, walking over and pulling the book out of your hand. "You can read this later."

Not pleasant, was that? How angry are you feeling at your spouse right now?

In preschool, we have to make a lot of transitions. So how do we do this smoothly?

Picture Schedule

The first thing we do is give children a concrete way to see what is going to happen in the class that day, using what's called a picture schedule. We have small cards with photos representing each of the things we do, and each morning we put the day's events, in order, onto a Velcro strip.

Since preschoolers do not understand time very well yet, these pictures are a very useful and concrete way for them to keep track of what is happening and what will be coming next, and to know that something they are waiting for *will* happen. It helps them to feel that the events of their day are more predictable and less arbitrary. So the picture schedule reduces anxiety, reduces questions and nagging, and gives the child a sense of order and therefore control. Beyond that, it teaches and reinforces the concepts of sequence, of left to right, and before and after.

Think about how you can use a picture schedule at home. Your child would probably have fun helping you think of photos you can take, and posing for them as well! You can take photos of your child cleaning up his toys, in the bathtub, eating dinner, putting on a coat, and so on. You can also take pictures of places you usually go—Grandma's house, your child's school, the grocery store, the park, and so on. You can also make a few cards to represent unexpected or special events.

Of course, your home picture schedule doesn't have to show the whole day. You could use it to show that today is a school day, or to indicate a sequence of events—for example, that a particular babysitter is coming (use her photo) *after* you go to the library and eat dinner; or that your child should get dressed *before* breakfast; or to reinforce the pre-bedtime routine.

Advance Warnings

The second technique we always use is to give the children advance warnings of impending changes. When it's five minutes before clean-up time, we let them know. We suggest to them that this is the time to be finishing up their drawings or puzzles. We discovered that when we ask the children to acknowledge the warning, they pay more attention to it. We simply say, "Show me your *five hand*" and they hold up the ASL sign for "five," which is just an open hand with the five fingers spread apart.

We also give a final one-minute warning (a one finger signal works well).

Often we use a visual timer to show the amount of time left. This really helps, because the children can prepare mentally and physically for the transition, rather than having it abruptly imposed on them out of the blue.

Another fun way to let the children know how much time they have left for their current activity is to play a song that lasts about three to five minutes. We say, "When the song is done, it will be time to stop what you are doing." Use the same song each time, so that they are familiar with it and know when the ending is coming.

How about using a song for the final three minutes before leaving for school in the morning? This is not just for preschoolers. Tina learned that her son's high school would loudly broadcast one minute of a popular song during transitions between classes. When the music stops you must be in your seat.

Signals

The third thing we do in preschool to make transitions easier is to use concrete visual or sound cues to tell the children that it is now time to change. At clean-up time, we turn off the lights, a signal which immediately gets attention, and then sing the clean-up song.

When it's time to come to group, we ring a bell—and you should see those children scurry over to the circle when they hear that sound! When it's time to line up to leave the gym, we blow a train whistle, since we call our line a train, and our line leader the engineer. When it's time to leave the playground, we blow the train whistle and go around calling loudly, "All aboard! Train 114 is now leaving the station! All aboard the lunch train!"

Counting is another simple device that helps children understand that it is time to move from one thing to another. But not counting up—that's too much like a threat, as in "If you don't come by the time I count to three, you'll be in trouble. One, two..." Instead try counting *down*, which is fun and interesting. When our class was taking a walk in the woods one day, we stopped at a little bridge that goes over a stream, and the kids became engrossed in throwing leaves into the stream and watching them float downstream.

Our ultimate destination was the big bridge that goes over Minnehaha Creek. Eventually, it was time to move along on our walk, but some of the kids didn't want to stop throwing leaves. We said, "Get on board the rocket ship! 10, 9, 8, 7, 6, 5, 4, 3, 2, 1... blast off for the big bridge!" Every kid jumped up, and off we all went.

At home, you can use visual or sound cues to alert your child about a transition. Even singing something like, "Scrub-a-dub, scrub-a-dub, I see bubbles in the tub" instead of saying, "It's bath time. Put your toys away," will get a better response from your child.

Rhyming often gets a good result. For example, we might say: "One and two and three and four, come and join me at the door." Or try singing, "Come and join me, come and join me, come and join me at the door. With your shoes and your jacket on, come and join me at the door."

It's amazing how children respond more readily to a request that is sung, chanted, or rhymed rather than stated. It sounds like you are more relaxed, and even ready for some fun yourself. Add a smile and they are ready to go.

You can use what your child is interested in to create these cues, and to make the changes more fun. For example, if your daughter loves fire trucks and wants to be a firefighter when she grows up, you can make a fire truck alarm sound to signal clean-up time. Add: "The firefighters have to hurry! They've got to get their toys put away super-fast, so they can slide down the pole and get to the fire!"

When her toys are cleaned up, you give her a high five and say "Good job, firefighter! Let's get going to that fire!" You can pretend she's getting into her firefighting clothes as she puts on her outside clothes. Then you jump on the fire engine (get into your car) and you're off to your destination with a happy child.

Do you have to do this every time? No, of course not. But it's a lot more pleasant to strap your little firefighter into her car seat than to struggle with a screaming, kicking child.

Let's remember, also, that it's important to respect what your child is doing at the time of the transition, and her feelings about that. So if you know your child is not going to be able to finish a puzzle she's started before you have to leave, you can acknowledge that she's been working hard on this difficult puzzle, and isn't that wonderful? You can tell her she probably won't have time to finish it before you have to leave in five minutes, and ask her what she'd like to do. Would she rather have you help her, or would she rather leave it just where it is so she can finish it when you come home? Warning her ahead of time, and giving her these choices, gives her some control, and greatly increases the likelihood that she will be more cooperative when the time comes.

Sometimes the problem, in making the transition, is that he hasn't had a chance to *start* doing something he wanted to do.

One day in our class, the easel was a particularly popular choice. When it was five minutes to clean-up time, there was still another child waiting to paint ahead of little Davis. At one minute to clean-up time, that child was still painting, and it was clear that Davis, standing there with his paint smock on, would not get a turn. When we told him that, he began to cry. Telling him he would have a chance to paint the next day did nothing to stop the tears or make him feel better. Then Tina suggested that she could put a note on the easel that said "Davis wants to paint." Davis watched her write out the note and tape it to the easel. This concrete indication that he would have a turn to paint later did the trick and he was able to move on to the next activity.

You might be surprised at how effective this simple technique is at home. Not only does it give your child a concrete cue that he will have the opportunity to do what he wants to do, it also acknowledges for him that you think what he wants to do is important. Plus, it has the added bonus of reminding you of what you promised. We're all busy adults, and it's easy to forget things like that.

When we walked into the classroom the next day, there was Tina's note to remind us, so that when Davis came in at the start of class time, we were able to say to him, "There's the note, telling us that you're going to be the first person to paint at the easel today." You should have seen Davis' beaming face as he picked up the paintbrush.

Tip: If you make a promise to your child about something he can do the next day, write it on a Post-It® note and put it where you both can see it.

Sometimes, your child just doesn't want to let go of what she's playing with; she's still emotionally involved with that object. Let's say we want the child to come and write in his letter journal, but he doesn't want to stop playing with his toy lion. We may suggest that he bring the lion to the table so the lion can watch him while he writes in his letter journal. So if you're going to the grocery store and your child doesn't want to stop playing with Dino Danny, why not invite Dino along?

Sometimes, we need to ask a child to temporarily stop doing something. For example, when we're trying to get all the children to the bathroom before we go outside, we have to interrupt each child while he is reading a book or drawing a picture, in order to have them use the bathroom one at a time. Invariably, they don't want to go. We have found that it helps a lot to say, "I will hold your book (or crayon, or whatever) while you use the bathroom, and will give it back to you as soon as you come out." Holding their object for them seems to make the temporary transition much easier for them than just saying the words, "You can finish your book after you use the bathroom."

TRANSITIONS ARE EASIER IF ...

- They are predictable and expected
- The child has an advance warning (remember to have her acknowledge it)
- There is a special signal to announce the transition
- There is an element of humor or fun
- You acknowledge their work and involve them in deciding how to conclude or continue it later (perhaps taking it along, or leaving a note about coming back to it later)

Cooperation

Ahmed offered this definition: "A volunteer is where you call on somebody and they come up and do what you want them to do."

Why can't kids just be more cooperative? Why does everything have to be such a struggle?

Well, think about what we really mean when we say a child is uncooperative. What we usually mean is, he is not cooperating with something that we adults want him to do that he doesn't want to do. It's never a battle to get a child to eat ice cream. You don't hear parents threatening, "Watch another hour of TV or you'll be in trouble, mister!"

So the first thing we have to ask ourselves, both as teachers and as parents, is how important is it that this child comply with my desire at this moment? In other words, it's the old maxim: *pick your battles.*

The classic situation in which you need to pick your battles is when the child wants to choose her own clothes instead of letting the parent pick out the cute matching outfits for her to wear each day. When we see a child walk through our classroom door in the morning wearing a pink and green flowered skirt, a blue and red striped shirt, and polka-dotted tights, we smile and tell her what a colorful outfit she's wearing. Sometimes the mother is embarrassed, but we let her know that we are happy that her daughter is expressing her own individuality so well. Always, we try to look at it from the child's point of view — and in her eyes, she looks fantastic!

Many parents believe that you should never negotiate with a child. We believe that these discussions teach good skills for working things out with other people, and show children that you respect them and their feelings. However, negotiating with a preschooler is a balancing act.

Children will sometimes try to discuss things endlessly, or become stuck in their position. The parent has to be in control of the ultimate decision. If you need your child to do something she doesn't want to do, you can offer choices or variations that are acceptable to you. For example, "Would you like me to read the story before you brush your teeth or after?"

Although there are times when the child cannot be given a choice, we find that children are much more likely to be cooperative if we also show her that we respect her work and her feelings. That means, acknowledging that she is engrossed in something, and letting her finish when possible. That means listening to him explain his reason for not wanting to comply with a request we've made, and responding thoughtfully, "I understand what you're saying." And then, if we still need him to cooperate, adding, "Unfortunately, that isn't a choice right now. I appreciate your help on this."

When Deb's son, Zack, was three years old, they were going to visit Grandma one day. Zack had picked up a couple of toys to bring along, but he didn't have his favorite stuffed bear, Aardbart, to which he was much attached. Deb feared that he would want Aardbart later, and would become very upset when he couldn't have him. But she couldn't talk Zack into bringing the bear. He just wouldn't cooperate. (His grandma probably would have said he was being stubborn.) Finally, after Deb had said for the third time, "Why don't you just bring Aardbart in case you want him later?" Zack looked her straight in the eye and said firmly, "It's *my life*." And you know what? *He was right.* He wasn't being sassy when he said this, he was just making a very good point. We should all remember and consider Zack's words, because ultimately, it *is* their life.

Young children are far more likely to be cheerfully cooperative when we clue them in about our expectations, and when we explain our reasons in a way that they can understand than when we throw demands at them in an abrupt and imperious way.

Let's say a mother has a special vase, a beautiful family heirloom that she's decided to put on display in the living room now that her son is past the toddler age. He is attracted to the lovely colors and picks it up. She yells at him: "Don't touch that! Put that down now!" He yells back, "No! I want it!" and runs away with it. Possible outcome: broken irreplaceable vase. Definite outcome: unhappy mom, unhappy kid.

On the other hand, if she sits down with her son, holding the vase herself as she shows it to him (and maybe lets him touch it while she holds it), telling him about its history and explaining that it is very delicate and valuable (preschoolers like important words) and that she really needs his co-operation in not touching it, the very likely outcome will be an intact family heirloom that they will all enjoy for years. This will go even better if she enlists his cooperation by emphasizing their mutual effort to preserve the vase: "I think this is so beautiful. I like the golden flowers here. What do you like about it, Peter? We're all going to try hard to be careful with this special vase."

Generally speaking, the least likely way to get a preschooler's cooperation is by locking into a head-to-head battle. The most likely way to get cooperation is by soliciting it in a friendly, respectful manner.

> **Developmental Asset #2:**
> Positive family communication

And of course, the adult takes care to understand the situation from the child's viewpoint: what she knows, what she's doing at the moment, what she needs explained to her and how it will feel to her.

Acknowledging that it might be hard or unpleasant for her to have to cooperate with what you want goes a long way toward alleviating a potential battle. Finally, the adult takes into account the temperament of each child. For those children whose first reaction to anything is automatically negative, give them extra time to come around, and extra help to look past the negative to other possibilities.

Building Cooperation Momentum

Speaking of helping our resistant children to be more cooperative, Professor John W. Maag, PhD, a specialist in Emotional/Behavioral Disorders and Counseling at the University of Nebraska, Lincoln offers advice that makes sense and that we have found helpful. Among the tips he shares in his talks and papers is a process of "Building Compliance Momentum." Maag explains that asking the resisting child to do two or three things that he likes to do, *before* asking him to do something he is likely to resist, builds a willingness to comply.

We have seen this work in our classrooms. For example, Rory was resisting sitting down for a writing practice to work on the letter C. We knew that he enjoyed using the electric pencil sharpener, so Tina asked him to sharpen a few pencils, which he readily did. When he brought them back, she said, "Thank you, now let's use one of them for your writing work." He sat down and did it. At home, for one example, you might tell your child: "Please eat your cookie and then give your brother a hug." And then: "Come upstairs and help me choose your pajamas."

Another technique advocated by Maag is to have the child make a small change in behavior rather than expecting the child make a complete change all at once. To go from refusing (or forgetting) to clean up her room to willing and thorough compliance is hardly realistic.

Having her make a small change (parking the toy cars in their garage before bedtime, for example) sets in motion the ability to make further changes. Without your making too big a deal of it, she discovers that it wasn't so over-whelming, or so frightening, or so difficult to make that first step. It seems logical that small steps are easier, but in our urgency to stop the frustrating behavior, we so often forget. Here are two examples of how Maag's advice for changing the resistance works.

At the age of six, Tina's son Nathan was very resistant to change of all sorts, so he was quite upset when it was time to replace the carpet and paint his room. Tina agreed to let him keep a small square of the old carpet, and to paint one wall of his room the color of the old carpet. He agreed to that solution and became much more accepting of future changes.

A classroom example which could as easily apply at home involves a four-year-old named Amy. Amy was also resistant to even small changes in her routines — like sitting at a different spot at the lunch table, or having a different kind of pizza. One day, she started to cry because the pizza she was given for lunch was not the kind she was used to. We noticed that she had a pear in her lunchbox, so on a whim, we offered to slice some pear onto her pizza. This worked, and she was then willing to eat it. Soon after that, a new child in our class sat in Amy's chair at lunch, so we suggested that Amy sit in the chair next to her, and praised her "flexibility" highly when she did. She is now willing to change her seat without protest.

Now, let's take a closer look at that particularly vexing problem: cleaning up. How do we move children from No to OK without a battle every day?

Cleaning Up

Can there be a harder struggle in the world than getting your child to clean up his toys? OK, we exaggerate, but sometimes it seems like it would be easier to get an octopus into a wetsuit than to get this one little four-year-old to put his toys away.

Because we are adults, we can see the benefit in the future of doing an unpleasant task now. Thus we can force ourselves to pick up a scrub brush and get that toilet clean, even when we'd rather be watching TV. Not so with preschoolers, who as we know, are very much centered in the here and now. Although some four-year-olds are orderly people who keep their rooms tidy, most don't seem to be bothered by living in a mess of toys all over the place. But we adults know that it is better for the child to live in a more orderly environment. Not to mention, those toys everywhere... they drive us crazy!

So, cleaning up is an area where we need to maximize the ease of the task for the child, in order to get the greatest cooperation and the minimum amount of struggle.

In preschool classes, the first way we do this is by keeping the materials in containers. Each set of construction materials has its own clear plastic storage container. Likewise, there's a bucket for the set of toy animals, a container for the lacing cards, a basket for the puppets, a rack for the puzzles, and so on. All of these things go on shelves, which is a very easy way for the children to store away and later find materials.

Everything has a Home

Imagine that in your kitchen you have a giant Kitchen Box. All your frying pans, baking utensils, casserole dishes, measuring cups, wooden spoons, muffin pans, egg beaters, meat thermometers, and everything else get thrown into one huge box. OK, we'll even give you two huge boxes. You can have another one for all the food. Sweep all that cereal, all those spices, all that flour and sugar, all those spaghetti packages, all those soup cans, and all the rest, out of your organized kitchen cabinets and into the big Food Box. Now, it's time to make dinner. Start rummaging!

So here is our suggestion: throw out the toy box. Instead, put shelves in your child's playroom and bedroom, and use clear storage containers or attractive baskets to hold the various items. As a reminder to the children, at school, we attach a small photo or symbol of the items belonging in each shelf or bin. Yes, it may be quicker to just gather all the toys up by the armful and dump them in a big chest. But this really does a disservice to your child.

One of our jobs, as parents and as educators, is to help these little people make sense out of the jumble of the world that they first experience. The toy chest hides the mess, but it also hides that toy that your child is looking for. What does he do? Toss all the toys back onto the floor until he finds the item on the bottom! With an orderly storage system for his toys, he can know where things are, he can find exactly what he wants the next time, and hopefully all the pieces will be there. And since he won't need to throw all of his toys onto the floor in his search for one specific thing, his room probably won't get as messy in the first place.

Tip: For toy storage, use shelves with numerous containers for each of the kinds of toys your child has.

Play is a child's work. It's how he makes sense of the world. It's his job to figure out how spatial relations work by building with blocks, and to discover how green is made by painting with blue and yellow paints, and to figure out what being a family means by playing with his toy lion family. But if he can't find the toy lion cub, underneath the stuffed bear, underneath the baseball mitt, at the bottom of his toy box, he can't do his job.

The Process of Cleaning Up

Our clean-up time comes at the end of about an hour of free choice time, during which the children may have been doing the art project, building a huge structure with blocks, working at the writing center, exploring magnets on the Discovery Table, doing a pegboard, playing airplane pilot in the dramatic play area, painting at the easel, playing a board game, or any number of other activities. Our room can be a pretty big mess by this time. As we look around the room, the task looks pretty overwhelming. And if it seems daunting to us, imagine how overwhelming it is to a preschooler!

We begin by giving the children a five-minute advance warning. Five minutes later, we turn off the lights and sing the clean-up song: "Clean up, clean up, everybody, every-where. Clean up, clean up; everybody do your share."

At home, when it's time to clean up the playroom after a long day of playing, if you just say, "Tommy, clean up this playroom," turn around and walk out, you may be asking more of Tommy than he can manage. You may have to stay with him, and get him started on one small task at a time. Start with the largest items, or the ones closest to him. "First, why don't you put all the cars and trucks away? Here's the tub for them." You may offer to help him with part of it.

Tip: Break down the clean-up task into small, manageable parts for your child.

We emphasize teamwork in our classroom. If you have more than one child in your family, you can use teamwork at home, too. Create your own team cheer to start clean-up time. Children working as a team gets the job done easier and also fosters social cooperation, which is an important learning goal for preschoolers.

When we see two kids working well together, we try to acknowledge this with a thumbs up and a "Good team-work, guys!" If your kids are using good teamwork at home, reinforce that. Siblings who are working together as a team and who think of themselves as a team, are more likely to cooperate than to fight, and are less likely to complain that they're doing more work than their sibling.

What about those days when it seems nothing is working? Sometimes, it takes a little pizzazz to get some cooperation. Up the fun quotient!

When we challenge them—"I bet you can't get this whole room cleaned up before the five-minute sand timer runs out"—a flurry of frenzied action suddenly erupts. Sometimes we challenge the kids to get the whole classroom cleaned up before a song on the CD player ends, and they respond with enthusiasm. Of course, if the room isn't all cleaned up at the end of the five minutes, you don't want to make your child feel like he's failed. Just say, "Boy, we sure got close, didn't we? Let's finish up this last bit right here, and then we're done." Clean up to music, and dance as you're putting the toys on the shelves.

Here's a time when puppets are especially useful. When we bring out our King of the Classroom puppet, and he asks the children to clean up his castle in his deep voice, they really get moving! If you choose a special puppet to be the King (or Queen) of the House, you may be surprised at how responsive your children are.

One thing you don't want to do, though, is make clean-up a competition between siblings. It may sound like a fun game to say, "Let's see who can put away more toys." But a clean-up time that ends with a winner also, by definition, ends with a loser, and that means you've got one gloating child, and one crying child angrily. Cleaning up should always be an occasion for cooperation, with mutual satisfaction and a job well done for everyone at the end.

You may feel like your children should just do what you say and you shouldn't need to use a song or a puppet to get them to cooperate. Don't think of it as giving in to them; think of it as working with them.

CLEAN-UP TIPS

- Keep toys organized in baskets or bins on shelves

- Give a five-minute warning with a visual timer, or a "Five hand" sign, and have them acknowledge the signal

- Signal the transition to clean-up time, such as with a flash of the lights or a short rhyme or song

- Break the larger clean-up task into small, discrete tasks

- Stay with your children as they clean up

- Put on lively music

- Encourage and compliment teamwork among your children

- Do not make clean up a competition

Jobs and Chores

We've got some really good news for you here. Preschoolers actually *like* to do jobs and chores! They feel important and valued. Not so for their older siblings, perhaps, but at this age, children want to do important work just like they see adults doing. There's no greater compliment for a preschooler than calling him a "big kid helper." So this is definitely the age to start having your children do small chores.

In our classroom we have a job chart, and one of the first things most children do when they walk into the room each day is to check the job chart to see if their name is there, and to find out what job they have. "Yes! I'm the door-holder today!" In fact, when we were discussing the topic of feelings one day at group time, and we asked the kids what made them sad, one boy said, "When I don't see my name on the job chart."

Of course, some of our jobs are fun ones that you wouldn't have at home, like being the line leader. But one of the most popular jobs in our class is Custodian. That kid gets to wash the tables, sweep the floor, and generally help out with the cleanliness of the class. We have a child-sized broom and a small whisk broom for the Custodian to use. Adult-sized brooms are really difficult for little children to manage.

In Montessori schools, there is an emphasis on "Practical Life," where the children do things like wash tables, sweep, carry water, and polish things, following prescribed steps. In traditional preschool classrooms, these skills are also developed and encouraged in the children as part of caring for and being responsible for their own environment.

One thing is undeniable: Little children love to scrub things. Whoever has the custodian job for the day will find his friends gathering around and asking him if they can help as he vigorously scrubs the paint from the art project off the table. In our classroom, the children use a spray bottle of soapy water, a scrub brush, and towels to dry the table. Please note that the children only use regular soapy water, not chemical cleaners that might be dangerous.

If you were to make a custodian kit for your child, putting these things in a bucket especially for him, you'd have a very happy cleaning helper.

Tip: Preschoolers love to do important jobs. Capitalize on that!

Of course, we don't expect the children to clean to our adult standards. We still have to finish off cleaning the table before snack, sweeping the floor, and so on. But we try to do it discreetly, when the children are busy with something else, so we don't hurt their feelings by implying that they didn't do a good job. Or, if we need to get the job done right away, we may ask if we can join them in finishing up. If we're working together as a team, in which they feel an equal part, they're very happy to let us get those last stubborn spots scrubbed up.

Do you know why we called the cleaning job Custodian? We like to use real world job titles in our class. It contributes to the child's feeling that he is doing a real, important job. Thus, our calendar helper for the day is called the Secretary, and the person who picks the song for us to sing at group time is the Choir Director.

You might like to come up with some real world job titles for your child's chores at home as well. When he sets the table for dinner, he can do his Waiter job. When he helps sort the laundry or fold towels, he can do his Dry Cleaner job. When she puts water in the dog's dish, she can be the Veterinarian.

Note: We consider being responsible for their toys to be just part of the daily routine of the child, not a specific job. Clean up time happens every day for every child, both at school and at home.

You can capitalize on your preschooler's natural inclination to try to make sense of the big, confusing world by giving her jobs that involve sorting and putting things in order. Preschoolers love to sort, classify and order things. Finding matching socks and putting them in pairs, and then sorting the paired-up socks into piles for mommy, daddy, brother and sister is a great activity! So is taking the clean silverware out of the dishwasher and putting the knives, forks and spoons in their correct places.

One other reason we get cooperation at preschool regarding chores is that the jobs rotate among the children. If the same child had to sweep the floor every single day, she might get tired of it and balk at doing it. You want your preschooler to do chores at home more for the purpose of ac-

> **Developmental Asset #30:**
> Responsibility

quiring responsibility and getting in the habit of doing household jobs, than for the actual results that her doing the job produces. Admittedly, you're not having her sort the socks in the clean laundry to make your day easier, because it probably takes more time than if you just did it yourself.

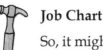 ## Job Chart

So, it might be a good idea to rotate your child's jobs at home, too. In fact, if you made your own job chart for your child, you'd probably see her rushing to check it every day with excitement. You can take your own photos or use pictures you find online to illustrate the jobs (a picture of a dog and a water bowl, a pair of socks, a set of silverware, and so on).

Of course, if you have more than one child, your at-home job chart will have a space for each child. Then, it's especially important to rotate jobs fairly among your children. If there are some jobs that only your older child can do, such as walking the dog, your preschooler will understand that his turn will come when he is older.

Oh, and one other thing about the jobs your child does at home. We mentioned that we have some fun jobs, like line leader (that's our Train Engineer.) Why not have a few just-for-fun jobs at home, too? How about the Pizza Delivery job? He can participate in ordering online, and when the pizza comes, he gets to bring it to the table.

Discipline

> *Harley was told to use his words rather than hitting his friend.*
> *"Okay," he said. "I'm working on keeping my good hands*
> *on my own body."*

"That child needs some discipline." How many times have you seen an out-of-control child and thought those very words?

We agree. Plenty of children need discipline. But when most people say discipline, what they mean is punishment. That's not what we mean. We don't punish children in preschool, in the usual sense of the word. Rather, we teach better behavior.

What that child really needs is to learn how to have self-control. What that child really needs is an understanding that when mom says no, it actually means no, rather than "take the whining and screaming up a notch and maybe I'll reconsider." That child needs an understanding of social conventions: It is simply not acceptable to run amuck in other people's homes, or to disturb the public peace with a temper tantrum, or to push another kid off the swing at the local park. What that child really needs is a lesson.

> **Developmental Asset #31:**
> Self-regulation

And that's exactly what school is for. We teach lessons. Discipline mostly means learning how to behave acceptably. The best kind of discipline is that which averts misbehavior before it happens, because the child has learned how to behave correctly. He has learned *self-discipline*.

When prospective parents ask us what kind of discipline we use in our class, what they mean is, how do we handle children who misbehave? They know we don't use physical punishment, of course. But do we use Time Out, or what do we do?

So let's say Amelia has grabbed a car from her friend Scott. But it's not the first time this morning, it's the third. We've already talked with Amelia about why it's not OK to take toys from other children. We've already told Scott to tell Amelia firmly, "I don't like it when you grab stuff from me." We express our confidence to Amelia that we know she knows how to play nicely with friends.

But then, as we're working with some of the other kids in another part of the room, we hear Scott crying. Oh no, now Amelia has pushed him down. After we tend to Scott, we take Amelia aside. "Amelia, you're having a tough day, aren't you?" She looks away angrily. "Amelia, I think you need some help cooling down. You look like you're really feeling mad right now, maybe THIS BIG mad, (stretching our arms wide). You know what? I want to help you calm down and feel better, but I can't let you hurt the other children in the class. You can sit on this chair over here for a few minutes, till you're more ready to play in the room without hurting anyone."

This is somewhat like Time Out, but it's not used as a punishment ("Go to your room, young lady! You're in Time Out!") When we need to remove a child from the group, it's to help her calm down and get back in control of herself again, as well as to protect the other children and the environment. It's always followed by talking with the child about what happened, rather than just saying, "OK, your Time Out is done. You can come out now." And if the child has hurt someone else, we always have her go back to that child to check on him to see if he's OK now.

Note: See the Social Competence chapter for why we don't require "I'm sorry" from the offending child, and the Emotional Competence chapter for anger management techniques.

Tip: Time Out should be used for short amounts of time to help your child calm her body down and regain self-control.

Time Out can be a useful behavior management technique, but it should be short and specific. One teacher mentioned to us that a parent was complaining that her child was having a very hard time at bedtime. In discussing it with the mother, the teacher discovered that he was often punished for bad behavior by being sent to his bedroom for extended periods. His bedroom had become a negative place for him. When they changed his time-out place to a specific chair, and also shortened his time out to a reasonable amount of time (a few minutes), the bedtime problems disappeared.

And if a child is so wild, so out of control that he goes ballistic when we tell him he needs to stop and sit down — if he runs around the room screaming at us and pulling stuff off the shelves and throwing things at other kids — then what?

Then he really needs our help in calming down, because he just can't do it himself. So if we can, we hold him on our lap and put our arms around him, gently but firmly holding him tightly. We tell him softly, "I'm going to help you calm your body down, because it's really hard for you to do that by yourself right now."

This is almost like swaddling a baby, a time-honored approach to calming crying babies. As we're holding him, we're saying, "Let's relax now. Take a deep breath with me. Good. Let's do another one." If he's fighting being held, we give him some space where he can't hurt anyone, and when we see that he seems a little more ready, we can try again to help him to calm down.

What Amelia doesn't need now is to be shamed by being labeled as a bad girl. What she doesn't need is to be compared to a child who is behaving well. ("Look, Luisa is sharing her toys so nicely. Can't you play nicely like Luisa?") What Amelia's brain will hear is that the adults in her life believe her to be a bad girl, a girl unlike the good girls. If this happens frequently enough, Amelia will decide that she is, in fact, a bad girl and will act accordingly.

If Amelia is a child who misbehaves frequently, we document her behavior so we can figure out what's going on with her. We might notice that there is a pattern. Perhaps Amelia misbehaves every time there is a transition. Then, we know that we really have to help her learn how to deal with transitions better. Maybe her behavior deteriorates

Behavioral Competence

during the half hour between lunch and nap. Hmm, we think. Maybe Amelia's tired; maybe she just needs to get on her cot right after lunch. It's easy to get caught up in the moment-to-moment details of living, whether in the classroom or the home, and miss the big picture.

Take a step back and try to figure out what's really going on with your child. If it seems like your child has been getting into trouble a lot recently, jot down a quick note each time it happens: when, where and under what circumstances. The explanation for misbehavior that just seemed naughty may become clear, and the solution may well present itself.

For example, you may notice that your child misbehaves often in the hour between arriving home from preschool and dinnertime. Is he hungry? Tired? Needing your attention after a long day of being away from you? Once you figure it out, you can determine if he needs a small snack in the car on the way home from school, or a bit of rest, or ten minutes of cuddling with you and reading a book before you begin to make dinner.

Tip: Document your child's misbehavior over several days to determine the underlying cause, and the remedy.

Natural and Logical Consequences

As an alternative to punishment, you may have heard the phrase "natural and logical consequences." As Gilbert and Sullivan put it in their famous opera The Mikado, "Let the punishment fit the crime."

Many young children are unaware that their actions have effects on others or direct consequences, or they have come to see the consequences as punishments unrelated to their actions. To help them become the thoughtful, responsible, and respectful people we want them to be, it is our task, as teachers and parents, to help them understand the consequences of their actions. To do that, we need to understand the consequences of *our* actions.

> **Developmental Asset #12:**
> Boundaries in childcare & educational settings

Often, children push our buttons. If we respond with an automatic, harsh, and accusatory reaction, they will learn to fear us and avoid us, but will not necessarily understand what they have done to cause that response. If we fall into the habit of imposing the same punishment, no matter what the infraction, they will not understand that some infractions are more serious than others. If we bribe them, promising a treat if they will stop whining, having a tantrum, or refusing to comply, then we are in fact, encouraging them to do more of the same. We are often asked, "So what are some *logical* consequences?"

We use natural consequences a lot in preschool, because they are logical and make sense. The natural consequence of refusing to put your coat on in thirty-degree weather is that you get cold. The natural consequence of refusing to put away the Play-Doh is to not be allowed to use it the next day.

Note: one day is enough. One day to a three-year-old is like a week to an adult. Also note: when the child comes to us the next day and says, "I really will put it away this time, please let me play with it," we respond, "I'm glad to hear you will put away the Play-Doh the next time you use it. But I told you yesterday that you would not be able to play with it today. You can have another chance *tomorrow*." Be prepared: This may precipitate another meltdown the first time (or two or three), but stick to your word and your child will soon learn that the consequence is real but that he gets another chance the next time.

A logical consequence, at home, might be that the action figures get put away for a certain period of time immediately after

> **Developmental Asset #10:** Safety

a child throws one at someone else. Assuming that the child has heard the rule about not throwing things in the house (and most have heard it many times), we don't give a second chance for this one.

This is a good time for adults to explain to the child: "My job is to keep people safe. Your job is to play safely. If you do something that is not safe, then you are done playing with that for today." You can either remove the child from the situation, or remove the toy from the child. This is a more logical consequence than sending a child to her room, or saying she can't go to Grandma's. Which reminds us: Don't say she can't go to Grandma's if you need Grandma to babysit tonight!

When you can see a misbehavior brewing, this is the time to explain to the child that if X happens, then Y will follow. For example, "If you continue to kick the other kids under the table at snack time, you will have to sit away from the others so you don't hurt them." This gives the child a chance to understand what the natural consequence of her actions will be, so that she can change them. If she kicks a child again, she is immediately removed to a small table to eat her snack by herself.

We do not recommend washing Kevin's mouth out with soap if he says a nasty word (a common threat heard in our childhood), but we have found it effective when a child is teasing another by using potty words to ask: "Do you need to go to the potty? Because I heard you using potty words. If you want to say those words, you can say them in the bathroom." One year, we kept a small chair in the bathroom, and several children did decide to go there so they could say some potty words that they wanted to try out. That was a logical consequence of our suggestion!

Explaining what the logical result will be if a specific misbehavior continues is different from threatening. The tone of voice is also important: the intent is to help the child understand, not to instill fear. Threats are a warning of punishment, and they tend to be vague and ineffective.

As an example, here's a typical scene at a park. Mom tells her child they have to go home now. The child keeps playing, ignoring mom. "If you don't come here right now, Molly, you'll be in so much trouble!" What does that vague threat mean to a four-year-old? Two minutes later: "I told you, get over here right now!" Molly keeps playing. Five minutes later: "I'm warning you, get over here right now or we won't come back to this park anymore!" (A consequence she is unlikely to stick to.)

Molly still keeps playing until she sees her mom take a few steps toward her, then runs over to her. Mom grabs Molly's hand and says angrily, "Next time you come when I call you, do you hear me? Let's go." What has this child learned? That she can play for at least ten more minutes after her mother tells her they have to go, and that mom's threat doesn't really mean anything.

A better scenario for both Mom and daughter would be this: Mom tells Molly that "We'll be leaving in 5 minutes, so please finish up your game," rather than abruptly expecting her to stop the play she is involved in. Five minutes later she says, "Our time is up. We are leaving now." Mom gathers her things, holds out her hand to Molly, and if necessary takes Molly's hand and leads her to the car.

If Molly doesn't comply, instead of vague threats it would be better to tell her in very specific terms what the natural consequence will be. "I need you to come when I call you. Please come over here right now, or we won't be able to come to the park the next time you ask." And then Mom needs to follow through. Follow-through is absolutely vital to helping the child learn better behavior. "Remember when I told you we couldn't come to the park the next time, because you didn't stop playing when I told you it was time to go home? You'll have to find something else to do today." Note that the consequence is that Molly will miss out on going to the park one time, not forever, as the mom at first threatened but would have been unable to follow through on.

OK, here is an exception to consistently imposing the logical consequence. If you have imposed a consequence and then your child (or a supportive friend or sibling) explains the circumstances surrounding the incident that just occurred, and you feel that the situation no longer makes the consequence logical, then admit that you have changed your mind, and then re-state the situation as you now understand it. This is respectful, and fair.

Be Proactive — Head Off Misbehavior

Sometimes, little children behave badly because they are bored or restless. For example, in our class we need all the children to use the toilet before we go outside. Usually during this potty time, the children are supposed to be doing puzzles or looking at books while they wait. But this is often a time when some children begin chasing each other around the room, screaming and laughing wildly. They just aren't able to sit and work quietly anymore. It helps if we start an active (but contained) game, such as Simon Says, or sing songs with a lot of action while they wait their turn for the bathroom.

Just like in our classroom, there are occasions in family life when the children become bored and misbehave. Typical times include at the grocery store, riding in cars, and at religious services—when you are likely to have the least tolerance for these distractions! These are usually times when the adult is engaged in an activity, but the child is not—he's just along for the ride with nothing to do, and even worse, Mom's attention is somewhere else, not with him.

In these cases, you'll get much more cooperation by giving the child something interesting to do. Try to engage him in a grocery store game. "Can you find something red in this aisle?" "Look at the back of this cereal box. Can you find the letters of your name on it?"

When your child is annoying his sister in the back seat of the car, it may well be because he's bored and he has nothing else to do. Play a car game, like "I Spy." Play a rhyming game. ("I'm thinking of an animal and it rhymes with 'how.' Can you guess it?") Put on some music that you and your children enjoy. When you have to be in places where your child will be required to sit quietly for a long time, bring quiet activities for her to do, such as a pad of paper and a few colored pencils.

Many parents find that having their child use an iPad®, personal movie-player, or other electronic device is useful at these times. While this may work, the more often you can do something interactive, where your child feels your attention, the more likely you'll help your child develop the ability to invent his own entertainment, and increase his willingness to be cooperative in the future.

What About Rewards?

We said we don't believe that punishment is effective in the long run, but what about rewards? Maybe you've tried offering your child a special treat if he is good for the whole grocery store shopping trip. Sometimes that works, but often it doesn't, because it's really hard for a little child to keep that goal in mind for such a long time.

An hour is an eternity to a four-year-old. Then, when your child does misbehave 15 minutes into the shopping trip, where do you go from there? Do you offer him another chance, and then another, and then another? This actually rewards him for misbehavior. Or do you tell him he's blown it, so no treat? Doing so often results in you spending the next 45 minutes dealing with his misbehavior, because all he knows is: There's no further incentive to behave, so why try?

It's not a bad idea to let your child pick out one special treat at the store, as long as it's not offered as a reward. You may find that if you don't tie it to 60 minutes of sitting quietly in a cart, it can keep your child happy and occupied. She picks a package of cookies in aisle three. Then you get to aisle five, and she wants cheese crackers. Now she has to decide: which to keep and which to give up. She knows the deal is, one special treat. That's the rule. By the time you check out, she puts the peanut butter crackers that were her final, for sure, best choice on the conveyor belt. She's spent her time weighing her choices, making decisions, and is now happy with her very special treat.

If you do want to offer your child a reward for behavior that you are especially pleased with and want to reinforce, don't make it a bribe held out to the child before the behavior happens; make it a natural consequence for good behavior *after* it happens. "You were so kind to Bethany when she played at our house today, and you shared your toys so nicely. I'm proud of you for being a good friend. You can have another friend over tomorrow if you'd like. Or if you'd rather, I could take you and Bethany to a park."

Note: you should not offer an object — a toy or a sticker — as a reward. The reward should be a logical consequence of her good behavior, just as children experience the logical consequences of bad behavior.

The difference between offering a reward for desired good behavior before it happens, and rewarding good behavior *after* it happens, is that the first method encourages good behavior only so that a reward can be achieved. If there's no reward, why be good?

Tip: Natural consequences can be offered for both bad and good behavior.

We want to see good behavior occur naturally. We want the child to feel an internal incentive to behave well. In fact, children are motivated to behave according to the norms of their society, just as they are intrinsically motivated to accomplish tasks successfully and to learn things. They don't need external rewards for any of these behaviors.

Recognizing children's accomplishments is fine, as long as the praise doesn't go overboard and is specific to what they did. For example, a teacher may notice that Mohammed has gone into the bathroom to turn off the water tap that was left running. She might say, "Thanks, Mohammed, for turning off the water when you noticed that no one was using it. You're a good citizen of our classroom." The teacher's or parents' pleasure in the child's good behavior, which they convey to the child in affectionate language, as well as the child's own positive feelings about herself, are far more reinforcing than any material reward.

Scientific research backs this up. Noted child psychologist Dr. Robert Brooks (reviewing the book *Drive*, by Daniel Pink) discusses a well-known study by Mark Lepper, David Greene, and Robert Nisbett about the consequences of giving rewards to preschoolers. The study compared a group of children who were offered rewards to do something they already liked to do (drawing), with a group that did not receive a reward for doing the same thing, and a group who unexpectedly got rewards after they did their drawings.

Dr. Pink found that children in the group who were offered contingent rewards later showed much less interest and spent less time drawing compared to the other two groups. Essentially, the promise of a reward turned the joy of drawing into a duty (cited by Brooks, Feb. 2010). Please see our website for more links to discussions about why rewards for desired behavior are not the best way to go.

Despite these findings, teachers do use incentives such as stickers sometimes, and you can, too. But they're mostly good for modifying a specific behavior — using the potty being the most popular one! Ultimately, the goal is for the child to be doing the behavior on his own. And yes, you can celebrate your child's accomplishments with physical rewards sometimes. Teachers do this when they decide to have a popcorn party for the whole class because they've done such a great job of playing cooperatively all week.

Parents can say to their children, "You guys have played together so nicely all week. It feels great, doesn't it? Let's celebrate by going out to your favorite restaurant tonight!" This physical reward ties in naturally to the positive behavior.

If you decide to do this at home, you may also discover a wonderful side benefit for yourself. When you devote your attention to trying to catch your child using good behavior, rather than mostly noticing and responding to bad behavior, your relationship with your child improves. You discover that he engages in a lot more positive behavior than you'd realized. With your focus off of the bad behavior, you find that you enjoy your child more. And with all the positive reinforcement you're giving him, you find him acting nicer to you, too.

Human beings are social creatures. When it comes to natural consequences for both good and bad behavior in social situations, most of the time for a small child, the natural consequences are built in. If you are nice to other kids, they want to play with you, they smile at you, they like you. If you are mean to other kids, the opposite happens.

Lying and Stealing

We'd like to say a few words here about two behavior problems that are especially intolerable to adults: lying and stealing. Those may be criminal offenses in the grown-up world, but for preschoolers, they're barely misdemeanors. Sometimes, children take toys from our room and try to hide them in their pockets to bring them home. Their parents find this very upsetting. But we are not too concerned, because we understand that preschoolers are at a stage in development where their desires overwhelm them, and their self-control is very rudimentary. Preschoolers still find it difficult to distinguish between fantasy and reality, between wishes and facts.

So, when a four-year-old says to us, "My mommy gave me a unicorn for my birthday, and I rode on it all day," we don't call the child a liar. She's not. She's just expressing her fantasy. While she probably knows that she doesn't really own a live unicorn, she sure would like to!

Jared, a child in our class, regularly enthralled the children at his table during lunchtime with tales of his pet cheetah. We didn't correct him with "Now, Jared, you don't really have a cheetah living at your house, do you? Cheetahs are wild animals. They're not pets. Where do cheetahs really live, children? That's right, in the jungle, or at zoos." All that would have done is squelch Jared's wonderful imagination and humiliate him in front of his friends.

Also, remember that preschoolers are just learning about the world, and often don't know enough to be able to distinguish the truth from fiction. Sometimes a child will assert that she went to Florida, or China, or some other faraway place, last night. They don't know time, and they don't understand distances. Maybe they went to Florida once. Maybe they're planning a trip for the summer. Maybe they read a book about China. So, sometimes young children are confused, sometimes they just wish something were so, and sometimes they really mean something other than the literal words they're saying. Many a preschooler has asserted firmly that his dad is so strong he can lift up his whole house. When they say that, they really believe it, because the most important truth to them at that point is that they have the strongest daddy in the world.

And sometimes they're protecting themselves. When you ask a three-year-old if he broke a glass, even if he's standing there with the pieces of glass around his feet and a guilty look on his face, he might say no. Why? Because he really, really wishes he hadn't broken the glass, and he doesn't want to get in trouble for it.

If we already know that a child has done something wrong, we never ask him if he has done so, because that's just inviting him to tell a lie. Instead, we say, "I see that you broke that glass. What do you think you should do about this?"

As for stealing, you may have seen that toddler T-shirt that lists the "Toddler Rules":

- If I want it, it's mine
- If I put it down but now you're playing with it, it's mine
- If I was thinking about playing with it, it's mine
- If I can take it, it's mine

Preschoolers aren't all that far removed from their toddler days. Many preschoolers give in to the desire to take something that they want. They do know that they shouldn't, but their grasp on the ideas of ownership and possession is pretty tenuous. Fortunately, they're usually obvious about it when they know they've done something they shouldn't. A preschooler will hide the little toy car behind his

> **Developmental Asset #29:** Honesty

back, inch his way out to his cubby, and say to us, "Don't look behind my back." We're pretty matter-of-fact about getting the item back from the child and reminding him that these toys belong to the class and have to stay here. He knew it. He just needed our help in going along with that rule.

If your child is lying and stealing at age ten, you've got a problem. At age four, you've just got a kid who needs you to help him figure out why sometimes fantasy is fine, but sometimes you have to say what is really true. You've got a kid who needs your help in learning how to resist doing what he wants to, when he knows he shouldn't.

Final Words on Discipline

✓ **Expect your child to behave well most of the time.** Children generally live up to their parents' and teachers' expectations. Good behavior is really the natural state. Most of the time in our class, most of the children are behaving appropriately.

✓ **Expect that misbehavior will happen sometimes.** No one is perfect, and little children don't have a lot of self-control, nor can they generally think through where their actions are leading them. They live in the moment, and they are subject to strong feelings, which they cannot easily control. At those times when you know that misbehavior is likely to happen, such as when your child is bored, or tired, or when you're making dinner and the kids are cranky, try to avert the behavior by giving them a few minutes of your attention or something calm and relaxing to do. They might even enjoy setting the table or helping you wash the carrots and potatoes, because it's a chance to be with you, and to do something you will appreciate.

✓ **Teach your child good behavior.** You can directly instruct your child on how to behave properly. Children come

> **Developmental Asset #11:**
> Family boundaries

into this world needing to learn many things: how to walk, how to use language, how to feed themselves. Learning how to behave properly is another item on that list. Just as children are intrinsically motivated to learn how to walk and talk, they are intrinsically motivated to learn how to behave well toward other people in order to be a part of their social group, whether it's the family or the classroom.

✓ **When your child does misbehave, give him a chance to correct his behavior.** If the misbehavior continues, it should be met with a natural consequence.

✓ **Follow through.** If you tell your child he can't have the candy, don't let him persuade you to give it to him through whining, pleading, crying or whatever means he has at his disposal. If you tell him that he won't have time for a bedtime story if he takes too long eating his bedtime snack, and then he fools around with his brother at the table for half an hour, put him to bed and don't read the bedtime story.

✓ **Don't threaten.** Scaring a child does him no good. Explaining a logical and appropriate consequence to your child if he continues to misbehave is different from threatening. Remember, you want to help your child understand your expectations so that he feels good about fulfilling them, not to make him comply out of fear.

✓ **Enjoy your child's good behavior.** Express your appreciation of it. Let him know you are happy that he behaved so well,

Developmental Asset #1: Family support

and be specific about what he did that was good. Also, enjoy your child's positive behavior by spending time with your child. Children crave their parents' attention, and it's much more pleasant to give your child attention when he wants to read a book with you while snuggled up in your lap, than it is to give him attention for pulling his sister's hair and making her scream.

Remember the kid who everyone agrees "needs some discipline?" The fact is, he knows he needs some discipline, too. He just doesn't know how to get it. It's up to us, his parents and teachers, to help him.

FIVE KEYS THAT OPEN THE DOOR TO GOOD BEHAVIOR

⚷ Consistency

⚷ Follow through

⚷ Treating your child with respect

⚷ Positive expectations

⚷ Reasonable expectations

6

Cognitive Competence

> *We were introducing the concept of "half" and asked our group of 17 kids to divide themselves in half. They kept scurrying back and forth between the 2 groups, but of course couldn't make it work. Finally, Braden lay down between them, with his head near one group and his feet near the other!*

If you had Superman's power of super-vision and could look inside your child's skull, you'd be astounded to see those neural connections forming at breakneck speed. Literally every day, your child is getting smarter.

How do preschoolers learn so much? Well, lots of ways.

✓ **Children learn by playing.** Maria Montessori said "Play is the work of the child." These words have become the foundation of early childhood education throughout the world, and you will see them on the first page of almost every preschool's parent handbook. In fact, if the preschool you're considering doesn't say "Play is a child's work" or words to that effect somewhere in its literature, keep looking. When a parent asks us at the end of day, "What did she do besides just play?" that's like asking "What did she do besides learn?"

> **Developmental Asset #17:**
> Play and creative activities

✓ **Children learn by observation.** Young children are keenly observant, in ways that we adults have forgotten to be. When our class passes by the flower garden on our way to or from the playground, it is always the children who spot the tiny new monarch caterpillars there, even though we teachers scan the bushes and flowers for the caterpillars, too. But we are also keeping one eye on the class, and part of our brains on other things. The children can focus on one thing with laser precision. It may seem like a contradiction that young children can also be so easily distracted, but really that's just the flip side of the same coin. If their attention is diverted to something else, they then focus on that to the

| Developmental Asset #21: |
| Motivation to mastery |

exclusion of whatever held their attention before. As we have said, young children are very much in the moment. They are not multi-taskers.

✓ **Children learn by imitation.** You may have learned the hard way that your child is often watching you and taking in what you're doing and saying, even when you think he's not paying attention. As James Baldwin has often been quoted as saying, "Children have never been very good at listening to their elders, but they have never failed to imitate them."

When we set up an office in our dramatic play area, we were amused to see one little girl with the phone propped on her shoulder, pencil poised in her hand as she pretended to write down things related to her business call. No doubt she'd seen her mother do the same thing when she visited her at her office.

When we had an airplane in dramatic play, Cassidy got onboard with her suitcase, stuffed it under her chair, and pulled out the pretend cell phone she'd put in her pocket. "Yes," she said into the phone, "I just got on the plane now." We were pretty sure she must have seen her own father do exactly that on their recent vacation.

✓ **Children learn by doing and experimenting.** When they build a block tower, putting one block on top of another until it topples over (often to their cries of delight) they are finding out about gravity, about engineering, about structural stability. You may see them doing this same thing over and over again. They are learning rules of constancy: that the same thing happens the same way each time. Then, after doing the same thing five times, they change something — perhaps by putting a smaller block on the top place on the stack — and change the outcome. Hey, it stayed up this time! Now what if another small block is put on top of that one? Yea, it fell down! Let's build it again! All of this repetition also helps them to imprint what they are learning into their brain. Zip! zap! Those neural networks are growing and connecting!

In the later section on science, we share some fascinating experiments that the children thought of themselves, as well as some experiments that we did with them, or that we put out for them to try. Whenever they see the picture card for "Experiment" on our daily schedule, they become very excited! Kids love doing experiments.

✓ **Children learn by reading.** When we read books to the children, or when they look at books with interesting illustrations themselves, they are picking up a lot. Every book teaches a child something, whether it's facts about the weather or dinosaurs, or how to be a friend, or simply how beautiful and joyous the language is. Children love books!

✓ **Children learn by direct instruction,** such as when we teach them how to tie their shoes, or how to look both ways before crossing the street.

They do listen to what we say, and direct sharing of information is one way for children to learn. However, especially with younger children, a little bit of talking goes a long way.

We have learned over the years that at group time, after about five minutes of the teacher talking at the kids, it all turns into "blah-blah-blah" for them, and most of them tune us out and turn their attention to something more interesting, such as the friend sitting next to them.

The reason we put this method of learning last in our list is that it is the least effective method of learning for young children. But when you think about it, isn't this often true for adults as well? How many of us have had someone tell us how to do something new on the computer? "Just right click the mouse and click on 'hyperlink and fill in the URL and blah, blah, blah…" When we sit down to the computer the next time, can we recall what we were told? Frustratingly, no. It's not until we *do* the actual procedure on the computer, usually several times, that we really learn it.

The famous developmental psychologist Jean Piaget discovered that **young children are active constructors of their own knowledge,** not just passive receptacles of knowledge to be filled by adults. He gave the example of the child who said the wind is made by the trees, because she saw the trees waving

> **Developmental Asset #22:**
> Engagement in learning experiences

their branches on windy days and concluded that they were creating the wind.

Piaget felt that adults do the child a disservice by correcting her and telling her how wind is really made. It is important for the child to use her brain to figure things out; it is not particularly important for her to know as a four-year-old the physics wind-flow patterns. This is far too abstract for her to grasp. We can feel reasonably confident that she won't be telling her 10th grade science teacher that the wind is made by trees waving their arms. In the meantime, respecting her and her attempts to understand and make sense of the world lead us to say something along the lines of, "That's a very interesting idea!" And really, when you think about it, it is a very interesting idea, and a reasonable conclusion. After all, when a person holding a towel or a piece of paper waves his arms, it makes a breeze. Good thinking, kid!

Children construct their own knowledge in every area of learning, whether they're figuring out numbers or grammar or whether something floats in the bathtub. Piaget said that children must construct their own understanding and do their own research in order to truly learn and understand something. He felt that adults actually do a child a disservice by teaching the child something rather than letting him discover it himself. He felt that the deeper learning one achieves on one's own stays with a person much longer.

Tip: Children learn better by doing than by being told.

Now, guess who agrees with these child-development experts about letting children figure out the world for themselves: some of our greatest geniuses ever.

Albert Einstein once said, "Play is the highest form of research." And the guys who founded Google agree. When Barbara Walters asked Larry Page and Sergey Brin what they mainly attributed their success to, they credited their preschool, where they learned to be self-directed and to think for themselves.

And if that's not convincing enough, listen to the guy your child probably considers the highest authority — Elmo! In his book, *My Life as a Furry Red Monster: What Being Elmo Has Taught Me about Life, Love and Laughing Out Loud*, Elmo's puppeteer Kevin Clash says:

> "It's tempting to be the source of all information for our kids. They ask so many questions, and we have

to resist the urge to just answer them all. The show ['Sesame Street'] is designed to demonstrate to kids that knowledge is power.

Kids love to feel in control and smart, and so does Elmo. It's Elmo's World because, well... it *is* Elmo's world, and he's in charge of his own learning and discovering. Because he has the freedom to explore and define his own mission, he's an energized and enthusiastic student of the world." (p. 181)

So, parents—put away those flash cards, and give yourself permission to stop trying to drill knowledge into your young child's head. Those videos that promise to make your kid smarter? They may be fun and entertaining, but they're not necessary; she's going to learn a lot more on her own.

Promoting cognitive competence in young children is easier than you may think, because children are biologically primed to learn things well and quickly at this age. It's a lot like when we travel to a foreign county: Everything is new and interesting and exciting. The whole world is new to a preschooler, and everything is fascinating. That's the best part of our job as preschool teachers: We get to share with these children in their wonder and excitement of discovery. We get to experience the world as new, too, with them— and so do you. It is a gift, and a privilege.

Language: Speaking and Understanding

> *Victor informed us, "My daddy works downtown in an ice scraper."*

We will never forget the day when Norman, a four-year-old in our class, looked at a sign above the door of the classroom across the hall and suddenly exclaimed, "Oh my gosh, that says Fiesta!" We were privileged to be there at the very moment when written language clicked for Norman, the moment when those letters formed a complete word in his brain. We can still hear the amazed tone of his voice that conveyed, "I can't believe it—I just read that word!"

Some of the most exciting moments for us as teachers, for you as parents, and, not least of all for the child, are those moments of the discovery of language! What does it signify? Nothing less than liberation! From the moment your baby points and asks "Dat?" ("What do you call that?") your child is discovering the power of language—the power to understand, to express his ideas and his needs, and to affect the behavior of others. Is there anyone on Earth who feels more empowered than a two-year-old saying "No"? Words are powerful. Just listen to the five-year-old engaging in the fine art of negotiating with her mother regarding her bedtime.

From before your child was born, you've probably been told to talk to your child, read to your child, and expose your child to language, literature, and music. All of this creates a rich environment for the acquisition of language.

You've been doing that. Maybe your child's interest in language is flourishing. She wants to look at books or be read to, surprising you with how much she understands, talking non-stop. Maybe you even wonder if it's time to teach her to read. Or maybe your child is very quiet and seems to be slower to talk or to acquire mature language than you expected. Or it may seem that you are the only one who can understand her garbled speech. You wonder at what age she should be able to pronounce the "sh" or "k" sound. She confuses "he" and "she," or tells you "I ate it tomorrow," and this worries you a little.

The most helpful thing that we, or you, can do to encourage language development is to provide all kinds of language experiences—in a natural and playful way—tailoring them to the stage of language development your child is at and just beyond that stage.

Moderating Volume

Are your children too loud, too often? Do you wish you could "adjust their volume"? You might try singing the song "John Jacob Jingleheimer Schmidt" with your child.

[Start very quietly:]

John Jacob Jingleheimer Schmidt –
His name is my name too.

Whenever we go out,
The people always shout:
"John Jacob Jingleheimer Schmidt!"
Da da - da da - da da da !

[Repeat from beginning, louder each time]

Usually the song is sung loudly at first, and then more and more softly. To help the children become aware of controlling the volume of their voices, we like to start singing the song very quietly and gradually getting very loud.

Children love to have permission to be very loud and are delighted to find that their teachers can be loud, too. Many teachers refer to an inside voice (using a volume appropriate for being inside) and an outside voice (using a volume usually reserved for being outside). Elementary school teachers sometimes use the numbers 1 to 5 for the volume appropriate in different situations, and "zero" means to "turn your voice off." Whatever terms you use, just be clear and consistent. By the way, it's fine to use words like volume and appropriate, as long as you also use the simpler words and/or demonstrate the concepts.

Rhyming

Rhyming plays a big part in our classroom as a multi-purpose teaching tool. Silly rhymes are good, because children can use the concept of rhyming without having to think of real words or perfect rhymes. In English, nothing rhymes with orange, but if you say to your child, "Do you want to eat a piece of fruit that rhymes with 'borange'?" he will be delighted if he figures it out and says, "Yes, I want an orange!"

We usually start with the children's names. For example, sitting in a group, or eating snack, we might say "Claron. Whose name sounds like Claron?" "Sharon!" the kids will reply. Saying "Nick Click would you pick up that stick?" will get Nick's attention when we want him to start cleaning up, and if he giggles he's more likely to cooperate.

The rhyming accomplishes multiple purposes. Nick hears the "ick" sound repeated and realizes it is a part of his name as well as other words. He may start to listen for and recognize other words that incorporate the sound. Recognizing similar sounds, and later recognizing similar letter sequences that make those rhyming sounds, are pre-reading skills. Another purpose for rhyming? The kids think it's fun, and because it is fun, they pay attention. And because they pay attention, they learn. Rhyme, rhyme, all the time.

There's a reason so many popular children's books are written in rhyme. Besides the Dr. Seuss books with their clever, intricate, and silly rhymes (try *Hop on Pop* or *Green Eggs and Ham* for a start), there are wonderful rhyming picture books and stories and poetry that are silly and fun to read over and over. Rhyme and repetition catch the children's ear.

When reading a rhyming book or poem, we suggest you sometimes pause before the rhyming word and have your child supply the rhyme. After he is familiar with the book, have fun changing the rhyming words for extra giggles and practice in making rhymes. "Hickory dickory dock, the mouse ran up the sock," or "There were three little bears sitting on pears."

If your child is beginning to recognize patterns of letters as words, she may enjoy the challenge of finding matching patterns of letters and sounds in rhyming words. Try writing a word like cat. After she tries to sound it out, she can erase the first letter, and either you or she can write another letter at the beginning. What word is it now?

Children also enjoy doing puzzles where two pieces fit together if the pictures and words on each piece rhyme with each other, such as fox and box or dog and frog. Teacher supply stores are good places to look for rhyming games and puzzles.

Vocabulary and Usage

One of the primary tasks of young children is to learn the vocabulary and the grammatical structures of their own language. Children acquire new words at an astounding rate—anywhere from eight to twenty-eight new words a day. Most of these words they pick up from context: Daddy says "Hand me that screwdriver" as he points to the tool.

Dr. Diane Beals of the University of Tulsa points out that mealtimes are an excellent opportunity for young children to expand their vocabulary, as long as you're careful to make the conversation about topics that your child might be interested in and to which he can contribute.

Children understand far more vocabulary than they can produce, so don't hesitate to use words your child hasn't used yet. Children pick up the meaning of words from repetitive usage by adults.

As we've mentioned, we also love to introduce big words to the class. We make it sound important and grown up: "Would you like to learn the BIG word for this line around the middle of the earth? It's the EQUATOR. Try saying it: equator."

It's not really hard for a child to learn big words of three or four syllables. A child we knew could say all the names of the dinosaurs by age three, because he had a big interest in them and he read dinosaur books often. "There's a parasaurolophus!" he'd say, amazing the grown-ups around him.

Little kids can learn big words about things they're interested in and about real concrete things. They're probably not going to learn the word politician, but they matter-of-factly refer to the chrysalis when our caterpillars form one. Here are some words we heard kids in our class use recently:

- Nocturnal
- Hydration
- Predator
- Carnivore

Likewise, children pick up the correct way to structure what they say—the grammatical rules—from hearing sentences spoken correctly. So, English-speaking children learn to put the adjective before the noun, and Spanish-speaking children learn to put it after.

Of course, the irregularities of the language escape most preschoolers, so they will say things like "runned" for ran. Rather than directly correcting them, we repeat back what they said with correct usage: "Yes, you ran very fast." They don't appear to notice, but eventually, they naturally produce correct language in all its nuances and irregularities.

The same holds true when your child can't pronounce something correctly. It may be cute when your child says "I want a possical" or "I like susgetti," but should you laugh at it, repeat it, or correct it when you respond to them? None of the above. Just restate their comment in a matter-of-fact tone, as if you heard them say it correctly, modeling the correct speech. "Would you like a green or a red Popsicle®?" or "I like spaghetti too."

It is common for preschoolers to be confounded by opposites. It seems weird when a three-year-old says "I'm going to go up the stairs" at the top of the stairs, and then walks down. But in her mind, up and down both signify movements on stairs, and she gets caught by the fact that she is now up at the top of the stairs. Four-year-olds will say "I want to take off my jacket. I'm too cold." What they mean is they want to become more cold, since they're too hot right now, but the words get reversed in their speaking.

Most of these language usage issues will resolve themselves naturally as your child matures, so they are nothing to worry about. But, if you're looking for another way to pass the time while driving in the car, or sitting in a doctor's waiting room, why not play some simple language games? You can play The Opposites Game. You can begin: "When the light is *not* on, it is…" Later, you can say, "The *opposite* of heavy, is …." Depending on your child's age, think of above/below, high/low, thick/thin, morning/ evening, easy/difficult, inflated/deflated, bitter/sweet, and so on. Believe it or not, this is actually fun for preschoolers. They find it challenging and therefore interesting.

Playing guessing games can help your child with vocabulary and learning to describe things by their size, color, texture and other attributes by using adjectives in your description. "I'm thinking of something that is cold, hard, and slippery." "It is cold, smooth, and it melts in your mouth." "It is furry and soft and curls up in your lap."

Language: Reading and Writing

We read Robert McCloskey's classic "Blueberries for Sal." Leah speculated on why there was no color in the illustrations. "Maybe all their crayons were broken, and maybe they didn't have markers back in those days. Because I remember you said it was written a long time ago."

Reading and writing go hand in hand in preschool. These two aspects of language usage are intertwined: children try to write words using the sounds they know letters

Developmental Asset #25: Early literacy

make, and they try to read signs they see by sounding them out. They write words by scrawling on a piece of paper shapes that look like what they see grown-ups write, and then they pretend to read them. They love to read books, over and over, and they love to tell stories by drawing pictures or by having adults write down their words.

Recognizing Letters

When children begin to recognize that specific shapes represent letters, or become curious about signs, words in books, and so on, it is a good time to start focusing on specific letters, and their sounds. Being the egocentric creatures that they are, children first are most interested in the letters of their own name. Susie might spot a stop sign as she's riding in the car and exclaim with surprised delight, "Hey, there's my letter S!"

What are things you can do at home with your child to help him learn his letters? First, fun stuff. Buy a set of letter-shaped cookie cutters for him to use with Play-Doh and in making cookies with you. When you make the cookies, you can spell out your child's name. At school we sometimes put out trays of shaving cream, pudding, finger paint or sand in which the children can write letters with their fingers. At home, you can squirt shaving cream onto the wall of the bathtub and let your child trace letters in it.

Before long you will find, as we do at school, that the children are pointing out letter-like shapes in their snacks or lunch. Small twist pretzels are especially fun as they break or bite pieces off to form letter shapes. Or they're noticing that a straight stick makes an "l" and a curved piece makes a "c." Then they begin spotting letters everywhere.

We notice the children frequently looking at the alphabet poster in our room. There are many beautiful alphabet posters available, and we suggest you put one on your child's bedroom or playroom wall.

There are also sign language alphabet posters. Associating the letter with its sign-language sign is a good way to firm up that letter knowledge in the young child's brain, and we have noticed that many young children actually learn the alphabet more easily by using that kinesthetic (muscle motion) connection. A bonus is that several of the signs for individual letters are useful to teachers, as they will be for you, too. Putting the "L" sign by your ear means listen. We use that one a lot! It's often much more effective than just repeating "listen!"

If you shake the "T" sign, it means "toilet." Your child would enjoy telling you she has to go potty by making and shaking the "T" sign. It's also a good way to discretely ask to go to the bathroom in a crowd of people!

Make an Alphabet or Rebus Book

In our classroom, we sometimes make alphabet books based on photos we take of the children. For example, we take a picture of Jack and Jenny jumping joyously to put on the "J" page.

You might have fun with your child creating your own alphabet book with photos you take at home or in familiar places. You can do single words or phrases, as long as you make sure your child, or people or animals important to your child, are in each photo.

For "X," always a tough one, you can have your child draw a treasure map with an "X" marking the spot. When you get to "Z," you can show your child zipping his coat. Or if you're lucky enough to live near a zoo, what fun you'll have taking a trip to the zoo with your child to complete the book.

Try making books for your child that feature him and those things, people, and places he loves—a book about your vacation, or a book about his favorite places to go, or holidays, or accomplishments ("Mikey can ride a bike!"), or the people in his extended family, or just use your imagination, and your child's imagination!

Keep it simple. You don't have to write great literature — just a few words with each photo. These custom books can be printed out for your child to look at and read with you, and they can also be put on your tablet, so that you can have several personal books for him to enjoy, right at hand, wherever you are. And don't forget the Feelings Book we suggested in the *Emotional Competence* chapter. All of these books starring your egocentric child and his interests will be excellent tools for learning letters and words! Plus, they make wonderful keepsakes of your child's early years.

A favorite story in our classroom is the rebus book that Deb puts together each year, starring the kids in the class. If you are not familiar with them, a rebus book is one in which small pictures are inserted in the text in place of some words.

For beginning, or pre-readers, these books are fun for your child to read side by side with you. You or a big brother or sister can read the text, pointing to the words as you go, and the child fills in the word as you come to each picture. The child helps to read the story and, by following your pointing finger, also sees how to read each word in sequence left to right and return to the left at each new line, a very important reading skill! Sometimes children actually begin to recognize the words, too.

You can find some rebus books in the library, but Deb has created one for you on our website that you can customize for your child by inserting your own photos of your children. You can also have fun making your own simple rebus book, inserting pictures of the faces of your family members or your child's friends, as well as pictures that you get from Google Images or other sources.

Word Recognition / Beginning Reading

Children vary considerably in when they acquire the ability to read, so while we don't teach reading in preschool, we are aware that our three- to five-year-olds will range from total disinterest in letters to already beginning to read.

To understand what makes the building blocks of reading, it helps to understand where the children are heading when they get to Kindergarten and first grade. First grade teacher Judy Cowdery says, "From day one of first grade I am teaching them both sight words and phonics. Quick recognition of sight words makes reading more fluent and enjoyable." So, we give the children plenty of opportunities to recognize words that they see over and over, as well as to learn what sounds the letters make.

Once they recognize their own names in writing, we find that they often begin to recognize their friends' names. We are frequently surprised when a child who (we think) doesn't yet recognize many letters looks at the job chart and blurts out, "Evan, you're the line leader today." Your child will be motivated to read and write family members' names.

In school when we read the Morning Message, they see the same words used frequently: "We will..." or "Let's make..." or the best one, "Happy Birthday to..." At home, you can put a whiteboard at your child's eye level that is just for her. You can write daily special messages for her to discover: "Today we will go to Grandma's house" or "What do you want to do today?" or, of course, "I love you." Children also love to find a written message in their lunch box from Mom or Dad.

One day, when a couple of children noticed that their own names began and ended with the same letter, we helped them find other names that also did so: for example, the L's in Laurel, the N's in Nathan, and the A's in Alexa. This is a teachable moment. The children expressed an interest, and we helped them extend it. This discovery by the children turned into a list of names and words that start and end with the same letter, which we posted on the wall. The children would run up to us each time they found one to add to the list: Mom, Dad, Ana, Alaska.

Things that begins to fascinate and confuse the children as they begin to recognize letters include:

- N sideways looks like Z

- M upside down looks like W

- d can be turned or flipped to look like p, b, or q

- Some letters look the same in both uppercase and lowercase

Once they start to recognize words, it is fun to note that noon spelled backwards is still noon, and MOM turned upside down is WOW! Isn't it fun to play with words?

Another piece of beginning reading that we can introduce in preschool is phonics — knowing what sounds each letter makes. Be sure to keep phonics fun rather than a drill. If your child is showing interest in letter sounds, she may be asking you frequently what letter a word starts with. Ask her what she thinks before telling here.

Don't worry if your five-year-old shows no interest in letter sounds. Many children are so preoccupied by other interests, whether it's riding a scooter or drawing pictures or building with construction sets, that they just put phonics on the back burner of their brains. That's OK.

Another good game for the car, or to play with your child while you're making dinner. "I'm thinking of a vehicle that starts with a D—DUH—and helps with construction." "Dump truck!" Or write a letter on her whiteboard and play, "Can you think of five things that start with this letter?"

Whether your child learns the letter sounds at age three, four, five or six, at some point the connections will be made in his amazing brain and it will all click, and your child will discover the joy of reading. Of course, there are some children who struggle with dyslexia or other learning disabilities, and if your child happens to be one of them, professional help is available.

Writing

Writing, for a young preschooler, may not be fun. Many three-year-olds do not yet have the necessary fine motor skills. Even by age four, writing letters can be difficult.

Many preschoolers just make a series of diagonal up and down lines for both "M" and "W," and depending on whether they happen to start at the bottom or the top of the letter, it can come out either way. Likewise, many preschoolers mix up "b" and "d" and can't really see the difference. In general, reversals don't carry significance for a young child. Just like a book is still a book when it's turned backward, and a fork is still a fork when they turn it upside down, a "b" is still a "b" in their mind even when they turn it backward. In fact, children at this age often write their whole name backward, starting at the right and reversing all the letters, without even noticing it.

Likewise, young children are not at first concerned with placement of letters on the paper. When Ariana writes her name, she might put the first three letters across the bottom of the paper, run out of room, put the next "a" and "n" on the left side, and then put the last "a" in the top right corner.

Also, it's very common for preschoolers to write each consecutive letter larger than the one preceding it, so that by the end of Ariana's name, the last "A" might be three times the size of the first. None of these things matter initially, and undue attention to them will only frustrate the child who is just learning to write.

Words on a page go from left to right, top to bottom. Learning the difference between left and right is a skill that applies to reading and writing, as well as to other things in life. We have a little trick for teaching which hand is the left hand. But the child has to recognize the letter L first (and know which way it faces). Hold both hands up in front of you (palms out), with your thumb and first finger making an L shape directly in front of you. Which hand makes the L going the correct way? L is for left.

Writing is both a physical skill and a cognitive one. Even if a child has a hard time physically forming letters, preschoolers can develop an interest in writing and an understanding that writing is a tool for communicating. We see this when they play at being a waiter, and pretend to write down food orders. They like it when we write down their ideas in class discussions and post them on a wall. They begin to realize that the words they see in books are a form of writing, too.

At home, keep a pad of Post-It notes handy. When Kara says she wants to go to the library, jot it on a note and let her stick it on the calendar. When Jason says he wants macaroni and cheese, let him see you write it on the shopping list.

Even though writing an actual letter to someone is becoming a lost art in this day and age, we encourage you to help your child write letters to far-away relatives. She can dictate it, while you write down her words exactly as she says them. If she draws a picture for Grandma, she may want you to help her sign it or put a note on it. Won't Grandma be thrilled when she gets a letter in the mail as dictated by her grandchild!

Some four- and five-year-olds who do have good fine motor skills become interested in writing letters and words. In fact, some preschoolers seem driven to write. You can encourage this at home by having a small clipboard with paper and pencil available. We've noticed that kids love writing on clipboards, doing surveys, taking your restaurant order, or copying words that they see.

We often see the children writing in the dramatic play area, making lists or pretending to write in an office. At first they are just making wavy lines up and down across the paper, imitating what they see grown-ups do. This is a good pre-writing skill and we are happy to see it. Some children write strings of letters and then ask us what it says. We try to sound out the string of letters and then say, "Well, that's a funny word, isn't it?" They happily agree.

When children can write letters and know what sounds the letters make, they can be encouraged to write simple words or short phrases. The child might write "PLZ GIV ME A BNA" for "Please give me a banana." This is fine—in fact, it's wonderful! We don't correct spelling at this point, since learning to spell, especially in English, comes much later. This child is well on the road to learning to read.

Another thing we do is to write down the children's stories. We may sit down with a group of four children at Halloween and say, "Let's make up a story about children going trick-or-treating." We hope that you will try it at home, too. Write down stories for your child that she dictates to you, encouraging her to say how it begins, have something happen, and then eventually come to an ending. She may want to create illustrations for her story as well, and will probably want to look at the finished product frequently with you.

We want children to understand that written words are important, and their written words are especially important. Deb can still vividly remember her parents help her first story ever, at age four, when she bounded into their bedroom early one morning to ask for help writing the words. The resulting book, written in purple, of which she was so proud? How the Bunny Stole the Carrots.

Introducing Other Languages

Introducing some of the vocabulary, songs, and sounds of other languages is another way to play with words. It also helps children realize that language is for communication and that there are many different ways to communicate.

Since both of us know some Spanish and a little bit of American Sign Language, we make it a habit to introduce words in both languages that relate to other things we are learning or doing. Using CDs available from the library, we help the children learn some simple or familiar songs in Spanish. And there are some songs we sing while signing the key words. "The More We Get Together" is a good one for this. The children take to it readily and enjoy learning new words. In the process, we let them know that children around the world sing and play and enjoy stories very much like they do, but using different words and ways of talking to communicate them.

Of course, we're not all fluent in two or more languages, but maybe you know a little bit of another language. Even if you don't speak a second language, you can look for bilingual children's books in the library. Many of these, like *Abuela,* by Arthur Dorros, *Isabel and the Hungry Coyote,* by Keith Polette, and *Mama Provi and the Pot of Rice,* by Sylvia Roa-Casanova, contain just a few words in another language and give a glimpse into another culture.

If you speak another language, your children will be all the richer when you share it. Often, parents wonder if their child will be confused by another language while her first language is still developing, but that is not the case. Young brains are very flexible, so they absorb and sort out languages readily.

Fun with Literature

We don't have to tell you that sitting close to you and listening to you read or tell a story is a very special time for your children. Hearing the emotions in your voice helps them understand and empathize with the characters. You bring the characters to life for them. Of course, children like their favorite books to be read over and over ... and over! We know that's a good thing, and we're sure you do too. But when you're tired of that book, you could agree to read that favorite book plus a new one you're excited to share with her.

A friend of ours had read his son Zack's favorite book, Louis Baum's *I Want to See the Moon*, so many times, he didn't have to look at the pages to read the book! Does this sound familiar?

When you and your child are thoroughly familiar with a book and maybe you are becoming pretty bored with it, you can surprise him by changing some key words in the story. Reading with a straight face, you might substitute your child's name instead of the character's name. Or you might change the description of a familiar object—"Clifford, the big purple dog" or "Cinderella lost her rubber slipper." "NO! It's a glass slipper!" he will howl.

Children love for us to be wrong even if they know we're joking. What are they doing? Enhancing their listening skills, realizing that word choices matter, that adjectives describe things, and even that grownups make mistakes.

We have found that certain books become favorites of the children in our class year after year. These often are the classics. James Marshall, who won the Laura Ingalls Wilder Award for his substantial and lasting contribution to children's literature, has retold Goldilocks and the Three Bears, Little Red Riding Hood, and many other tales in a delightful fashion that the children adore.

They also like books about big things—dinosaurs and giants for example, as in Deb's favorite, *Abiyoyo*, by Pete Seeger. They love wordless books with wonderful illustrations, such as those by Caldecott Award-winning author David Wiesner.

There are thousands of wonderful books for preschoolers. We share a few of our favorites on our website. One type of book we do not recommend are those based on popular toys, movies or TV shows. These are usually just poorly-written commercials for the product, in our opinion.

When we read, we tell the children the names of the author and illustrator. We let them know when we are reading them one of *our* favorite books. We take our time with the stories, letting children point out things that they notice, asking them questions about what they think, or what will happen next. Sometimes we ask, "Why do you think that?" We give them time to answer. Specialists say that you should wait between three and fifteen seconds for children to absorb a question and decide to answer. Resist the urge to answer for them!

It is important for children to see adults read. Seeing that you make time for reading, that you enjoy reading, and also that you read and write to gain information from the newspaper, magazines, cookbooks, your mail makes the idea of reading both important and special for your child.

Other ways you can help children enjoy literature are:

✓ **Provide a book corner.** We recommend a mix of fiction and non-fiction books for children (on construction, animals, art, travel, professions, sports, and so on).

In your home, it would be nice for your child to have a cozy little book corner of her own. It's also important to store and display her books on bookshelves which are inviting and which keep the books from getting wrecked. Or if you don't have room for a bookshelf, you can keep the books in a plastic bin or a nice basket, so that she can easily look through them to find the one she wants.

✓ **Listen to stories on CDs** (which may be borrowed from the library)

✓ **Listen to poems** with eyes closed. Books of poetry usually have fewer illustrations, so we tell them: "Close your eyes and listen to the words and create the pictures in your head." Afterwards ask them what they saw. Often, they have noticed details or imagined things that surprise us.

✓ **Make up variations on familiar stories** with your child. A fun example: We asked the children to re-tell *The Three Little Pigs*, by picking a new environment and new animals. They came up with a wonderful story called *The Three Little Crabs and the Big Bad Shark*. After the crabs defeated the shark, the story ended with, "Then the three little crabs had a crab party to celebrate. The only problem was they popped all the balloons with their crab claws!" Aren't preschoolers creative?

You might also try a variation on the popular book, *If You Give a Mouse a Cookie* by Laura Numeroff. "If you give a ____ [your child picks an animal] a ____ [your child picks an object]. What would happen? Then what?" Be sure to write down your children's original stories, with each scene on a different page, and then let them illustrate it. You, too, will be impressed by your amazing preschooler!

Tip: When building your child's home library, don't forget the classic picture books, like *Make Way for Ducklings* and *Blueberries for Sal* by Robert McCloskey.

Appreciation for great literature, both poetry and prose, begins early. Help your child choose books with engaging stories, interesting dialogue and vocabulary, and wonderful illustrations.

The child who eagerly asks for *Cloudy with a Chance of Meatballs* at age four becomes the child who devours the Harry Potter books at age 10. The child who reads and rereads *Jumanji* at age five becomes the young woman who reads and rereads *I, Robot*.

The child who carries *Stellaluna* with him everywhere at age three becomes the young man who treasures *Call of the Wild* as a teenager.

Once you get into the habit of reading often with your child, you will both find that you don't want to give that up! Many parents we know (ourselves included) continued to read with their kids long after they had learned to read by themselves—and eventually the children read long chapter books to their sleepy moms and dads, as we nodded off to sleep!

Math

> *Wesley told us "My birthday is Thenember 14" (an interesting combination of "number" and "November").*

OK, everyone, let's have some fun now — let's do *math*! What? Math isn't fun? Math is hard and boring? Clearly, you are not four years old. Preschoolers find numbers just as intriguing as butterflies and books. Preschoolers' curiosity knows no bounds and their desire to be powerful knows none either. Bigger is better ... and bigger is a math concept.

As high school test scores come in from around the world, there has been a growing realization for some time now that American students need to catch up to educated children in the rest of the world in their knowledge and competence in math and sciences. Parents, schools, and governments are focusing on improving the curriculum, increasing the rigor, and pushing kids ahead. We want our children, right from the start, to buckle down, study and learn more, and be driven to excel. But the best and deepest learning, and the most lasting drive must come from internal motivation and a sense of personal competence.

The preschool years are the time, we believe, to instill that sense of competence, of curiosity, of investigation, and self-motivation. We encourage and capitalize on the fascination with mathematical concepts and the power that preschoolers feel when they can de-

> **Developmental Asset #21:**
> Motivation to mastery

scribe their world in mathematical terms. In preschool, we strive to make math and science a natural and necessary part of our everyday experiences. We seek to instill a life-long interest in mathematical competence. In preschool, math is exciting and fun.

When preschoolers begin to realize that they can express things in terms of numbers—"I can jump a thousand twenty-hundred-eighty-ten inches"—they feel powerful. When they measure ninety feet down the school hallway and realize that an apatosaurus was *that* long, they feel awe. And when they realize that ten and ten more is twenty, or that they can share their ten blocks equally by giving five to a friend, they have gained new powers to manage and explain their world. There is pride in Emilia's face as she figures out that when her little brother is four, she will be six. In preschool, math is everywhere, math is hands-on, math is real-life, and math is powerful.

Where do we find math and what does it look like to a preschooler? Math is everywhere in our classrooms and in our conversations. It occurs in the natural course of play; in books and songs and signs on the walls; in making comparisons and making predictions; in discussions of time; in games and artwork; in making and observing patterns and geometric shapes, sorting, and sequencing. Children engage in math activities naturally and the teachers facilitate their understanding by putting names to things, by asking questions, or by helping them to figure it out again.

In mathematical terms, the basic concepts, usually grasped in this order, are:

- Counting by rote

- One-to-one correspondence

- Understanding that a number represents a quantity of things

- Geometric (shape) awareness

- Sequencing

- Seeing and making patterns

- Making comparisons

- Measurement

- Understanding parts of a whole

- Manipulating objects and numbers to add and subtract or to make new shapes

Predicting and estimating can also be introduced to preschoolers.

One-to-one correspondence, although it seems obvious to us as adults, is a big step in early math awareness. With one-to-one correspondence, you can match each object in one set of things to exactly one object in another set. More abstractly, you can touch and count objects, so that the number 1 refers to one object and 2 refers to the next object.

As children count sequentially, lining up and touching the objects helps them realize that they should count each object only once. They then can touch and count a small group of objects and identify the set as the last number they counted, finally matching a written number to that number of objects.

One activity preschoolers enjoy is counting out small buttons, crackers, and so on to match the number written inside a muffin tin or the number of dots on the dice. There is a gradual and natural progression to understanding these concepts, much like a baby must realize that her hand is part of her own body before she can use it purposefully to pick up peas or get a spoon to her mouth. But there is also an inter-connectedness, not only between the math concepts, but between math and music, language, reading, art, and thinking skills.

Of course, the preschoolers we see discovering a mathematical awareness at school are doing so at home, as well. We know that you are probably delighting in your child's numerical discoveries, too. Let's look at some of them.

Here are some examples of math questions and discoveries in our class.

Rahma holds up two grapes from her lunch and asks the others at her table: "Which one is bigger: the big one or the small one?" She laughs when Robby says, "The big one is bigger!"

Hallie says "I have 15 Cheerios. How many do you have?" "Is 15 more than 10?" Hallie and Henry decide to eat them one at a time together. Hallie discovers that she has five more.

Jody uses interlocking cubes to make a long symmetrical line of colored cubes — the pattern of colors repeats from the center, going toward both ends. She then breaks it in the middle, puts the two halves next to each other and comments that she has "upside down patterns." They are the same, but one sequence starts at one end, one at the other.

Chuck sorts a small pile of seeds into groups of each type, counts to find out that he has seven different kinds of seeds, then uses glue and the seeds to make patterns with the seeds.

Alicia adds an X on the chart where we are keeping track of how many days until the tadpole gets legs, and then announces that it has been 13 days so far.

At home, listen to your child's comments and questions. When you notice that Carla is lining up the peas on her plate, ask her how many peas she has. If Denny is arguing with his little brother over who has more of the blocks, or cars, or action figures, ask them to figure out how they could make sure they both have the same number? Will they line them up together and compare? Can they put them all in one pile and then deal them out, one to each, then one more to each, and so on. What should they do if there is one left over?

Tip: When your child asks you a math question, ask her to try to figure it out first, rather than just giving an answer.

Speaking of counting, there are dozens of cleverly illustrated picture books that introduce children to counting to 10, or to 100, or counting by 2s, 5s, and 10s, finding matched pairs, and so on.

Our website has suggestions of books and games that engage children in counting and math. The Internet has an ever-increasing supply of mostly free online math games of all kinds, for all ages.

Check our website for books and games that we like because they challenge and engage the imagination. Try out the games yourself first. Look for games you can download and play off-line, or ones that are on education sites, without ads. Always watch and supervise your young child at the computer.

But before we get carried away with the entertainment the Internet affords, let us tell you more about the amazing ways that children discover math in their real-world daily life.

Geometry and Patterns

Preschool is the age when most children learn the names of shapes, including some fairly difficult shapes, such as oval and hexagon. The circle is the easiest shape to learn, while the rectangle can be difficult for many children.

Drew shows us a design he has made on a geoboard, a board with pegs in a square grid. He points out that he had stretched two rubber bands from corner to corner, making a large X, and then he used rubber bands to make a triangle in each part of the X. We show him that if he outlines the board with rubber bands, each part of the X also makes a triangle. He then sees that he has four large and four smaller triangles, or eight triangles. That's geometry, counting, classifying, and adding — all in one manipulative activity.

Please see our website for a photo of a geoboard. You can make a geoboard at home by hammering nails at regular intervals into a square piece of wood or plywood A 9 x 9 inch square is a good size. Or you can buy a geo board at school supply stores. Your child can make lots of designs by hooking colorful rubber bands around the nails.

Tip: A geoboard and colored rubber bands are a great thing to add to a special quiet activities kit that you can pull out when it's time for your child to calm down, or for children who have outgrown their nap but still need some quiet time each day.

Another geometry exploration happened when we introduced the idea of writing cards or letters to send in the mail. We gave each child an envelope and a piece of paper. We asked, "What do you notice about the envelopes?" and "How can you fold that paper to fit it in your envelope?" The children replied: "The envelopes are different sizes and shapes." "Mine is a rectangle." "The flap is a triangle." "Mine is long." "Look, I can fold it two ways and it fits in the envelope." This led to a lot of interest in paper folding.

To reinforce the names of shapes, we talk about them in the context of the children's world. You can do this too. Questions you can ask include:

- **At lunch**: "Is there something square in your lunch?" "Can you find a triangle?"

- **While driving**: "What shape is the Exit sign?" "What shape is a Stop sign?"

- **At a playground**: "Let's draw a circle in the sand." "Do you see a diamond shape in the fence?"

Tip: While you're making dinner, send your child on a shape hunt. "Go find three things that are circles, and come back and tell me. Now find three triangles in the kitchen."

Of course, a great toy for learning about geometric shapes, as well as other math concepts such as fractions and patterns, is a good set of wooden blocks. This tops our list of excellent toys for home as children can discover new and more complex ways to use them for years.

Also fun and appealing in their color and beauty are sets of parquetry blocks: thin, flat geometric pieces children can assemble onto a board or to make their own patterns. These small colorful wooden triangles, squares, rectangles, and diamonds can be made into endless designs and patterns. Deb kept a basket containing a couple of hundred parquetry blocks on her coffee table at home for years, and even adults who visited would be drawn to them and begin arranging them in complex and beautiful designs on the coffee table.

Learning to recognize, repeat, and create patterns is important. It leads to facility with math, music and reading.

Like we do in school, you and your child can hunt for or spy patterns in art, in ceiling tiles, in windows, in picture books, on the piano keys, on a fence, in the garden. Don't forget to notice the shapes, too!

You can help your child identify patterns in music, too. By singing songs with repeating lines and simple repeating rhythms, children incorporate the patterns and rhythms into their brains.

With rhythm sticks, we play a game where one person taps a quick pattern, maybe just three or four taps, and the others try to copy it. They love to take turns creating the rhythm. They learn to hear syllables in words as we (and then the children) tap out the syllables in their names: Co-ry, Bri-an-na, E-liz-a-beth. In music class one day, our class practiced drumming their names. Later, hearing about eight or ten rapid drumbeats coming from an adjoining classroom, Taylor commented, "Whoever is doing that sure has a long name!"

Another way you and your child can explore visual patterns is to set out a few stamps and stamp pads, or use beads to string on pipe cleaners. Show your child how to make simple repeating patterns with the stamps or beads, and then ask her to suggest or make her own patterns.

Comparing, Ordering and Measuring

As children begin to expand their vocabulary they love to learn new words. We don't just talk about short and long. We demonstrate the concepts:

- We use Play-Doh to make snakes that are short and long, and longer

- We curl up small and then stretch to be tall, and taller

- We compare our pretzel sticks to see which is taller

- We'll play with a tray full of buttons to sort them by size and talk about which ones are small, medium, or big. If we find some that are even smaller, we'll decide if they are tiny or miniscule.

You can do this at home, and then start a game by asking questions, such as: "What is something that's tiny?" "Can you think of something tinier than that?" "What is the tiniest thing you can think of?" "What is something large?" "Even larger?" "How about something that's *huge*?" "Even larger — something humongous?"

You can enjoy this game anytime, anywhere, with any type of comparison: "Think of something light as a feather, a little heavier, heavier than that; the heaviest thing you can think of."

Young children really enjoy sorting and classifying. Your child will be delighted when you ask him to line up the boots in order from smallest to biggest. He will enjoy sorting the coins in the coin jar, or lining up his toy animals by size.

The next step is to compare more-subtle differences, and sort items accordingly. After that, some children may be able to classify objects with more than one common attribute. You can make a simple Venn diagram on a large piece of paper, drawing two large circles that overlap in the middle, and call it "The Sorting Things Out Game." As a first step, have children sort things like rocks or toy cars into two groups, ignoring the overlap in the middle. You can offer this game with many variations. Believe it or not, this is really fun for preschoolers.

When your child has mastered this, try adding in the overlap. If you find a jar of buttons at a garage sale, pick it up! Kids love playing with and sorting buttons.

Another day you and your child might have picked up fall leaves that can be sorted by color and size. Or you could sort family photos into "cousins", "people who live far away" and in the middle, "cousins who live far away"? This is very challenging for four- and five-year-olds. If your child finds it frustrating or too hard, don't push it. Also, refrain from correcting mistakes.

Tip: Sorting and classifying activities are not only fun and challenging for preschoolers; they also develop math, language and higher thinking skills, including the important executive function skills.

A step past the ordering of objects from smallest to largest is to measure things. We keep several measuring tapes in our room, and the children often use them to measure things, and each other. They're not always accurate about getting the starting point of the tape at the beginning of the object. Sometimes we help them do so, but usually we just let them explore the measuring tape on their own and get a feeling for what measuring something means. An inexpensive measuring tape and a ruler would be great toys for your child. Of course, the thing they are most interested in measuring is themselves.

You have many opportunities to use measuring when your child helps you cook or bake at home. Cooking also involves beginning use of fractions, offering a very concrete, visual way for the child to see that two half cups make one whole cup.

Since children are very interested in the weather, you and your child could keep track of the temperature each day, or use a rain gauge to measure rainfall and a ruler to measure snowfall.

Counting

Let us count the ways that children love to count! They endlessly enjoy favorite songs and poems, such as:

"One, two, three, four, five. Once I caught a fish alive.
Six, seven, eight, nine, ten. Then I let it go again.
Why did you let it go? Because it bit my finger so!
Which finger did it bite? The little finger on the right."

We all love the counting backward songs such as "Five little monkeys swinging in a tree," "Five green and speckled frogs," and "Five little ducks went out to play." Of course you can start with any number. A simple and fun way to keep on track and illustrate the subtraction process — and you can do this at home — is to print and cut out small pictures of monkeys, frogs, ducks, and so on.

You can also buy stickers of monkeys, frogs and ducks, and attach them to Popsicle sticks to make stick puppets. Start with all the monkeys and let your child take one away after each verse. You can put these in your car fun kit, since singing songs while driving is a wonderful alternative to watching videos all the time.

A favorite job in our classroom is Accountant. The children love to count the days on the calendar or the number of children in school today.

If you have a job chart at home, Accountant would be a fun job to add. Ask your child to count how many people will be eating lunch, and then to figure out how many plates to put on the table, or how many sandwiches to make for the picnic. Or you might say, "Oh, accountant, I need to know how many books we are checking out of the library today. Will you please count them?"

Snack and lunch times offer many opportunities for counting, adding, and comparing. Although we are apt to initiate the counting discussion, the children often bring up the questions themselves. "How many crackers can I take?" "How many people have apples today?" "There are five girls at this table and four at the other table. We have more girls." You can find similar opportunities at home, too. Of course, the key in all these situations is to make it natural, fun, and game-like. You don't want to be quizzing your child relentlessly, or forcing counting on him when he's not interested.

Don't be surprised if your child skips thirteen and fifteen when learning to count in the teens. It is extremely common. Shouldn't they be "three-teen" and "five-teen" anyway? One child counted correctly to nineteen, but the next number was "ten-teen." What good logic!

Predictions and Guesses

To help your child learn to estimate and make predictions, you can ask your child questions like:

- "How many steps do you think it is from here to the bathroom?"

- "How many raisins do you think you can fit in your hand?"

- "How many days do you think it will be until the butterfly comes out of the chrysalis?"

- "How many cups of water are in that pitcher?

- "How many days until the tomatoes are ripe?

You can write down the guesses, and then count to find out the actual number. Decide together if the real number was more or less than the guess. Also decide if the prediction was close or not so close.

One reminder: Children learn best when they are ready—when they have mastered the preceding steps, when their brain is ready, when their muscles are developed, when they are mature enough, when they are rested. So in all of these activities, take the cues from your child, and do the activities only at the level she is ready for, and for the amount of time that she can remain interested. And remember, preschoolers are concrete visual thinkers. They can't think of numbers abstractly in their heads very well. They need real objects and real numbers with which to work.

Most preschoolers can't add or subtract in their heads. A few can do it using the number 1. But most children can use objects, or their fingers, or a number line, to figure out adding and taking away.

You can use your own number lines, perhaps to represent the number of juice boxes in the pantry, the number of days until a fun activity, or the number of times your child has done a chore this week.

This is just the starting point! All these number games can be done using numbers larger than 10 or 20 when your child is ready. Start where he feels competent, and move on, enticing him to make that next step ahead. We love to see the amazement on the children's faces when they begin to discover and to manipulate large numbers. In turn, we are continually surprised by *your amazing children!*

Number Literacy

Just like we provide a print-rich environment to foster print awareness and pre-reading skills, we provide a number-rich environment with number puzzles, bingo games, a sign telling how many pretzels to take for snack, and a number chart.

Your child can find a lot of numbers at home, too:

- Days on the calendar

- Page numbers in the books you read with your child

- House numbers

- Numbers on a phone or on the TV remote

Discovering or pointing out these numbers when occasions arise, and giving your child the chance to play with numbers by using an old phone or hand-held calculator, provide natural ways to practice recognizing numbers. In fact, if she can memorize her home phone number or your cell phone number, that's a good safety idea.

On the highway and at the grocery store, you can play number games with your child such as:

- "Spot the Numbers" — 1 to 9 in order

- "Numbers Up and Down" — spotting the numbers 1 to 9 and then 9 to 1

- "Double Numbers" — spotting 00, 11, 22, and so on

- "My Number" — how many 4's (if your child is four) can you find in the next 10 minutes?

You can make up your own variations on these simple but engaging games. And an added bonus is that kids who are looking out the car window avidly seeking numbers aren't getting into fights in the back seat.

Game stores carry dice of many kinds, some with more than six sides. We suggest getting a few with dots and a few with numbers. Inventing dice games such as "Which is more? Which is less?" or "Add the dots" or "Hop ____ times" can be an easy way to engage your child while you prepare dinner, feed the baby, wait to be served at a restaurant, or just spend some one-on-one time with your math-loving child.

How much fun can you have with math? Let us count the ways …

Science: Learning About the Natural World

One morning, we were huddled around the computer, watching live video from a webcam at a nature preserve in South Africa. It was evening there. As we watched the impala at the watering hole, Tyler, ever observant and curious, asked, "If there's only one sun in the sky, how can it be going down in South Africa when it's coming up here?"

Does your kid like to collect rocks? Many of our students do. One day, several of the children in our class were collecting rocks on the playground, and filling their pockets with these treasures to bring home. As we watched them excitedly showing each other their beautiful rocks, we realized that an interest in rocks was growing. Then one day one of the children asked us, "Are rocks alive?"

Hmmmm. Very good question. How should we answer that?

Our response was, "What do you think?" Well, that child wasn't sure, but he thought maybe they were alive.

The next day when the children came to group time, we told them we'd noticed that a lot of them were interested in rocks, and we wondered if they'd like to learn more. They responded enthusiastically. We asked them what they'd like to learn about rocks. At the top of the list we wrote "Are rocks alive?" They also wanted to know things like how rocks are made, and what rocks are used for.

The next three weeks were absolutely fascinating, not just for the children, but for us as well. We explored rocks in many different ways. We took walks in the woods to hunt for rocks. The children drew pictures of rocks, and they made beautiful art sculptures from rocks.

> **Developmental Asset #22:**
> Engagement in learning experiences

We got a lot of books from the library about rocks for the children to look at. We put a large basket of rocks on the Discovery Table, so the children could weigh them on a scale, examine them, and sort them in various ways.

And most importantly, we let the children figure out for themselves if rocks were alive. At the beginning of our rock project, the class was split about 50-50 on whether they thought rocks were alive. The children had a wonderful discussion about what makes something alive. This is what the group came up with: Things that are alive move, talk, make sounds, move by themselves, grow and get bigger, eat food and drink water, and have things inside themselves like stomachs and bones.

Then, we gave each of the children two rocks, and told them to try to figure out if their rocks were alive. The experiments they did on their own were wonderful. One child was determined to find out what was inside, since the group had said that living things have hearts and stomachs inside their bodies. He spent a very long time, first banging on one rock with another to try to get it open, and then chipping away at his rock with a hammer and chisel, with our help for safety reasons. His perseverance was incredible! The children rolled their rocks, tossed them, talked to them, banged them on each other, examined them with magnifying glasses, and more.

Afterward, we asked each child what he thought: Are rocks alive? Several children were unsure, some decided they were not alive, and some were firmly convinced that they were alive. And they had very good reasons for thinking so. They'd put on their list that things that are alive make noise—cows moo, dogs bark. Well, when they banged their two rocks together, they made noise! They'd said that things that are alive move—people run, fish swim. Well, when they rolled the rocks, they moved! They'd said that things that are alive grow from small babies to bigger adults. Well, they found little rocks and they found similar big rocks, so it looked like some rocks had grown!

The group got together again to continue the lively discussion. When one boy observed that his rock was hard, another responded with excitement: "Yeah, 'cause bones are hard! The things that are hard are alive!" Another boy made a further comparison to human bodies by noticing that rocks have holes that look like mouths. In fact, many of their observations involved how rocks compared to themselves, as when Julia asserted that her rock could stand up by itself, and so could she.

Another child said that the white in her rock was like bones, and the red was like blood. When one child said that rocks don't have teeth or tummies, so they can't eat, that argument was countered by Eli who said that rocks live in the ocean and so they drink ocean water. The final argument in favor of rocks being alive was an unexpected one: Morgan said, "I think it's real because my dad knows all about rocks because when he goes hunting he sees rocks and he shoots them. You shoot things that are alive."

At the end of our extensive rock learning project, the children were left to their own conclusions. We never said to them, "Those of you who figured out that rocks are not alive are right." It really didn't matter that more children fell into the "rocks are alive" camp at the end of our study than at the outset. What mattered was the excitement of learning that they had experienced. What mattered was that these children were *learning how to learn*, how to explore and investigate their world. It was very empowering for them to realize that they could figure things out for themselves!

And in some ways, it was rather charming that these little children could believe that rocks are alive. To a small child, the whole world is wonderful and amazing and filled with the spirit of life.

Now, what would have happened if we had just answered that child's question in the first place? What if, when we'd gotten back in from the playground, we'd sat down with the group and said, "Peter wants to know if rocks are alive. The answer is, no. People, animals and plants are alive. Rocks are not alive."

In an obituary about Allan Sandage, "who spent his life measuring the universe, becoming the most influential astronomer of his generation," we found this comment:

> We may never know the fate of the universe or
> the Hubble constant, he once said, but the quest
> and discoveries made along the way were more

important and rewarding than the answer anyway. "It's got to be fun," Dr. Sandage told an interviewer. "I don't think anybody should tell you that he's slogged his way through 25 years on a problem and there's only one reward at the end, and that's the value of the Hubble constant. That's a bunch of hooey. The reward is learning all the wonderful properties of the things that don't work." (Overby)

So, what would have happened if we'd given our inquisitive preschoolers the straight answer? The result would have been: end of discussion. End of story. End of scientific inquiry. End of interest. End of learning.

Grownups really like being the ones with the answers to all the questions children have. It's very pleasurable to be able to share our knowledge with our children. But the important message that we want you to take from our rock story is this: *You don't always have to be the Answer Person.*

That's not to say that you can't answer any questions your children ask you. If you're walking along and your child takes your hand and looks up into your eyes and says, "Daddy, why do flowers smell so nice?" you can give her a smile and a little squeeze of the hand and say, "Well, Alicia, flowers smell good because they need to attract bees that will pollinate them."

But consider responding sometimes, "Why do you think flowers smell nice?" You might find her answer far more interesting.

Or consider saying, "I wonder if all flowers smell nice. Let's check out the flowers we pass on our walk, and when we get home let's check the flowers in our garden." Alicia will get to experience the thrill of scientific exploration, and you'll get to enjoy that thrill with her.

If you want her to learn about bees and pollination, consider suggesting that the two of you sit together and watch the flowers in the garden for a while and see what happens. It will be a far more memorable and meaningful learning experience for her to see the bees flit from flower to flower than to hear you lecture about it.

Tip: When your child asks you an interesting question, instead of giving her the answer, ask her what she thinks, or say, "I wonder how we could find out."

Sometimes it's fun to spark the discussion by asking your child an interesting question. After talking about how water goes from the clouds to the ground when it rains, Tina asked the children to think about how the water could get back up into the clouds to make more rain. The children hadn't realized that the same water goes back up to the clouds, naturally assuming that clouds make their own water. Now they were intrigued, and they had some great ideas.

One child suggested taking a spray bottle outside and spraying water up into the air. Another child objected that it wouldn't go far enough, and said maybe you'd need a longer hose. One boy boldly asserted, "I would go up in an airplane and then I would go out on the wing and pour the water into the cloud." Later, Tina introduced a new word to the children: evaporation. Since they'd all had experience with wet clothes and wet hair drying out, it made sense to the children that water evaporates into the air.

Eighty years ago, Jean Piaget called children *"young scientists."* An exciting method of preschool teaching, called the Reggio Emilia approach (named after the Italian town where it originated) also considers children to be young scientists, who are eager participants in constructing their own learning. No doubt about it, young children are driven to explore the world, to construct their own knowledge, to be investigators and theorists. It is our job as teachers, and your job as parents, to foster this.

We have noticed, after many years of teaching, that some topics particularly fascinate preschoolers. Insects are huge. We have done extended explorations in our class about monarch butterflies and caterpillars, spiders, mosquitoes, and even acorn weevils!

This last one we happened on by accident when the children brought a load of acorns in from the playground one day. We put them on the Discovery Table in a basket. Several days later, we heard a child exclaim, "Look at the worms!" Underneath the basket we found many wriggling, quarter-inch white grubs. How did they get there? This was a fascinating mystery to explore. The existence of acorn weevils was news to the teachers as well!

Again, the children were young scientists who observed and learned things for themselves. For example, they wondered how the worms got into the acorns. It was four-year-old Laura, who noticed that there was a tiny hole in each acorn. "Maybe it crawled in through the hole," she guessed. She also theorized that maybe they grew from the nut inside the shell. Once, she found a shell with two holes, and theorized that there might be two larvae inside.

After the children speculated and explored for a while, Deb found a book at the library and brought back pictures showing the life cycle of the acorn weevil, which lays its eggs in acorns for the larvae to feed on when they hatch out. They were fascinated by the close-up picture of the adult female, with the long proboscis she uses to drill a hole into the acorn through which to lay her eggs. Laura was right!

The children spent a very interesting couple of weeks collecting acorns and breaking them open to look for the larvae. They now knew to look for acorns that had holes in them in order to find the larvae. It was fun to see the excitement spread to other classes, too, as our kids searched the playground and cracked open the acorns.

The acorn weevil project brings up another point. Very few children are innately repulsed by anything in nature. It's all fascinating! Not one child thought the little wriggling white larvae were gross, but plenty of the adults who saw them did. Actually, several of the little girls held them in their hands, petted them, and crooned, "Oh, they're so cute!"

We try really hard not to pass our prejudices about anything in nature on to the kids, and we hope you will, too. For example, Deb adored our friendly, white rat, Sweetie, a favorite class pet that several children liked to carry around in the pocket of their sweatshirts. Tina admits that she avoided contact with Sweetie, but she never let the kids notice. If they had, she would have explained that while she herself had some nervousness about rodents, most people did not.

Tip: Try not to pass on your fears or squeamishness about the natural world to your child.

Over the years, we have noticed that preschoolers are universally interested in very small things (insects, little rocks, minnows, frogs) and very big and powerful things (dinosaurs, sharks, volcanoes, trains, garbage trucks).

They're interested in natural phenomena around them: weather, trees and flowers, water. They're interested in light and dark, in shadows, in colors. They're interested in physics: how things move, spin and roll; how things fall; how simple machines work. We are as excited as the kids when they discover catapulting! Placing that long board across another board and stomping hard on the end to make a little stuffed animal go flying high into the air? Thrilling!

We know that we've really succeeded in creating little investigators when the children come up with their own experiments. Two five-year-olds initiated their own soggy experiments when they noticed a cookie getting soggy in their milk at snack time. They wondered if a carrot would get soggy if left in water. So, on their own, they got a small cup, filled it with water, and put in a carrot from their lunch. Then they asked us to help them write a sign to put beside it: "Soggy Experiment. Do not touch." They checked it each day.

Other kids got interested. We asked them if they wanted to test other things, and they said yes. So, they got many cups of water and put them out on the Discovery Table. They, along with some other children who had become interested, put everything from pieces of wood to potato chips to chocolate chip into the water cups.

After about a week, we asked them to give a report to the class on the results of their Soggy Experiments. The two girls were very proud and confident as they stood in front of the group with photos and drawings and told their classmates what they had learned.

Please enjoy your little scientist. Discover the world anew with your child. Do experiments, ask her questions, go to museums and nature preserves, read books together, draw pictures and make models.

Get tools to help your child explore nature especially good magnifying glasses. You can explore your own neighborhood. Scoop up water from a nearby lake or river and examine it closely with that magnifying glass. We had a five-year-old who could spot one-eighth-inch mosquito larvae floating in the water from the creek near our school. Value nature with your child.

And above all, keep in mind the key concept from this section: *You don't always have to be the Answer Person.*

Learning About the Human World

> *During a lunchtime conversation, DeMarcus informed us, "If you see Rudolph's red nose, then that is North."*

Whenever one child says, "I live in Minnesota," a chorus rings out: "I live in Minnesota, too!" with some children insisting adamantly that "No, *I* live in Minnesota." They know their place in the world, and they each claim it as their own. As we know, at this age, children are very egocentric: the world revolves around them. But they are also curious to learn about a wider world and how it relates to them.

Learning About Their Own Society

In preschool, we don't formally teach Social Studies. We approach the topic as a part of learning about the immediate environment as well as one more opportunity to open the children's eyes and engage their imaginations.

Our goal is not to have a child identify twenty countries on a map or to know what Benjamin Franklin did. It is to have a child with a growing understanding of how his immediate world functions, and of his place in a wide world of great diversity and possibilities. They are the explorers. You are their guide.

So where do we start? We try to approach learning about the social environment the way the kids do, starting from how their immediate world relates to their lives and experiences.

As you might expect from our previous discussions, preschoolers approach the world from an egocentric, concrete, and visual point of view, they have great imaginations, and they love to pretend. That is why preschool classrooms have a dramatic play area. Children can try on adult roles and explore professions. They practice social and familial relationships, and play-act the roles of salesperson and customer or doctor and patient.

Does your child like to pretend to be a kitty? A baby? Does she want to be the Mommy? Does he want to put on his firefighter or superhero costume every day? Does he want to serve you a meal from his pizza restaurant?

Children are trying out roles to figure out what they feel like. You can help to deepen their understanding and extend their interests by joining in the conversation: "Did the kitty hurt her paw? Should we take her to the vet?" "What do you think firefighters do when there isn't a fire? How could we find out?"

When we talk with the children about adult jobs, we use the real words for them, such as veterinarian and police officer. If your child is a dinosaur fanatic, tell her she is a paleontologist. If he's really into bugs, call him an entomologist.

When our class expresses an extended interest or gets involved in a guided project, we look for opportunities to take a field trip. This is something you can do too, but you won't need a bus or caravan of cars to transport 15 or 20 children!

If your child is curious about where her food comes from, find out if there is a working farm in your area that you can visit. Go to the farmers' market, and let her meet and talk to the people who grow the food. Or there might be a bakery where they are willing to show you how they prepare the bread dough in huge vats and bake the cupcakes in pans with 36 cups. The library is always a good field trip.

You might find non-fiction videos on various places, habitats and professions such as road construction, fire-fighting, and airplane pilot. We look for videos that show real-life people and places. The children are fascinated to see the power of a real bulldozer, the beauty of a living rainforest, the height and symmetry of the Eiffel Tower, and the enormity of a real airplane. Thanks to a dad who is a pilot, Tina's class in Phoenix got to examine several jumbo jets in an airplane hangar!

On TV, you can check PBS or cable channels such as the Discovery Channel for topics of interest to your child, but be sure to watch it with him, ready to answer questions or interpret information, or to turn it off if the program turns out to be confusing, scary, or inappropriate for your child. Children sometimes tell us details of the inappropriate programs they watch, and sometimes the scary nightmares they have had afterwards.

Diversity

In their play, the children mimic the family roles that they see at home and that they learn about in stories and movies. They also learn from their peers that not all homes and families function the same way. At school, we try to vary and add to their explorations

Developmental Asset #34: Cultural awareness and sensitivity

by introducing household items, clothing, and toys from other cultures into the dramatic play area, especially those representative of the families in our school. We also serve ethnic foods for snack. If you've been sticking with the same old hamburger places that are your child's favorites, we recommend trying out restaurants representing a variety of cultures.

As long as you are enthusiastic about the food and the experience, your child will probably follow your lead. We had a child in our class who ate out frequently with her parents at many types of ethnic restaurants. When we were polling the children on their favorite foods one day, she surprised us with her list: broccoli, sushi, and calamari!

Tip: Expand your child's awareness of other cultures, as well as her palate and her healthy food choices by going to many ethnic restaurants. Assume she will try and probably like some new foods, and convey this with a matter-of-fact and positive attitude.

By combining these experiences with reading good children's books set in other cultures, as well as folk tales from various countries, and inviting families and friends to share their home experiences, we help the children to role-play and explore with curiosity, interest and empathy.

Rather than teach diversity, preschool teachers treat all the variations they encounter in their classrooms, neighborhoods, pictures, and stories as natural ways that people can be different, and likeable — in their abilities, interests, tastes, homes, clothing, habits, languages and customs.

If you don't know a lot of people from other countries or cultures, perhaps you have at least one friend or relative who grew up or has lived in a place far different from your own. If they are willing, invite them to tell some stories from their own experience to your family.

Interestingly, in terms of appreciating diversity, we've been impressed with how easily young children accept all kinds of differences among people, as long the adults around them do, too. They see so many new aspects to the world every day that variations seem natural.

Our school serves many young children with disabilities, and we can tell you that these children are readily accepted, whether they are in a wheelchair, or can't speak clearly, have medical issues, or have trouble sitting still for more than a moment.

All of these children are played with as friends by the other children, and are regarded as the individuals that they are. They are just Tony or Kendra, not "the kid in the wheelchair," and the fact that they are in a wheelchair is just one of the characteristics of that friend, not the defining aspect.

Learning About the Wider World

Where is that train that we keep hearing going to, and what is it carrying? When your friend Padma moved here from India what transportation did she take to get here? Where do bananas grow and how do they get here? Let's look at a map or the globe and find out.

The children love it when we take out the globe. They love to find where we live. When you look at the map, always start by pointing out where you live. Then find the other place. Point to the features on the map or globe as you trace the path between them. Do you have to cross over the mountains? Is it past the farthest place you have driven to? Can you find the blue areas? Are they rivers, lakes, or the vast oceans? Could you get there by car? Could you take a boat? How long would it take to drive or fly? The world widens before your child's eyes and at the same time becomes more comprehensible.

Did you ever have a pen pal? When Tina moved to Arizona, her new class became pen pals with Deb's class in Minnesota. They exchange drawings, photos, and newsy letters written or dictated by the children. Not only is it exciting to receive the mail, the kids are always delighted to learn that both classes have raised butterflies from caterpillars and that both classes have a favorite puppet friend named Gabby!

The kids in Deb's class are amazed that the children in Phoenix are playing barefoot in the sand in February, and the kids in Tina's class are fascinated to see Deb's class playing in mounds of snow. The photos and letters stay on the bulletin board for months, where the children often go to study the pictures and to wonder what their pen pals are doing.

If your child has a cousin or a friend, near in age but far in distance, it could be fun if he started a pen pal relationship, either by regular mail (better for young children) or by email. He might have fun sending some pictures of his world to share with his distant pen pal. Plus, having pen pals is a great way to promote language skills in your child!

Often, an interest in the wider world begins when we invite the children to send pictures or write letters to someone they know who lives far away. We have also invited parents to ask far away relatives to send postcards to us at school.

As the cards come in, the classroom job of Mail Carrier becomes highly coveted. We read each note to the whole class and then attach it with a ribbon to the place it came from on a large wall map. We have both a U.S. and a world map on the bulletin board. Before long, children want to find the places themselves. Some can read the names, some look for a clue like the first letter on the name, and some remember where Florida was the last time. But we were quite surprised one day when Grace asked: "Thailand. Is that close to China?" It was not a random guess; it was an educated guess. Her interest had been sparked, and she was paying attention. Like we keep saying, preschoolers are amazing. We just need to help them uncover and develop their abilities.

How can you apply this at home? If you have friends or relatives who travel, ask them to send your child a postcard. When you travel, even if she is with you, mail her a postcard from your trip—she'll love reading it when she gets home and remembering your vacation. Or, let her pick out a postcard and send a note to herself. She'll have fun receiving the card in the mail and reading her own letter to herself. (Yes, it's that old egocentric nature coming into play again!) Most likely, she will also enjoy keeping a map at home showing where the cards came from, or keeping the postcards in a small photo album. If you travel for work, be sure to bring your child a postcard for her collection.

Tip: Kids love getting and sending letters and pictures in the mail! Expand your child's literacy development and culture awareness via the U.S. Postal Service.

If you don't have opportunities to travel, and if you don't have relatives all over the world, you can still spark an interest in the bigger world. Just start with a map, a few pictures from a travel magazine or downloaded from the Internet, some stories, some questions. Who knows where it will lead? In our classes, our investigations of the wider world have often led to an extended interest in maps.

Maps

Deb noticed one week that several of the children had begun drawing maps. Of course, many of them were treasure maps. In fact, if you ask your child what is the purpose of maps, he is likely to say what the kids in our class always say: to find treasure. So we decided to do a study of maps.

This met with skepticism from some of our fellow teachers and from parents.

After all, maps are a very difficult concept—even for many adults. A two-dimensional line drawing represents a three-dimensional space on a very different scale. A map bears no obvious relationship to a city; and a state or country is too big to even see. So how can we know its shape? Turn a street map around or mount it on the wall and it doesn't even point you in the right direction. Well, we discovered that four- and five-year-olds *can* begin to understand maps.

We started by looking at the symbols on a map—all kinds of maps. Look at a street map. What are the black lines? Where are the railroad tracks? What does that blue part mean? Where is our school? How are parks shown on a map? We noticed that if buildings are drawn, they are just little squares. Then we gave the children a simple drawing of some streets. We asked them to draw a school on one corner, a park on another, a house on another. They could draw cars on the street. They could label it. It became a kind of picture-map.

Next we asked them to draw a map from the school to their house. It didn't matter that they didn't actually know the route, nor that most drew a big school, one or two long squiggly lines and then a small box for a house. They knew what they were drawing. "Here is the stop sign and then you turn," explained Haley. "My dad is at my house," wrote Blake. "It's a long way," said Maria.

Next, we did something really fun that you can do, too. We drew a very simple treasure map of our school. You can do it for your house or neighborhood. The map featured lines for hallways, zigzags for stairs, symbols for doorways, and arrows to show which way to go. We started at our classroom door, and followed the map all the way to the X, where we found a small treasure box, filled with candy.

Looks like the kids were right after all—maps are for finding treasure!

Another map activity that you can do at home is to hang up a map of your local area, and mark where your friends and the people in your extended family live. You can also mark the places you and your child frequently go, such as the grocery store, the park and library.

At school, we mark the location of the kids' houses on a local map, along with photos of each child's family. They frequently go to the map to trace the lines between school and their friends' and their own houses, saying "This is how I get to school," or "You live here and I live here, so we're really close."

Kids love maps. Even if they can't always mentally translate the abstract symbols on maps to reality; even if they have a hard time understanding that Mexico is several thousand miles away from Canada while Canada is only several hundred miles from Minneapolis; even if they cannot conceive of what a mile is; even if they have a hard time grasping the difference between states, cities and countries—still, children love looking at maps and drawing maps.

Give your child some maps—of your town, your state, the world, of the national park you visit and your regional park. As you're driving around in your car, give your child a map and let her pretend to follow along. Who knows—maybe she'll find some treasure.

Discovering the Human World

- Help your child explore family, social and work roles through dramatic play. Ask questions.

- Take a field trip to see how they work at – the bakery, the fire station, the animal shelter, the hairdresser. Call first.

- Explore other cultures. Read storybooks with realistic illustrations or photos. Talk with people you know who are willing to share their own experiences.

- Find a pen pal. Write letters and postcards to someone who lives far away. Find where they live on a map.

- Explore maps. Find the places that you go, places where grandparents live, places that you read about.

- Use the Internet to find webcams that show where you live or pictures of places your child is curious about. You can look at Broadway, the Alps, Venice, or Juneau, Alaska, to name just a few.

- Watch non-fiction videos, PBS, or the Discovery Channel *with* your child, and talk together about what you see.

Time

We were talking about how dinosaurs went extinct millions of years ago. Leslie said, "My mom and dad were born long before me so they saw the dinosaurs."

"I'll meet you by the slide at 10:15," four-year-old Mandy says to her friend Allison as she checks her watch. "OK, that's good for me," Allison replies. "That'll give us fifteen minutes before my class is scheduled to go back inside at 10:30."

How absurd did that conversation sound to you? Much more realistic is this one, overheard at the lunch table recently: Ali said, "I went to the zoo with my grandma tomorrow." Jonah responded, "Cheetahs are my favorite animal." Jonah did not notice that Ali should have said yesterday. In fact, even if Ali had said "yesterday," she might just as well have meant last week or last month.

Time is very nebulous to a preschooler. Anything that's not here and now is difficult to get a handle on. We often hear the kids mixing up yesterday and tomorrow, and we often hear them using yesterday to mean any time in the past, and tomorrow to mean anytime in the future. Even harder to understand is the idea of long ago. For a toddler, reality begins with their existence. For a preschooler, they understand that there was a time before they were born, but their mental construct of the past pre-themselves is limited.

The future is equally as nebulous for a young child as the past. When John said, "I wish we could keep Sweetie (our pet rat) forever," we asked him how long is forever? He confidently replied, "Twenty days."

Children do understand the passage of days as being spaced by sleeping at night for a long time, so rather than saying that something will happen the day after tomorrow, often preschool teachers tell children that it will happen in "two sleeps."

Although most four-year-olds can tell you their birth date, that doesn't mean they have any concept of what that really means. When we asked the kids if anyone could say what the word month meant, they all defined it as special days. That's because what was salient for them was that special days—their birthday and holidays—are named by or associated with the month that they occur in.

Some of the older children do begin to understand the days of the week. They know that Saturday and Sunday are stay-home days, or they know that their friend comes to school on Tuesdays and Thursdays, so if we say it's a Monday, they realize that their friend won't be coming that day. We sing a "Days of the Week" song to help the children learn the names of the days.

Sticker Chart

In our classroom, we mark time with our Sticker Chart, a big rectangle with one square for every day of the school year. Each day, a child puts a sticker on the chart. The children are able to see the passage of time concretely as the chart fills up slowly with stickers.

We use stickers that relate to the topic we're learning about or a special activity of the day. On field trip days we put a school bus sticker on the Sticker Chart. When we're learning about pets, the children put on stickers of dogs and cats. The week of Halloween, they put on jack-o-lantern stickers. We have found that the children go back to the Sticker Chart repeatedly over the course of the school year.

We'll see them standing there alone or with a friend, pointing out stickers: "That's my birthday." "Remember when we went to the apple orchard?" "I was Batman on Halloween." They can see very clearly how long ago certain events took place. The Sticker Chart increases math skills as well. We often see the children counting the squares on the Sticker Chart.

You can let your child have his own calendar, which will be a personalized Sticker Chart for him. Kids love stickers, so why not buy a bunch of stickers and let him put one on each day? If you don't want to spend too much money, you can use stars or other cheap stickers that come on large sheets for most days, but then use some special stickers for special days.

You can buy holiday stickers, birthday stickers, stickers that show travel pictures (planes, suitcases, vacation destinations), and other stickers that could be used to mark special days in your family.

Write on your child's calendar upcoming special days, such as when he's going to Grandma's house. Put the calendar up on his bedroom wall at his eye level. He will look back through it as he remembers the past, and look toward what is coming in the future.

Then, when he looks at the zoo animal sticker and says, "I went to the zoo with Grandma tomorrow," you can show him that tomorrow means the next blank day after today, and you can say "this is yesterday" as you point to the square before today.

Tip: Give your child his own personalized calendar, and make it easy to take down off the wall to look at past and future days.

Now, what about time within the day? Terms like hour and minute are arbitrary constructs which mean little to a young child. Most three-year-olds think that a minute is about a second long, because they know it's a short amount of time. We try as teachers to be accurate in our use of these terms. When we say "clean-up will be in five minutes" we really try to stick to five minutes. One-minute and five-minute sand timers are fun for kids, and a very concrete way to show that length of time. Eventually, after many repeated experiences, the child will get a general sense of how long five minutes is.

As you may remember from the *Transitions* section of Chapter 4, we use visual timers to literally show the passage of time. Until they understand time, digital clocks are useless for children. Analog clocks and watches, with faces that show the hands moving around the clock dial, are concrete and a better way for the child to begin to learn to tell time, when he's ready.

The bottom line when it comes to time is, give it time. Keep it concrete and based in reality for a preschooler, and eventually — when they're six or seven or eight and their brain has developed to a point of readiness — the abstract words hour, year, September, last week will make sense.

Cognitive Competence

7

Creative Competence

> *Haley was working at the art table when a classmate sat down next to her. Haley looked up and stated, "This is my art house, and I have a guest."*

What do you suppose Pablo Picasso was like as a child? Was he painting all over his mother's walls? How about Yo-Yo Ma? Was he pounding out original compositions on his kitchen pots and pans when he was two? Was Jim Carrey acting out great comedic characters for his classmates in elementary school?

The short answer is, yes. All of these creative individuals showed talent early. By around age 8, Picasso was drawing well, Yo-Yo Ma had already performed for President Kennedy, and Carrey was doing hilarious comedy bits. What they had in common was that they were all recognized for their talent and encouraged in it, by their parents and by their teachers. Of course, many creative people have succeeded despite obstacles and without encouragement, but how many others were squelched by lack of support for their talents?

One of our favorite children's book illustrators is James Marshall. As a child he loved to draw. That is, until his second-grade teacher told him one day that he had no talent for drawing and he should never bother drawing anything again. He immediately stopped drawing, and did not draw again until he was a young adult. James Marshall went on to have a successful career writing and illustrating dozens of beloved children's books, and received the Caldecott Honor award in 1989 for children's book illustration.

So, do you have a creative child? Chances are you do. On the whole, children are pretty creative people. In every class, every year, we've had amazing artists, performers, builders, and story-tellers. Creative people are often said to think outside the box. Young children are often creative thinkers because they are not yet aware that there is a box!

There are lots of ways to be creative, too. It's not only in the artistic fields of music, writing, visual arts, and drama. The men who created Google were incredibly creative! So was Thomas Edison.

Ever heard of Percy Spencer? The next time you pop a bag of popcorn in your microwave, you can thank him for inventing the microwave oven. Despite having dropped out of grammar school in the early 1900's, Percy Spencer made it into the Inventors Hall of Fame because of his insatiable curiosity and his drive to learn things for himself. He called it "solving my own situation." He was indeed a highly creative person — and also the embodiment of Piaget's belief that children learn best when they figure things out for themselves.

Encouraging Your Little Artist or Inventor

> As we left the playground, Deb closed the squeaky gate. Emily remarked, "That's a funny noise. It sounds like a trumpet with a tummy ache."

In our classroom, we express our natural admiration for some of the works of art that the children produce, but we don't go overboard. If you tell your child that every single painting he makes is fantastic, even when he just strokes the brush across the paper a couple times and then walks away, he will know that your praise is hollow and doesn't really mean much. Rather than just praising the beautiful painting, we try to comment on a specific

> **Developmental Asset #38:**
> Self-esteem

aspect of the painting: "I like the way that little splotch of red contrasts with the blue and the darker colors." Or, "That's interesting the way you alternated yellow and green dots in that pattern."

This applies to all your child's creative endeavors. We might say, "That was an interesting little bit of music you played on the keyboard. It sounded fast and exciting!" A frequent preschool teacher's comment is: "Tell me about… (your picture, block structure, and so on.)" This lets the child know of our interest, and allows the child to express or interpret her work.

The best way to encourage creativity in young children is simply to give them plenty of opportunities to be creative, and to let them know that you value their exploring and trying out different things. That's why the easel is always available to use in our room, and many paintings are produced each day. That's why a musical instrument is always out on the music table. That's why a variety of building materials are available to use every day. That's why the dramatic play area is open every day.

By treating their work with respect, we further let them know that we value what they are doing. If a child is halfway done with a construction made of LEGOs at clean-up time, we let her save it to continue working on at the next opportunity. When we display the children's artwork, we often put construction paper behind it to frame it.

Sometimes we take photos of the children's block structures, or of the complicated patterns that they make with the pattern blocks.

Tip: Taking photos of large things that your child creates that you can't save, whether from boxes and toilet paper tubes, or from blocks, or a chalk drawing that covers your whole driveway, shows him that you value his work and creativity.

An important key to fostering creativity is to keep the materials and instructions open-ended. This means that many outcomes are possible. You may be very pleasantly surprised and impressed when your children come up with ideas you never thought of.

Both Deb and Tina have worked for many years with the creative problem-solving organization, Destination Imagination®. D.I. provides challenges each year for children from preschool to college-age to solve, and those challenges are all very open-ended, with limitless possible solutions. Over the years, even the youngest kids we've worked with have amazed us!

You know how you can give a kid a gift, and then he spends five minutes with the actual item, and an hour playing with the box it came in? Boxes are an open-ended kind of material.

Play and creativity go hand-in-hand in preschool. We share with you below the list of our favorite toys and play materials. Not surprisingly, these materials are open-ended and can be used over and over in many ways. These are the

> Developmental Asset #17:
> Play and creative activities

things that we see the children taking out and using most days.

All of these toys also enhance children's social skills, cognitive skills, and problem-solving skills. They also have the benefit of being interesting to children of many ages. Your child will use these toys year after year, increasing in the sophistication of his play with them as he grows older. And since older children like these toys as well, the children in your family will enjoy playing with them together.

Great Open-Ended Toys and Play Materials

- A good set of wooden blocks

- Large cardboard blocks that look like bricks, or colorful foam blocks

- Construction sets such as LEGO, Magna-Tiles®, Lincoln Logs®, and Tegu™ magnetic wooden blocks

- Toy vehicles; baby dolls; stuffed animals

- Realistic-looking small toy animals, especially in family sets (for example, a wolf family)

- Bucket of various-sized rocks (for making animal habitats and other constructions)

- Human figures, including multi-ethnic families and various occupations

- Pattern blocks (also called parquetry blocks)

- Creative games: classics, such as checkers, chess; simple card games, and others. Some of our favorites: *P is for Popcorn, Junior Labyrinth*™, and *Cariboo*™

- "Imagination Box" or basket—where you toss your paper towel tubes, fabric scraps, pieces of foil, sticks, small boxes, yarn, paper cups, rubber bands, bottle caps, old CDs, and so on

Don't worry—your child does not need all of these to be creative!

Let's look at that Imagination Box a little further. Before you throw something out, ask yourself if it could go in the box. Keep the Imagination Box available at all times, and then step back and watch your kids go to town.

On days when it's too hot, too cold, or too wet to go outside, challenge your kids to use the materials in it to create something—a bridge between two chairs, a tower six feet tall, a monument to something, a hole for an indoor mini-golf course, a new sport...whatever!

Brainstorming

Brainstorming is a crucial activity for developing creative competence. You can have fun playing the "What could this be?" game with your children, using ordinary objects. For example, you could give them a paper towel tube, and let them come up with many different things it could be. Their first answers will probably be ordinary— they'll play it like a horn, or use it like a telescope. But after they've used up the ordinary, their fertile little minds will move to the extraordinary.

The paper towel tube turns into Pinocchio's nose, or the Holland Tunnel for ants, or a wormhole to another dimension, or a chin support for a person who's sick of always being told to "keep your chin up."

Sometimes you can play brainstorming games that look for unusual or fun answers. You can give your child a key and say "What could this be a key to? What else? What else?" You and your children can think up ways you could feed a giraffe, or what an ant would say if it could talk to you. This is another bit of fun you could have on a car ride.

Brainstorming develops your child's thinking fluency skills, which will be critical to his success as a worker in the rapidly changing 21st century. We try to do a brainstorming exercise with our class at least once a week — sometimes the wacky open-ended games, but usually just generating a list of as many things as the children can think of in a particular category.

If we're learning about machines, for example, we might ask them to think of machines in their houses. When we learn about shapes, we draw a huge circle on a whiteboard and challenge the kids to fill it up with things that are round.

You can play the Categories game with all your children, where someone names a category, and then you take turns trying to think of things in the category without repeating anyone's answers. Categories can be anything from kinds of cookies to things found in a forest to names starting with the letter T, to whatever.

Most children won't grow up to be creative geniuses on the level of Leonardo da Vinci, of course. But each one of us is a more fulfilled person if we can use our creativity. It is deeply satisfying for some people to knit a sweater, especially if they put their own touches into it.

A gardener is happy when he plans and produces a beautiful flower garden. A person who loves visual design may enjoy putting together wonderful scrapbooks of family memories. Many people are very creative in the kitchen. And of course, these days many people like to create their own websites and blogs on the Internet.

Outlets for creativity are important, both for adults and children. Human beings need to express themselves as individuals. You do, and so does your child.

FOSTERING YOUR CHILD'S CREATIVITY

- Use specific comments and questions, rather than general praise

- Keep open-ended materials (cardboard tubes, pieces of cloth, and so on) on hand

- Do brainstorming games and exercises

- Treat your child's creations and ideas with respect

Artistic Creativity

Annika, painting at the easel, finished a lovely picture of herself standing next to a tall flower. She was about to put her name on it when she stopped and said, "Miss Deb, write my name on it — Mrs. Van Gogh."

Annika made us smile, and it also pleased us that she felt so proud of her work that she wanted to sign it with the name of a famous artist.

The first key to increasing a young child's artistic creativity is simply to have the materials available for him to use whenever he wants. Many of our children draw or paint every day. It takes a lot of paper to keep our classroom's artists in business! Fortunately, in addition to the supplies of construction paper and drawing paper in the school's art supply room, we get donations from the parents when their office gets rid of old letterhead or other paper.

We suggest that you keep a box near your home printer into which you can throw paper that's still usable, so the kids can draw on the back. This is good for the environment, and good for your pocketbook. You could also have a supply of nice drawing paper for when your child wants to draw something special.

If possible, you could establish an art area in your children's playroom or bedroom, with a small table, a shelf with art supplies, and a spot for her to put artwork that needs to dry. If you don't have room for that, you can put art supplies into a portable bucket with a handle, and she can bring them to the kitchen or dining room table (which you can cover with newspaper or a cheap plastic tablecloth for messy projects.)

There are two kinds of art that preschool teachers do with their classes, known as process art, and project art. each other. Project art involves all the children producing a specific end product, and the results generally look very similar to each other. This tends to be a good exercise in following directions but it doesn't leave a lot of room for creativity.

Process art is open-ended, and no two finished products look alike. Finger-painting is process art, and is greatly loved by most preschoolers!

A SELECTION OF ART SUPPLIES

- Drawing materials: markers, crayons, colored pencils, oil crayons such as Cray-Pas®, gel pens, and chalk

- Lots of paper, (may include scrap paper, wrapping paper, and so on)

- Child-sized scissors, including ones that cut ripples and other patterns

- Rolls of colored tape (masking tape comes in a lot of colors)

- Colored tissue paper

- Glue sticks, or non-toxic, water-based glue

- Stamps and stamp pads

- Watercolor paints

- A shoebox of scrap materials (junk mail, Popsicle sticks, cotton balls, and so on)

If you are looking for a new art activity, try one of our favorites. Give your child colored tissue paper, which she can tear or cut however she likes. She can put it on a white piece of paper and then brush liquid starch (found in the laundry section of the supermarket) over the tissue paper. This not only sticks it on the paper, it also makes it shiny.

Layers of colored tissue paper on top of each other produce different colors, and the results look rather like stained glass.

Using natural objects leads to unique and imaginative art, and children love the process. Let them collect some sticks, leaves, bark, pinecones, small rocks, and so on. They can glue them onto paper or cardboard to create pictures or designs. They can glue or tie them together to create a sculpture or a hanging mobile. They can look at them and draw or paint what they see. They can put a piece of paper on top of them and use chalk or a crayon (broadside) to make a rubbing of the textures and an image of the object.

Children really enjoy the freedom of process art. Let them experiment with colors, tints, shapes, composition, design and form. Value the process: This is where your child engages in experimentation, uses her imagination, and works within her own style. In this process, there is no right or wrong result.

Young children can be incredible artists. If your child is already an enthusiastic artist, you probably have quite a collection of his art at home. We both have several works of art, produced by our own children and by children from our classes, displayed in our homes. Do we do this just to be nice to the kids? No. It really is good art. Some of the world's greatest artists, such as Paul Klee and Juan Miró, have a child-like quality to their work, and a child can have a truly artistic eye.

Painting

Has your child gone through a period where almost all of his paintings ended up swampy green? This generally happens with two- to three-year-olds, although many four-year-olds are still in this phase. This happens when the process of painting — putting different colors of paint on the brush and moving the brush on the paper — is more interesting to the child than the outcome. So eventually, all the colors get blended together and the result is that swampy green color. They ought to name a paint color "preschool green," because it always ends up that same color. However, the child is still proud of what he has made, and still wants his name on it, and is still eager to bring it home and show it to his parents.

Sometimes it's OK to intervene as your child is painting. If a painting is really lovely, but the child looks like she's on the verge of making it into a big green splotch, we ask her to stop and step back and look at her painting. We help her notice things about it ("Look at how that long white line down the middle made all those colors lighter.") Then we ask her if she thinks the painting looks like it's done. If she says no, we tell her that she can keep working on it if she'd like, but that if she really just wants to keep painting, we can get her another piece of paper and she can do another painting. Usually, that's it — the child isn't ready to stop painting yet — and so she happily starts a new picture and we put her beautiful painting on the drying rack.

Here's a fun way to get water color paints for free and teach your child about the environmental benefits of using things that are bound for the trash. Save all your child's used-up, dried-out washable markers. When you've collected a few of each color, put them in baby food jars with water. You and your child will be amazed by how much color goes into the water. Let your child use a dropper to drop the colored water onto paper towels watching the colors blend.

Tip: take photos of your child's paintings or drawing and turn your favorites into screensavers for your computer, cell phone or tablet.

Speaking of photos, here's a fun art project that we do, which you can do at home. Make black and white photos of your child, your family members, your house, your pets, your garden… whatever you and your child like. Print out the photos, and let your child color them with highlighters and pastel markers.

If you print the pictures on plain paper rather than photo paper, your child could also use crayons, colored pencils, or watercolors on the black and white pictures. It's also fun, as well as interesting artistically, to print more than one copy of the same black and white photo, and ask your child to color each one differently.

For example, on a picture of himself standing in the garden, he can color in the background, but leave himself in black and white; on another copy, he can color himself but leave the background untouched; and on a third, he can color everything. Or you can leave one photo black and white, and display it in a frame side-by-side with the one your child hand-colored. These might make a fun gift for grandparents.

Drawing and Coloring

Many children love drawing. They especially love drawing pictures of their families, which are the center of the universe for them. Drawing is a good activity when your child needs to be quiet and occupied in a public place, or on a long car ride. If you give your child her own little tote bag with a drawing tablet, pencils, and perhaps a set of colored pencils as well, it will be easy to take with you, and she'll be delighted! She will feel like an important and serious artist.

Drawing is great for increasing your child's powers of observation. Drawing pictures is often a part of the learning experience in our classroom. Your child may protest that he can't draw real objects. But if you ask him to take it one step at a time and to observe specific details, he may amaze himself and you with what he produces.

When we got our pet rat, Sweetie, we sat down with the children at the art table, put his cage in the middle of the table, and asked them to carefully observe him. What shape is his body? What color are his eyes? How long is his tail? How many toes does he have? Their drawings were amazing!

Often, a child who has not developed much fine motor control just enjoys the act of what adults call scribbling and so he makes drawing after drawing. It's not until we ask him "Tell me about your drawing" that we discover there is a lot more going on.

One day when Tina asked Ruston about his drawing, he looked at his work and described what he saw: "a storm in a circle"! In another, he discovered, "This is Saturn!" and indeed his overlapping ovals did evoke that planet. (It might be tempting to tell him what *we* see, but it is far better to let the artist describe what *he* sees.)

Nevertheless, children often get frustrated that they can't draw something which they'd like to, and ask us to draw it for them. Please resist just picking up the pencil and drawing for your child. Sometimes, sadly, we have had parents grab a pencil and take over their child's drawing when the child is actually satisfied with it. Please, if you notice that your child's picture of a bird is lacking wings and that bothers you, but your child is happy with his picture, take a deep breath and let it go.

Be sure to have your child draw with more than just markers, which are rather crude art tools. You can't shade with markers, you can't make different thicknesses of lines, and you can't erase. A good pencil like Ticonderoga® with an excellent eraser is a must.

Many children enjoy coloring books, although we're not fond of encouraging coloring within the lines. Children can get value from coloring pre-drawn pictures by experimenting with color, and in using fine motor skills. And coloring can be a relaxing activity for children.

You can find interesting coloring books at good children's toy stores, museums, bookstores, and art supply stores. Some coloring books have geometric patterns and designs to color. We found one that had black and white line drawings of famous paintings. Or maybe your child is a dinosaur aficionado, and you can find a good coloring book with realistic drawings of dinosaurs.

CREATING ART

- Encourage open-ended "process" art. Value the experimentation and imagination involved. Allow your child to use his own style. Remember the Many Kinds of Kids!

- Help your child to *observe* what she's drawing, talk about it, and then let her draw it

- Resist the temptation to draw for your child, or to fix what he is creating

- Show your child that you value her art by saving it or finding ways to display it or taking photos of it

3-D Art

Your child will have a wonderful time creating sculptures at home from many found materials: wood scraps, macaroni, rocks, sticks, buttons, cardboard, and so on. You can use old boxes for a sturdy base. Make sure you get non-drip craft glue, in a bottle that's not too hard for little hands to squeeze.

One fun project is to put spaghetti into water colored with food coloring; let it absorb the color, and then lay out the flexible strands in squiggles and other shapes on foil or cookie sheets. When the strands dry and harden, they can be put together and glued into sculptures or mobiles.

And speaking of mobiles, these are another kind of 3-D art that kids love to make. All you need is sticks and string, and an imagination! Lots of things can be hung from mobiles, from feathers glued on small paper plates to plastic forks and spoons decorated with glitter, to whatever else you, or your child, can think of! Plus, mobiles have an added kinesthetic appeal, since they move.

Play-Doh is a fun material for preschoolers to work with. However, they generally have a hard time making actual things out of it, beyond a snake or a ball, so don't expect your child to create sculptures from Play-Doh or clay. Play-Doh is more of a sensory experience for young children.

Many Ways of Appreciating Art

We've talked about your child as an art producer. What about as an art appreciator? We like to introduce our children to works by great artists. We display art books (found on sale at bookstores or at the library) on our bookshelves. There are many good books about art specifically for preschoolers. But we find that the children enjoy looking at art books intended for adults as well.

We think that recognizing some works by famous artists is a part of cultural knowledge that even young children can acquire.

One day we were looking at James McNeill Whistler's famous painting, familiarly known as "Whistler's Mother." We asked the children to tell us about the painting. They impressed us with their perceptive thoughts. Zachary said, "Maybe she wants to go outside." Everly said, "She might be thinking about flowers." Tony, noticing the darkness of the picture, said, "It looks like she's probably in jail." Madison, picking up on the sadness of the figure, said, "Maybe she doesn't have any food." Alexi, continuing on this theme, said, "Maybe she doesn't have none stuff in her house except a picture."

We choose a few artists who have a distinctive style for the children to explore in more depth. Vincent van Gogh is a good choice. Children like his bright, vibrant and colorful paintings with their broad brushstrokes. They like swirly pictures, like "Starry Night," and his beautiful sunflowers, and his wavy trees. Many preschoolers are able to recognize his style when they see new works by van Gogh. Other favorites are Mary Cassatt's charming paintings of mothers and children; Rene Magritte and his surrealistic pictures (the children love spotting the weird things in the book *Dinner at Magritte's)*; and Edgar Degas.

Can four-year-olds be taken to the art museum? Yes! In our class, we read a children's book about Andy Warhol. The children did an art project you can do with your child. We took a photo of each of their faces, photocopied it six times, and pasted them together on one piece of paper like Warhol's picture of Marilyn Monroe. They colored the faces all different colors, producing their own Pop Art. Then we took a field trip to the Minneapolis Institute of Art, where the children were ecstatic to discover a huge painting by Andy Warhol!

If you have museums or galleries in your area, please take your child and enjoy the artwork with him. Of course, prepare him first, with a discussion of proper behavior in art museums: quiet voices and no touching the art. And plan to keep the visit brief. Stop and look at a few that he is interested in, and talk about them. Be sure to mention the name of the artist and the title of the artwork. Or ask your child to guess what a picture might be called before you tell her the title. What does he think is happening in the picture? What colors does he like in it? Would he like to visit that place? Has he ever seen a blue horse before? When his interest lags, it's time to leave; you can come back again another day and see some more.

The illustrations in many children's picture books are as evocative as any great work of art. When you are reading books with your children, please be sure to appreciate the art as well as the words.

You and your child might like to try out the techniques used by the illustrators of some of your favorite children's books. It looks like Patricia Polacco dresses the characters in her books by cutting out pieces of wrapping paper or wallpaper for the clothes. Leo Lionni often uses cut or torn paper, along with some paint or chalks, to make his pictures. And, of course, to imitate Crockett Johnson's *Harold and the Purple Crayon,* you would just need a brown and a purple crayon or marker.

Every child is an artist. Even if your child doesn't turn out to be the next Picasso, the chance to express herself, and to understand and appreciate art, is so important. Making art is a purely joyful experience. In fact, we'd probably all be happier if we took some time out to finger paint!

Dramatic Creativity

Drew was playing in the dramatic play area. He looked at Tina and said, in all seriousness, "A man's gotta do what a man's gotta do." "What's that?" asked Tina. "Clean the dishes and cook," he replied, putting on an apron.

"You be the mommy kitty, and I'll be the baby. Sita can be the sister kitty." Preschool teachers hear kids say things like this every day. Young children love to pretend! This is going to be the most familiar part of our discussion, as you have probably witnessed your own child in plenty of dramatic play situations. Maybe your daughter has even been called a "drama queen."

Role-Playing

Like most preschools, every classroom at our school has a dramatic play area. In our curriculum room there are many tubs filled with materials for dramatic play, which we take out one at a time: the post office kit, the circus kit, the bakery kit, and so on. Of course, the most popular dramatic play theme is housekeeping: dishes and food, brooms and telephones, baby dolls and high chairs. Preschoolers especially love to reenact family life.

Dramatic play can occupy a good deal of time for young children in a productive and positive way, fostering imitation, imagination, and innovation. If you give your child opportunities for dramatic play, he will be happier and so will you.

The best dramatic play toys that you can have at home are the housekeeping ones. You can buy some plastic dishes and toy food, but you can also save empty food boxes, used milk cartons, grocery bags, and so on for the pretend play.

Don't worry about needing expensive play kitchens, either. You can find useful items at yard sales, or you can convert large boxes into child-sized stoves and refrigerators, by using a utility knife, some markers and some tape.

Of course, all kids like to have baby dolls for pretend play. And we do mean all kids: boys and girls. In our classroom the boys like to pretend to play Daddy almost as much as the girls like to pretend to be Mommy. And what more important role should they act out than being caring, loving parents?

Other fun accessories are costumes. Kids love to dress up, of course, and the shinier and more spangled, the better. Here again, boys love it too. When we put out the jewelry or the dance costumes, which are made of satin and loaded with sequins, many of the boys have fun putting them on. And, it may surprise you, but it's true – no child ever makes fun of them for it. At this age, it's all OK and the kids really don't think anything of it beyond "Hey, Joe, I want a turn with that costume."

Capes are easy to make and instantly transform a child into a superhero. Long colorful silky scarves are good for dancing as well as dress-up. Old costume jewelry and your worn out dress shoes are great. Crowns are fun, and can be made from cardboard and aluminum foil and decorated with glitter by your child.

You can devote a shelf or a bin to dramatic play items. Instead of throwing out that old cell phone, put it in the dramatic play bucket. Better for the environment, and hours of fun for your child. Same thing for the handheld vacuum that breaks, and the computer keyboard that you replace.

Use your imagination as you scour your home, and garage sales if you like that kind of thing, for fun dramatic play props. The best thing about secondhand props is they're either free or really cheap! So it doesn't matter if they break, or if your child doesn't play with them very often.

Tip: Children love to play with real things that they see adults using—old cell phones, used computer keyboards, flashlights, keys, old cameras.

Children also engage in dramatic play when they use small toy animals, stuffed animals, puppets, princess dolls, dolls that replicate family members, doll houses, action figures, and so on. And when the children are acting out their own scenarios, these puppets, stuffed animals and dolls feel very real to them.

One day, Reid came up to Deb with a policeman puppet hanging limply between his thumb and fingers. "This guy is fake," he announced. "What do you mean?" she asked.

Developmental Asset #14:
Adult role models

Reid stuck his hand up inside the puppet and moved it as he said in a gruff voice, "You're under arrest." He gave Deb a satisfied look. "Now it's real," he asserted.

Children's dramatic play may look simple, but there is so much more going on behind the scenes. As they emulate your behavior as a parent, and that of other community members, they are observing adult role models. As they imagine themselves as successful adults, they are developing a positive view of their personal futures. Your children are engaged in planning and decision-making and cooperative social interactions. Dramatic play with a diverse set of materials and friends increases their cultural awareness and self-identity.

Performing

To take dramatic play one step further, let's talk about performing. Do you have a little actor in your family? Do the Halloween costumes get used all year? Has your patio become a stage? Or does your child act out scenes from movies and favorite books and perform them for an audience of his dolls and stuffed animals?

Tina's grown children still remember the hours they spent creating and rehearsing dramatic scenes with family friends we saw just once a year. This began when they were about four years old. Indulge us while we tell you about some dramatic productions created by our preschool classrooms to emphasize the surprising imaginations and abilities that can emerge when these young children are given the opportunity to perform.

These next stories dramatize some of the amazing ways in which the children in our classes have expressed their collective creativity. Every year we put on a Spring Performance for the parents. It is a big deal in our room. Parents and other teachers are always surprised at what the children accomplish. We spend about a month on it. The children love every minute of it and are highly involved in the whole production. It's a big task, but we are always confident that the children can do it.

We let the children vote on the story they will act out. We brainstorm with the children on what we would need for props, scenery, and costumes for the plays, and how we could make them. We also talk about how we will stage the play.

Sometimes these kids astound us with their great ideas — like the time we were trying to figure out how to make a book disappear on stage. One five-year-old suggested camouflaging the book by painting the back side white and then holding it in front of a white background, flipping it from front to back when it was supposed to disappear. Like we say, preschoolers are amazing!

After the planning, we make all the stuff. This takes several weeks, and is great fun for the kids. For example, when we did *The Little Engine That Could,* the children painted boxes for the train cars and the various engines. They wore these by cutting out the bottoms and fastening strings to put over their shoulders.

We brainstormed with them on how to make the wheels, and two girls found pie plates to trace around on paper and then cut out. Other kids drew the spokes on the 44 wheels. The kids wanted a long train track, so we rolled out a very long piece of paper and they worked for days putting black tape across it to make the rails.

All of this wonderful activity not only encourages creative thinking, it also promotes good teamwork. The children work together to create the plays. When they're ready to do the performance, they feel a real sense of ownership and pride in what they've accomplished. One year, we even made a nine-foot crocodile out of boxes for the Peter Pan play!

After the sets and props are done, it's time to practice. We act out the story over and over and over so that all the children have a chance to act out all of the roles. By the way, many of the boys will want a chance to be Cinderella and many of the girls will want to try out the role of Prince Charming. And that's just fine.

Then it's finally time to do the show for the parents. Surprisingly, some very shy children light up the stage and do a fantastic job of acting, because they are pretending to be something else, not themselves. Many actors claim to be painfully shy in real life. The smallest, quietest child in the class played the giant in *Abiyoyo*, and to see him stomping around and roaring so fiercely was a delight! Others choose to do small parts — they can handle only one line, and are so proud of themselves for doing it. For those who don't want anyone looking at them, there's always the behind-the-scenes role like being the prop-master who pulls the rope that raises the sun.

Sometimes, we go even further in letting the children create their plays by letting them write the scripts as well. The younger children need help, of course, but we've been surprised at how well the five-year-olds can create plots and write dialogue.

One summer, a group of five-year-old students did a Destination Imagination primary-level challenge. The challenge was to create a skit in which someone uses a map to find something that's been lost. This group really blew us and their parents away with their creativity! We expected them to make a treasure map and find lost treasure. After all, they'd been drawing treasure maps and pretending to hunt for treasure all year. But no, they came up with something far more creative: They had a dragon lose his fire, so he needed to follow the map to find a campfire.

When two boys both really wanted to be the dragon, we were all prepared to trot out the standard preschool teacher's solution, if necessary: How about two dragons? But they came up with a much more interesting idea all by themselves, creating a two-headed dragon by cutting two holes in a large piece of cloth and draping it over both of them.

So, are we really suggesting that you have your child put on a full-scale production?

Not necessarily. Kids also enjoy putting on a show on a smaller scale for you and maybe the grandparents, or the neighbors. They can create some costumes and find a few props and act out a familiar story in a few hours. And their time would be much better spent working together co-operatively creating their own show than sitting passively in front of the TV watching a show someone else made.

Tina still remembers a Thanksgiving Day tradition from her own childhood. While the adults prepared dinner, the children created and rehearsed a short play, which they performed for their parents after dinner. The adults each paid the performers a penny, and sat in a row of chairs as the audience.

Perhaps the biggest effect of having the kids create their own dramatic production that they perform in front of an audience is the huge boost in self-esteem. Deb ran into a former student several years after she left our school. Olivia's eyes were shining as she said to Deb, "Remember when I was Snow White in your class?"

FACILITATING DRAMATIC PLAY

Provide props and ideas for dramatic play:

- Kitchen and food-related items, a small table, pretend stove, pots and pans

- Family life: dolls, baby items, small broom, old cell phone, message pads, and so on

- Costumes to take on adult roles or fantasy characters: shoes, purses, scarves, men's ties and jackets, capes, crowns, costume jewelry

- Items related to various professions: hats, aprons, lab coats, hard hats and tools, restaurant menus, airline tickets and maps, doctor or dentist items, and so on

Creative Competence

Musical Creativity

> *A Beethoven symphony was playing on the CD player. Raya stood up and pretended to bow an instrument and declared, "I'm playing a shello."*

"You hit it or you bang it or you shake it," JC explains when asked how instruments make music. "Can we have music in our Quiet Restaurant?" asks Madison. It is one of our lunchtime treats to pretend we are in a quiet restaurant, using polite manners, and listening to music.

Whether Alice and Ahna are singing while playing the piano they have just constructed by lining up narrow blocks like a row of piano keys, or Claire, wearing a long dress, is standing on a bench and singing into a toy microphone, the mantra of many preschoolers might be "Sing, sing, sing, I've just got to sing."

Whether musically talented or not (and we are not), we, their teachers, sing along too, because music speaks to young children. It's been said that music is the universal language, and we teachers use it to connect with our students.

Does your child have a favorite song, or favorite album that you've heard or sung or played hundreds of times? Maybe you have been singing lullabies to your child since before he was born.

We all respond to music with our bodies, imaginations, emotions and voice. Preschool children incorporate the rhythms, rhymes, melodies and words of songs into their sponge-like memories. We capitalize on this to help your children exercise their minds and bodies, to express themselves, to relax and be joyous.

Singing has countless benefits. Whether done by an accomplished performer, some-time choir member, operatic shower singer, or someone who can barely hold a tune or remember a lyric, singing is good for human beings. Many studies have demonstrated that singing reduces stress levels, releases endorphins in the body, and increases the oxygenation of the blood.

There are many great CDs or collections of fun, creative songs for kids, with topics that cover all interests, from dinosaurs ("We Are the Dinosaurs" by Laurie Berkner) to whales ("Baby Beluga" by Raffi) to sports ("The Playing Field" by Grover Washington, Jr.).

It's fun to sing along with these songs, and it's also fun to make up your own songs using common tunes. You don't know many songs? You're not good at inventing them? The key to creating songs is simple: If you know a few familiar children's tunes, use the same tune with new words. This makes it easy to sing and remember. Listen carefully to "Twinkle, Twinkle, Little Star" and the "ABC song" — same tune.

So, for example, if you and your daughter are out for a walk, and she's pointing out things that she sees, you might put it into song (using the ABC tune): "Janie found a little rock, then she saw a cute little dog. She found a flower with a ladybug, she said hello to our neighbor Sam. Janie and Mommy are having a walk, all the way around the block." Notice that we didn't try to rhyme everything. For a simpler song, you could use the tune for "Mary Had a Little Lamb" and sing, "Janie found a special rock, a special rock, a special rock. Janie found a special rock and put it in her pocket."

We enjoy doing fun variations on favorite preschool songs, just to spice things up. Everybody's favorite song about body parts, "Head, Shoulders, Knees, and Toes," can be used in many ways. First, touching each part of your body as it is named teaches the words for body parts. Later, you can change the body parts, naming new ones: hair, eyebrows, elbows, and hips, for example. You can practice singing in a very high or very low voice. "The Itsy Bitsy Spider" is a fun song to do this way. You can vary it with the Great Big Spider (big voice), the Very Scared Spider (scared voice) and so on.

Is your child drumming with his fork on all the dishes and furniture? You can get some simple-to-use, expressive musical instruments like bongo drums, maracas, a xylophone or a small keyboard. Or use chopsticks or wooden spoons on the bottom of an empty coffee can for drumming. Kids love homemade maracas (or shakers) especially if they can help make them and decorate them. As we mentioned in the section *Make your own music*, you can put a handful of dry beans (or a half cup of rice and a few small pebbles, or some pennies) into a 12 oz. plastic bottle, screw the top on and secure it with lots of tape. Hold it by the neck and shake.

There are so many ways to enjoy music. Let your child dance with chiffon scarves, sing into a toy microphone (a decorated toilet paper tube with a tennis ball attached on top will do), drum along with a rock song, or listen to Chopin during quiet time.

At the library, the bookstore, in your music collection, or listening to the radio, be sure to look for music of many styles and cultures. You'd be amazed how much the children in our classrooms love to hear New Orleans Jazz, Zydeco, or music from Bolivia, Mexico, or China.

With all the prerecorded ways we have to experience music, it's easy to forget the power of experiencing music up close and personal, in a live performance. Seeing a person make the music before their eyes, with the bow going up and down on the violin or the cymbals crashing is mesmerizing to a young child.

You don't have to start out with a two-hour symphony performance. Orchestras often give short children's concerts. Local high school band or choir concerts can be a reasonably-priced way to expose your child to live music performances. Look for free outdoor concerts, with the added benefit that you'll often see small children dancing joyfully and with abandon in front of the musicians.

Stories Told in Music

And then there are stories told in music. Indulge us while we tell you our story about "Peter and the Wolf."

One day, we discovered that we both loved the music and story of Serge Prokofiev's "Peter and the Wolf'" and decided to introduce it to our class. Little did we know how it would capture their imaginations! There are many good versions of this musical story. We introduced the one performed by the Philadelphia Orchestra, which is narrated by David Bowie.

On the first day, we listened to the music while looking at the pictures in a book. Although the recording lasted 27 minutes, the children were rapt. Afterward we asked them what they thought. We were impressed by how well they'd paid attention and how thoughtful their comments were. Madison said, "I thought the wolf would eat the bird." "I was scared if Peter was going to get the rope tight on the wolf's neck and he could choke," said Sidney. "I didn't like it when the little boy climbed up the tree 'cause I was afraid he'd fall out and get an owie," said Anastasia. Luis piped up: "I wish we could go see wolves. I was sad that the wolf ate the duck."

Adan said, "When it was the big boom, that scared me! I went like [gasps, jumps]."

The recording begins with an introduction of the musical instrument and melody for each of the characters. We listened again to the instruments that represent each character in the story. Soon, the children started identifying the instruments and characters as they heard them.

That week, we listened to several different versions of the story that we found at the library. The music was always the same but the narration was different, and the story details varied. We also looked at several illustrated books and even the Disney animated video. The children commented on the differences. "The wolf is a different color." "The duck didn't get eaten." "They took the wolf to the zoo so he could be safe."

On the last day of our "Peter and the Wolf" week, we asked the kids to lie down with their eyes closed and picture in their minds what was happening while we played another version, this one narrated by the musician Sting. They listened, frequently commenting, reacting, and acting out their responses. When Peter's music was heard, many kids cried excitedly, "That's Peter!" When they heard the bird's music: "The bird! The flute!" Anastasia cried, "He's running in the meadow." Adan, hearing the duck's music, called out, "I can see her!"

Gabriel added, quietly, "When I picture the duck swimming, I think about my lake."

When it came to the exciting part where Peter shouts, "Look out!" to the bird, as the cat is about to pounce, all the kids spontaneously started drumming their feet. Then when the grandfather's slow music came on, they began drumming their hands slowly on the carpet.

Then we heard the wolf's music. They all cried out, "The wolf!" Raya, trying not to be afraid, said, "I'm not even picturing this part!" Ty was brave. "I'm picturing that Peter is taking a picture of the wolf." Sidney sniffed, "I smell something. I smell the wolf!" Luis imagined, "I feel like the wolf is coming into the room." Lin asserted bravely, "I'm not scared of wolves."

For the remainder of the school year, we had frequent requests from the children to listen to "Peter and the Wolf." They often wanted to hear it during lunch, and in the middle of a conversation, someone would break in: "Uh, oh, here comes Grandpa. I hear the bassoon," or "Look out, the hunters are coming!"

Knowing the children in our class as we did, and being used to having them take us by surprise with the things they were able to do, we still continued to be amazed at the depth of their interest, enthusiasm, and thinking, as a result of being introduced to this music. Like we said, music *speaks* to children. You don't have to look for four versions of "Peter and the Wolf," but we do recommend enjoying "Peter and the Wolf" with your child, unless you think he would be too frightened by it.

By the way, there are a number of good children's books sold with CDs included, where an accomplished actor reads the story with dramatic intensity and often with background music that enriches the storytelling. And there are several books with CDs that tell stories about music. Some of our favorites are:

- *Mole Music,* by David McPhail, a sweet and beautifully illustrated story of a mole who learns to play the violin but never realizes the profound impact his music has on his neighbors

- *Mama Don't Allow* by Thacher Hurd, a hilarious book featuring an alligator swamp band

- *The Jazz Fly,* a lively story that incorporates jazz even in its amazing illustrations, narrated with music by its author, Matthew Gollub

Another kind of music children love that tells a story is ballet. "Swan Lake" and "The Nutcracker Suite" have captivated children for generations. We enjoy spending a week or two exploring various kinds of dancing with our classes. Often we get videos from the library showing a ballet performance, Irish dancing, tap dancing, Mexican folk dancing, and so on. The kids dance along. Hint: it's fun to tape coins onto the bottoms of their shoes to turn them into tap shoes.

Dancing and moving to music is a great way to enhance your child's physical competence and confidence. Repeating rhythms, he gains control and coordination. Moving to the music—marching, gliding, and swaying, she gains balance, agility, and an awareness of her position in space.

Once you get started, and see how much your children and their friends enjoy making their own music, you will think of many more ways to include music in your daily routines. Give them an opportunity to listen to a wide variety of quality music including the music of other languages and cultures. Encourage them to express themselves in music and movement, and you will see how eager your child is to play and hear more. Don't be surprised if your child asks to listen to "that jazz music" or "music for our Quiet Restaurant." Listening to the radio, he may exclaim, "That's an oboe, like the duck in Peter and the Wolf!"

One final thought: If you happen to be a person who keeps the TV on much of the day, even as background noise, think about turning it off and putting on music instead.

Music *is* the universal language, and it's one that all children speak naturally.

8

Our Amazing Preschoolers

How could Michelangelo paint the ceiling of the Sistine Chapel? We posed this question to our class. We had looked at pictures of the frescos covering the huge curved ceiling, which Michelangelo had taken four years to paint 500 years ago.

After a few moments, their ideas began to pour out. "He could use a truck," Drew suggested. Jade realized he would need something much bigger. "Use a giant wagon, which is as high as a blue whale standing on its two back fins," she said. Sita tried to envision it: "Maybe a tall, tall, tall, tall, tall, tall, tall, tall, tall, tall ladder. Like one hundred and fifty-four. I want to do that!" We suggested that she might be able to go see the painting at the Vatican someday. "Can you give me a map?" asked Sita, ready to go.

Sita wasn't the only one who thought it would be pretty cool to be able to paint a mural on the ceiling, so we did the next best thing: we taped some large sheets of paper under our low preschool tables and the children worked in pairs, under the tables, lying on their backs like they imagined Michelangelo to have done. They chattered as they worked and we took notes.

Alice and Tess decided to draw a rainforest. Tess told us: "It's fun but it's not easy to do it when you're lying down. Alice agreed: "It's difficult for me and Tess. It's hard to make a beautiful tree." Brian said, "It's hard. Very uncomfortable with my head. It's really hard to draw ourselves." Hearing that, Jade gave him and JC a pillow. JC thanked her, and Brian quipped, "I bet Michelangelo didn't use a pillow."

When they were done, each pair showed their mural to the class. Raha and Malia said: We're drawing a cat and dog going to the park. That one is facing that way, and the other one is facing this way." Alice explained, "It's a rainforest. This is the lion; these are the trees. The "R" is for "rain." Kelli, our youngest student, explained, "This is a storm and everybody needs to get into the house."

Then they decided that they needed to put their drawings up on the ceiling of our classroom, which was about fourteen feet high.

JC wondered how we would get the pictures up there. Drew had two ideas and asked if he could draw them, because they were hard to explain. He made two drawings. On one, we were using a ladder. On the other, someone was standing on a very tall stack of books. A ladder seemed safer. Jade suggested "we could borrow a ladder from the guy that changes the light bulbs." Three children went off to ask the custodian if we could borrow his ladder. Soon Drew, JC, Brian, and Andy were helping us to measure a long strip of paper, taping the drawings onto it, and (very importantly) helping to guard the very tall ladder as Tina climbed up.

Are you just a little bit surprised at the way the children worked together to come up with these solutions? We were. And we were thrilled to see how thoroughly the children were engaged in this activity. They really tried to imagine Michelangelo, way up at the ceiling, painting that vast fresco. They showed empathy for the difficulty of his task. They used a lot of their prior knowledge in deciding what to paint on their murals, and they showed poise and confidence explaining their work to their classmates. We *know* that these children are capable of all this. *And yet they continue to amaze us.*

Our final story comes from another group, another year. It demonstrates how children exhibit the competencies we've discussed throughout this book.

Our class of 18 exuberant, delightful four- and five-year-olds was learning about maps. We decided to make a map of the school forest, so we grabbed a large piece of poster board and a marker, and out we trooped. We stopped at the entrance to the woods, held up the poster board for all to see. "What should we put on the bottom at the beginning of the forest?" we asked.

The children looked around, and spotted the sign marking the entrance. "Put the sign on!" We drew the sign. "Which way does the path go?" we asked. The children pointed ahead. "That way!" We drew the path proceeding straight up the poster board.

Along the way, we stopped to note landmarks. "There's a bench! Put that on!" We questioned them as to how we should draw the bench, and they examined it closely, noting the X-pattern on the back. Susie spotted a tree curving over the path and said it looked like a bridge. "Yeah, it's a squirrel bridge!" Benjy said. We drew the bending tree branch going across the path and then asked, "Does this bridge have a name?" "The squirrel bridge!" they all chorused.

When a side path diverged, we stopped and asked which way that path should go off from the main path. They all pointed to the left. Kevin lifted up his hand to make the sign for "L" and said, "It goes left. And make the bench that's over there at the end." "Good eyes," we said. "Does that bench look different than the other one?" The kids ran over to it. "Yeah," said Benjy, "it's more wrecked. There's a broken piece on the back." We drew the bench with a broken back.

A little further down the path, Ginger stopped. "There's a monarch butterfly!" she exclaimed with delight. "It's Greenie!" We smiled. Our class had raised several monarch butterflies from caterpillars that the children had found in the school's flower garden. The last one they'd named "Greenie," and every time they spotted a monarch flying outside, they were sure it was our very own Greenie.

"Put the monarch on the map!" Ginger said. We asked the children, "If we come back out here tomorrow, do you think that butterfly will still be here?" They all said no. We explained, "Maps are made so other people can use them to figure out where to go, right? If we put that monarch on the map, and then tomorrow some other kids come out here and use our map to find things, then those kids would think the butterfly would be here, and it probably wouldn't be. So on maps, you just put things that stay there, that can't move."

By this time, the monarch had indeed flown away. All the kids yelled "Good bye, Greenie!" Mary Lou piped up. "Look, Greenie was on milkweed." She pointed out a patch of milkweed. "Can we put the milkweed on the map?" "That's a very good idea," we agreed.

We continued on our way through the school forest, stopping to draw on the map where the path crossed another path, where it ended in a swamp, and many other points of interest. As we got to the end of the path, one little guy looked at us with a scowl on his face and protested that we hadn't written anything on the map that he'd said.

We responded, "We're all working together. But we can see you want to have your own part in this map, too. What do you see that we should put on?" He looked around, trying hard to find something new, and then his face brightened as he pointed to a tree deeper in the woods. "Put on that tree. It's the biggest one." He beamed as we drew the tree on the map and labeled it, "The Tallest Tree."

As we were admiring the map with the children, Mercedes suddenly bent over an old decayed log, and stood up with her hands tightly cupped together. "I found a frog!" she said with delight, as the children gathered around to see and touch it. It leaped out of her hand, and everyone jumped back and laughed.

Finally, we came to a new part of the school forest that the children hadn't seen before. An Eagle Scout had recently designed and built a natural playground. Stumps were set in the ground close together at various heights; an up-and-down balance beam created from a log sawed in half; and a seven-foot-tall tent had been created from a large number of big sticks leaning together. "Wow!" the children yelled with delight, and ran to explore this new wonderland.

Some of the children began using their physical skills, walking or crawling over the balance beam. Some jumped up and down off the stumps, or leaped from one to another.

Several children were drawn to the stick tent, and huddled inside it. "I'm a bear!" Hadley declared. "I'm a hibernating bear," said Ben. We'd learned about bears in our class a few weeks ago, and the children were remembering what they learned, as they pretended to forage about and eat imaginary berries off the bushes. "Let's make the bear cave bigger," proposed Shane. Several of them began searching the nearby underbrush, looking for big sticks to add to the stick tent. Lars tried to drag a thick, ten-foot-long stick, but it was difficult. He called to his friend to help. As they carried the stick together, Lars said proudly, "We're using teamwork!"

Meanwhile, Kendra picked up two small sticks, sat down at a stump, and began drumming on it. Janie, intrigued, found two sticks and joined her. Shane became the third drummer. Now we really had some interesting musical rhythms going. Astrid and Ruben picked up two sticks, leaped onto the stumps, and pretended to play them like guitars while making guitar-like sounds. Then Anusha got into the act, picking up another stick, stepping onto the stump next to the guitar players, and playing her stick like a saxophone.

An audience was gathering for this nature rock band performance. Hannah said, "They need a singer," jumped onto the stump stage, and started singing a song from one of her favorite TV shows. The rest of us clapped and moved our bodies, enjoying this amazing impromptu performance.

As you can see, in real life, what children do cannot be neatly separated into compartments. As we spent a wonderful hour in the school forest with the children, they were using and developing all of their competencies.

Certainly, their **cognitive competence** was growing! They were thinking on a deep level, learning and discovering for themselves, problem-solving, and working together as a team to transform the school forest they were walking through into a two-dimensional representation on the map. They were learning about the natural world, as they examined the frog and explored the forest. They were recalling things they had learned in the past, and incorporating them into this day, cementing the knowledge that they'd acquired about monarch butterflies and bears into their brains.

They could see us writing words on the map, and were increasing their **language competency**. We were using intriguing vocabulary — words like "intersection" and "decayed."

Their **social competency** was increasing, as they used imaginative play together in the natural playground, pretending to be bears and rock stars, and playing follow-the-leader on the balance beam. They were learning to do collaborative planning and work, as we all worked together to create the map.

Their **emotional competency** was being enhanced, as well. Did you notice how Lars overcame his frustration at not being able to move the huge stick, and enlisted the help of a friend? And our little friend who was feeling left out managed to find a way to feel satisfied that he had contributed an important part to the group effort.

And of course, the children's **creative competency** bloomed! They were engaged in dramatic enactments of bears: "You be the mommy bear, and I'll be the baby. Me hungry, Mommy. Me want berries." Their musical skills and enjoyment soared as they drummed and played their own rock band music.

This was a particularly enjoyable and satisfying day for us as preschool teachers. But we must say, every day, it is a privilege for us to spend time with these amazing preschoolers—your amazing children!

And so, in conclusion, parents, we encourage you to nurture the blooming competency of your children in all areas of their development.

Share *your* wisdom and experience and especially your enthusiasms and interests. Nurture *your child's* enthusiasms and curiosity, knowing that children are driven to learn and to master new things, whether it's making it all the way across the monkey bars, mastering the letter sounds so they can read the words, exploring how caterpillars turn into butterflies, or figuring out how to make friends.

Your child is driven to learn, driven to become part of her social group, driven to succeed. You also play a vital role in this: You can help your child capitalize on his natural strengths and competencies.

Set reasonable limits and boundaries for trust and safety. Give your child the tools, the time, and the trust, to grow — in her own unique and amazing way.

Ask plenty of questions, like: "What do you think? How do you think that works? How could you solve that?" Answer the questions that he *needs* to know right now, but not *all* the questions. Remember: Sometimes questions are more important than answers.

Enjoy your child! Enjoy this incredible time of growth and development. Your preschool child is amazing!

Find more resources and ideas on our website:

www.youramazingpreschooler.com

Works Cited

ASLU (American Sign Language University) ©2014 William Vicars, Ed.D. Images used by permission. http://www.lifeprint.com/

Baldwin, James. quote: "Children have never been very good listening to their elders, but they have never failed to imitate them." Retrieved from web 22 July 2015. http://www.britannica.com/biography/James-Baldwin/article-supplemental-information

Brooks, Dr. Robert. web. 15 Feb 2010. "The Complexities of Motivation: The Uncertainty of Predicting Behaviors — Part 1," citing Daniel Pink, *Drive: The Surprising Truth About What Motivates Us*. New York: Penguin, 2011. Retrieved from web 20 July 2015. http://www.drrobertbrooks.com/monthly_articles/1002

Clash, Kevin, with Gary Brozek. *My Life as a Furry Red Monster: What Being Elmo Has Taught Me about Life, Love and Laughing Out Loud*. print. Crown Archetype, 2006. p, 181.

"Face Saving," International Online Training Program On Intractable Conflict. Conflict Research Consortium, University of Colorado, © 1998. web 1 July 2015.

Greene, Dr. Ross W. *The Explosive Child: a New Approach for Understanding and Parenting Easily Frustrated, Chronically Inflexible Children*. New York: HarperCollins Publishers, 2014. 5th edition.

Hewitt, Deborah and Sandra Heidemann. *The Optimistic Classroom: Creative Ways to Give Children Hope*. St Paul, MN: Redleaf Press, 1998, 2002.

Kurcinka, Mary Sheedy. *Raising Your Spirited Child: a guide for parents whose child is more intense, sensitive, perceptive, persistent, and energetic*. New York: HarperCollins Publishers, 2006.

Louv, Richard. *Last Child in the Woods: Saving Our Children from Nature-Deficit Disorder*. Chapel Hill, NC: Algonquin Books, 2008.

Maag, John W. "Dealing with Children's Opposition by Building Compliance Momentum." Maag writes and speaks frequently on this topic; a two-page summary can be accessed online from the KansasASD.com TASNBehaviorSupports.com, Aug. 2013 newsletter. Find at: http://kansasasd.com/nletter_attach/kisn-newsletter33A41C3B31.pdf

Overby, Dennis. "Allan Sandage, Astronomer, Dies at 84; Charted Cosmos's Age and Expansion," [obituary] *The New York Times*. web. 17 Nov. 2010.

Piaget, Jean. "Some Aspects of Operations." published in Maria W. Piers, ed. *Play and Development*. New York: W.W. Norton & Co., 1972.

Tarkan, Laurie. "Benefits of the Dinner Table Ritual." *The New York Times*, May 3, 2005. web 19 July 2015.

Appendix A

40 Developmental Assets® for Early Childhood

Search Institute® has identified the following building blocks of healthy development—known as **Developmental Assets®**—that help young children grow up healthy, caring, and responsible.

Support

1. **Family support**—Parent(s) and/or primary care-giver(s) provide the child with high levels of consistent and predictable love, physical care, and positive attention in ways that are responsive to the child's individuality.

2. **Positive family communication**—Parent(s) and/or primary caregiver(s) express themselves positively and respectfully, engaging young children in conversations that invite their input.

3. **Other adult relationships**—With the family's support, the child experiences consistent, caring relationships with adults outside the family.

4. **Caring neighbors**—The child's network of relationships includes neighbors who provide emotional support and a sense of belonging.

5. **Caring climate in child-care and educational settings**—Caregivers and teachers create environments that are nurturing, accepting, encouraging, and secure.

6. **Parent involvement in child care and education –** Parent(s), caregivers, and teachers together create a consistent and supportive approach to fostering the child's successful growth.

Empowerment

7. **Community cherishes and values young children –** Children are welcomed and included throughout community life.

8. **Children seen as resources –** The community demonstrates that children are valuable resources by investing in a child-rearing system of family support and high-quality activities and resources to meet children's physical, social, and emotional needs.

9. **Service to others –** The child has opportunities to perform simple but meaningful and caring actions for others.

10. **Safety –** Parent(s), caregivers, teachers, neighbors, and the community take action to ensure children's health and safety.

Boundaries and Expectations

11. **Family boundaries –** The family provides consistent supervision for the child and maintains reasonable guidelines for behavior that the child can understand and achieve.

12. **Boundaries in child-care and educational settings –** Caregivers and educators use positive approaches to discipline and natural consequences to encourage self-regulation and acceptable behaviors.

13. **Neighborhood boundaries**—Neighbors encourage the child in positive, acceptable behavior, as well as intervene in negative behavior, in a supportive, nonthreatening way.

14. **Adult role models**—Parent(s), caregivers, and other adults model self-control, social skills, engagement in learning, and healthy lifestyles.

15. **Positive peer relationships**—Parent(s) and caregivers seek to provide opportunities for the child to interact positively with other children.

16. **Positive expectations**—Parent(s), caregivers, and teachers encourage and support the child in behaving appropriately, undertaking challenging tasks, and performing activities to the best of her or his abilities.

Constructive Use of Time

17. **Play and creative activities**—The child has daily opportunities to play in ways that allow self-expression, physical activity, and interaction with others.

18. **Out-of-home and community programs**—The child experiences well-designed programs led by competent, caring adults in well- maintained settings.

19. **Religious community**—The child participates in age-appropriate religious activities and caring relationships that nurture her or his spiritual development.

20. **Time at home**—The child spends most of her or his time at home participating in family activities and

playing constructively, with parent(s) guiding TV and electronic game use.

Commitment to Learning

21. **Motivation to mastery**—The child responds to new experiences with curiosity and energy, resulting in the pleasure of mastering new learning and skills.

22. **Engagement in learning experiences**—The child fully participates in a variety of activities that offer opportunities for learning.

23. **Home-program connection**—The child experiences security, consistency, and connections between home and out-of-home care programs and learning activities.

24. **Bonding to programs**—The child forms meaningful connections with out-of-home care and educational programs.

25. **Early literacy**—The child enjoys a variety of pre-reading activities, including adults reading to her or him daily, looking at and handling books, playing with a variety of media, and showing interest in pictures, letters, and numbers.

Positive Values

26. **Caring**—The child begins to show empathy, under-standing, and awareness of others' feelings.

27. **Equality and social justice**—The child begins to show concern for people who are excluded from play and other activities or not treated fairly because they are different.

28. **Integrity** — The child begins to express her or his views appropriately and to stand up for a growing sense of what is fair and right.

29. **Honesty** — The child begins to understand the difference between truth and lies, and is truthful to the extent of her or his understanding.

30. **Responsibility** — The child begins to follow through on simple tasks to take care of her- or himself and to help others.

31. **Self-regulation** — The child increasingly can identify, regulate, and control her or his behaviors in healthy ways, using adult support constructively in particularly stressful situations.

Social Competencies

32. **Planning and decision making** — The child begins to plan for the immediate future, choosing from among several options and trying to solve problems.

33. **Interpersonal skills** — The child cooperates, shares, plays harmoniously, and comforts others in distress.

34. **Cultural awareness and sensitivity** — The child begins to learn about her or his own cultural identity and to show acceptance of people who are racially, physically, culturally, or ethnically different from her or him.

35. **Resistance skills** — The child begins to sense danger accurately, to seek help from trusted adults, and to resist pressure from peers to participate in unacceptable or risky behavior.

36. **Peaceful conflict resolution**—The child begins to compromise and resolve conflicts without using physical aggression or hurtful language.

Positive Identity

37. **Personal power**—The child can make choices that give a sense of having some influence over things that happen in her or his life.

38. **Self-esteem**—The child likes her- or himself and has a growing sense of being valued by others.

39. **Sense of purpose**—The child anticipates new opportunities, experiences, and milestones in growing up.

40. **Positive view of personal future**—The child finds the world interesting and enjoyable, and feels that he or she has a positive place in it.

Appendix B

Useful ASL Signs For Young Children

The ASL alphabet uses an easily-learned hand sign for each letter of the English alphabet. These alphabet signs are often used to describe how to do other signs for words and phrases (as in: use the "B" hand). Some words are simply made by using the first letter of a word in a particular gesture, as in: hold up the "T" sign and shake your wrist to mean "toilet". Knowing the signed alphabet is also very useful for spelling out a name or word once children are learning to spell.

You can find charts for the ASL hand sign alphabet on our website:

www.youramazingpreschooler.com

You can also find posters or printable versions by doing a web search for "sign language posters," or at Lakeshore Learning or other school and teacher supply stores.

Very clear photos of the ASL alphabet signs are also found on the Lifeprint.com website at:

www.lifeprint.com/asl101/fingerspelling/abc.htm

On the following pages, you will find some of the ASL signs that we have found most useful in our classroom. You may find them helpful at home as well, or out in the community when you want to give a gentle, silent signal to your child, or where she might want to communicate silently with you.

The following notes and images are adapted from www.Lifeprint.com. © 2014, Dr. William Vicars. Used by permission.

For more ASL-related material, visit www.lifeprint.com

WAIT

The sign for "wait" is made by holding the hands up and off to the side a bit. Wiggle the fingers.

STOP

The sign for "stop" is made by extending your left hand, palm upward. Sharply bring your open right hand down to your left palm at a right angle.

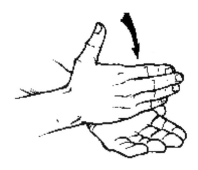

SIT

The sign for "sit" uses a single motion. Bend the first two bent fingers of your right hand and "Sit" them on the first two outstretched fingers of your left hand. If you use a double motion it means "chair."

MORE

The sign for "more" uses flattened "O" hands (thumb and all finger tips meet). Bring both "O" hands together.

PLEASE

The sign for "please" is made by placing your flat, right hand over the center of your chest. Move your hand in a clockwise motion (from the observer's point of view, use a circular motion towards your left, down, right, and back up) a few times.

I'M SORRY

The sign for "sorry" is made with your right hand closed in the "A" sign (thumb is next to fingers). Rotate your hand on your chest using a couple of clockwise motions. This sign can also be used to mean "apologize" or "regret." Make sure to use a "sorry" facial expression:

THANK YOU

The sign for "thank you" is made by starting with the fingers of your dominant hand near your lips. Your hand should be a "flat hand." Move your hand forward and down in the direction of the person you are thanking. Smile so they'll know you mean it.

YES

The sign for "yes" uses an "S" hand (fist). Memory aid: Think of the fist hand as representing your head. When you raise and lower your fist, bending at the wrist it represents your head nodding "yes."

NO

To sign "NO," snap your first two outstretched fingers down onto your thumb. The sign "NO" can use either a polite double motion or a more-firm or definite single motion. A firm, solid "no" (as in a command) uses one motion.

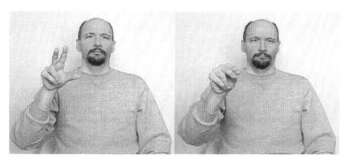

POTTY / TOILET / BATHROOM

The sign for "bathroom" is made by forming the right hand into the letter "T." (Thumb sticks up between the first two fingers of the closed hand.) The palm side is facing away from you. Shake your hand side-to-side a couple of times. Some people use a twisting movement instead of the side-to-side shake. Either is fine, but I prefer the side-to-side shake.

"Do you need to go to the bathroom?" is a frequent question in households with children and/or developmentally disabled folks. To ask, just tilt your head forward a bit, raise your eyebrows, and do the "toilet" sign.

LOUD / TOO LOUD:

To do the sign for "loud" point to (or touch) your right ear and then shake your fists back and forth at shoulder level.

To indicate "too loud," grimace while you make the sign.

Material courtesy of Dr. Bill Vicars and www.lifeprint.com
For more ASL-related material, visit www.lifeprint.com

56289574R00183

Made in the USA
Charleston, SC
14 May 2016